Safety Symbols

These symbols appear in laboratory activities.
They alert you to possible dangers and remind
you to work carefully.

General Safety Awareness Read all directions for an experiment several times. Follow the directions exactly as they are written. If you are in doubt, ask your teacher for assistance.

Physical Safety If the lab includes physical activity, use caution to avoid injuring yourself or others. Tell your teacher if there is a reason that you should not participate.

Safety Goggles Always wear safety goggles to protect your eyes in any activity involving chemicals, heating, or the possibility of broken glassware.

Lab Apron Wear a laboratory apron to protect your skin and clothing from harmful chemicals or hot materials.

Plastic Gloves Wear disposable plastic gloves to protect yourself from contact with chemicals that can be harmful. Keep your hands away from your face. Dispose of gloves according to your teacher's instructions.

Heating Use a clamp or tongs to hold hot objects. Test an object by first holding the back of your hand near it. If you feel heat, the object may be too hot to handle.

Heat-Resistant Gloves Hot plates, hot water, and hot glassware can cause burns. Never touch hot objects with your bare hands. Use an oven mitt or other hand protection.

Flames Tie back long hair and loose clothing, and put on safety goggles before using a burner. Follow instructions from your teacher for lighting and extinguishing burners.

No Flames If flammable materials are present, make sure there are no flames, sparks, or exposed sources of heat.

Electric Shock To avoid an electric shock, never use electrical equipment near water, or when the equipment or your hands are wet. Use only sockets that accept a three-prong plug. Be sure cords are untangled and cannot trip anyone. Disconnect equipment that is not in use.

Fragile Glassware Handle fragile glassware, such as thermometers, test tubes, and beakers, with care. Do not touch broken glass. Notify your teacher if glassware breaks. Never use chipped or cracked glassware.

Corrosive Chemical Avoid getting corrosive chemicals on your skin or clothing, or in your eyes. Do not inhale the vapors. Wash your hands after completing the activity.

Poison Do not let any poisonous chemical get on your skin, and do not inhale its vapor. Wash your hands after completing the activity.

Fumes When working with poisonous or irritating vapors, work in a well-ventilated area. Never test for an odor unless instructed to do so by your teacher. Avoid inhaling a vapor directly. Use a wafting motion to direct vapor toward your nose.

Sharp Object Use sharp instruments only as directed. Scissors, scalpels, pins, and knives are sharp and can cut or puncture your skin. Always direct sharp edges and points away from yourself and others.

Disposal All chemicals and other materials used in the laboratory must be disposed of safely. Follow your teacher's instructions.

Hand Washing Before leaving the lab, wash your hands thoroughly with soap or detergent, and warm water. Lather both sides of your hands and between your fingers. Rinse well.

From Bacteria to Plants

PRENTICE HALL Science Explorer

PEARSON

Prentice Hall

Boston, Massachusetts
Upper Saddle River, New Jersey

From Bacteria to Plants

Book-Specific Resources

Student Edition
StudentExpress™ with Interactive Textbook
Teacher's Edition
All-in-One Teaching Resources
Color Transparencies
Guided Reading and Study Workbook
Student Edition on Audio CD
Discovery Channel School® Video
Lab Activity Video
Consumable and Nonconsumable Materials Kits

Program Print Resources

Integrated Science Laboratory Manual
Computer Microscope Lab Manual
Inquiry Skills Activity Books
Progress Monitoring Assessments
Test Preparation Workbook
Test-Taking Tips With Transparencies
Teacher's ELL Handbook
Reading Strategies for Science Content

Differentiated Instruction Resources

Adapted Reading and Study Workbook
Adapted Tests
Differentiated Instruction Guide for Labs and Activities

Program Technology Resources

TeacherExpress™ CD-ROM
Interactive Textbooks Online
PresentationExpress™ CD-ROM
ExamView®, Computer Test Bank CD-ROM
Lab zone™ Easy Planner CD-ROM
Probeware Lab Manual With CD-ROM
Computer Microscope and Lab Manual
Materials Ordering CD-ROM
Discovery Channel School® DVD Library
Lab Activity DVD Library
Web Site at PHSchool.com

Spanish Print Resources

Spanish Student Edition
Spanish Guided Reading and Study Workbook
Spanish Teaching Guide With Tests

Acknowledgments appear on page 214, which constitutes an extension of this copyright page.

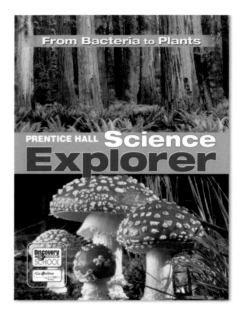

Cover
Ferns grow among giant redwood trees in Redwood National Park in California (top). Although these colorful fly agaric mushrooms might look harmless, they are extremely poisonous (bottom).

ISBN 0-13-203517-0
5 6 7 8 9 10   10 09 08 07

Program Authors

Michael J. Padilla, Ph.D.
Professor of Science Education
University of Georgia
Athens, Georgia

Michael Padilla is a leader in middle school science education. He has served as an author and elected officer for the National Science Teachers Association and as a writer of the National Science Education Standards. As lead author of Science Explorer, Mike has inspired the team in developing a program that meets the needs of middle grades students, promotes science inquiry, and is aligned with the National Science Education Standards.

Ioannis Miaoulis, Ph.D.
President
Museum of Science
Boston, Massachusetts

Originally trained as a mechanical engineer, Ioannis Miaoulis is in the forefront of the national movement to increase technological literacy. As dean of the Tufts University School of Engineering, Dr. Miaoulis spearheaded the introduction of engineering into the Massachusetts curriculum. Currently he is working with school systems across the country to engage students in engineering activities and to foster discussions on the impact of science and technology on society.

Martha Cyr, Ph.D.
Director of K–12 Outreach
Worcester Polytechnic Institute
Worcester, Massachusetts

Martha Cyr is a noted expert in engineering outreach. She has over nine years of experience with programs and activities that emphasize the use of engineering principles, through hands-on projects, to excite and motivate students and teachers of mathematics and science in grades K–12. Her goal is to stimulate a continued interest in science and mathematics through engineering.

Book Author

Jan Jenner, Ph.D.
Science Writer
Talladega, Alabama

Contributing Writers

James Robert Kaczynski, Jr.
Science Instructor
Jamestown School
Jamestown, Rhode Island

Evan P. Silberstein
Science Instructor
The Frisch School
Paramus, New Jersey

Joseph Stukey, Ph.D.
Department of Biology
Hope College
Holland, Michigan

Consultants

Reading Consultant

Nancy Romance, Ph.D.
Professor of Science
Education
Florida Atlantic University
Fort Lauderdale, Florida

Mathematics Consultant

William Tate, Ph.D.
Professor of Education and
Applied Statistics and
Computation
Washington University
St. Louis, Missouri

Reviewers

Teacher Reviewers

David R. Blakely
Arlington High School
Arlington, Massachusetts

Jane E. Callery
Two Rivers Magnet Middle
School
East Hartford, Connecticut

Melissa Lynn Cook
Oakland Mills High School
Columbia, Maryland

James Fattic
Southside Middle School
Anderson, Indiana

Dan Gabel
Hoover Middle School
Rockville, Maryland

Wayne Goates
Eisenhower Middle School
Goddard, Kansas

Katherine Bobay Graser
Mint Hill Middle School
Charlotte, North Carolina

Darcy Hampton
Deal Junior High School
Washington, D.C.

Karen Kelly
Pierce Middle School
Waterford, Michigan

David Kelso
Manchester High School Central
Manchester, New Hampshire

Benigno Lopez, Jr.
Sleepy Hill Middle School
Lakeland, Florida

Angie L. Matamoros, Ph.D.
ALM Consulting, INC.
Weston, Florida

Tim McCollum
Charleston Middle School
Charleston, Illinois

Bruce A. Mellin
Brooks School
North Andover, Massachusetts

Ella Jay Parfitt
Southeast Middle School
Baltimore, Maryland

Evelyn A. Pizzarello
Louis M. Klein Middle School
Harrison, New York

Kathleen M. Poe
Fletcher Middle School
Jacksonville, Florida

Shirley Rose
Lewis and Clark Middle School
Tulsa, Oklahoma

Linda Sandersen
Greenfield Middle School
Greenfield, Wisconsin

Mary E. Solan
Southwest Middle School
Charlotte, North Carolina

Mary Stewart
University of Tulsa
Tulsa, Oklahoma

Paul Swenson
Billings West High School
Billings, Montana

Thomas Vaughn
Arlington High School
Arlington, Massachusetts

Susan C. Zibell
Central Elementary
Simsbury, Connecticut

Safety Reviewers

W. H. Breazeale, Ph.D.
Department of Chemistry
College of Charleston
Charleston, South Carolina

Ruth Hathaway, Ph.D.
Hathaway Consulting
Cape Girardeau, Missouri

Douglas Mandt, M.S.
Science Education Consultant
Edgewood, Washington

Activity Field Testers

Nicki Bibbo
Witchcraft Heights School
Salem, Massachusetts

Rose-Marie Botting
Broward County Schools
Fort Lauderdale, Florida

Colleen Campos
Laredo Middle School
Aurora, Colorado

Elizabeth Chait
W. L. Chenery Middle School
Belmont, Massachusetts

Holly Estes
Hale Middle School
Stow, Massachusetts

Laura Hapgood
Plymouth Community
Intermediate School
Plymouth, Massachusetts

Mary F. Lavin
Plymouth Community
Intermediate School
Plymouth, Massachusetts

James MacNeil, Ph.D.
Cambridge, Massachusetts

Lauren Magruder
St. Michael's Country
Day School
Newport, Rhode Island

Jeanne Maurand
Austin Preparatory School
Reading, Massachusetts

Joanne Jackson-Pelletier
Winman Junior High School
Warwick, Rhode Island

Warren Phillips
Plymouth Public Schools
Plymouth, Massachusetts

Carol Pirtle
Hale Middle School
Stow, Massachusetts

Kathleen M. Poe
Fletcher Middle School
Jacksonville, Florida

Cynthia B. Pope
Norfolk Public Schools
Norfolk, Virginia

Anne Scammell
Geneva Middle School
Geneva, New York

Karen Riley Sievers
Callanan Middle School
Des Moines, Iowa

David M. Smith
Eyer Middle School
Allentown, Pennsylvania

Gene Vitale
Parkland School
McHenry, Illinois

Contents

From Bacteria to Plants

Discovery SCHOOL **VIDEO** Living Things

Discovery SCHOOL **VIDEO** Viruses and Bacteria

Discovery SCHOOL **VIDEO** Protists and Fungi

Discovery SCHOOL **VIDEO** Introduction to Plants

Discovery SCHOOL **VIDEO** Seed Plants

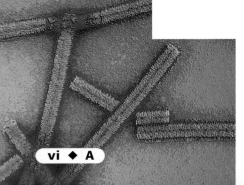
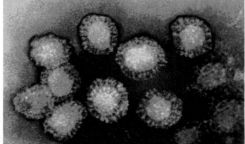
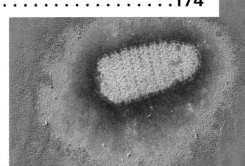

Reference Section

Enhance understanding through dynamic video.

Preview Get motivated with this introduction to the chapter content.

Field Trip Explore a real-world story related to the chapter content.

Assessment Review content and take an assessment.

Get connected to exciting Web resources in every lesson.

$SC\overline{LINKS_{\text{TM}}}$ **NSTA** Find Web links on topics relating to every section.

Active Art Interact with selected visuals from every chapter online.

Planet Diary® Explore news and natural phenomena through weekly reports.

Science News® Keep up to date with the latest science discoveries.

Experience the complete text-book online and on CD-ROM.

Activities Practice skills and learn content.

Videos Explore content and learn important lab skills.

Audio Support Hear key terms spoken and defined.

Self-Assessment Use instant feedback to help you track your progress.

Activities

Disease Detective Solves Mystery

The Colorado Health Department had a problem. Seven children had become sick with diarrhea, stomach cramps, fever, and vomiting. Within days, another 43 people had the same symptoms.

Tests indicated that they all had become infected with salmonella. Salmonella are bacteria that are usually transmitted through foods such as contaminated meat or eggs.

How did these children become infected with salmonella? To find the answer, Colorado health officials called in Dr. Cindy Friedman. Dr. Friedman works at the Centers for Disease Control and Prevention (CDC), a United States government agency that tracks down and studies the transmission of diseases throughout the world.

Cindy Friedman studies outbreaks of diseases in groups of people rather than in individuals. Her specialty is infectious diseases, illnesses that spread from person to person. She has investigated outbreaks of disease in such places as rural Bolivia in South America, Cape Verde Islands off the coast of Africa, and a Vermont farm.

Career Path

Cindy Friedman grew up in Brooklyn, New York. After receiving a B.S. in biology at Purdue University, she earned an M.D. at Ross University on the Caribbean island of Dominica. She is a physician and investigator in the Foodborne and Diarrheal Diseases Branch of the Centers for Disease Control and Prevention (CDC).

A salmonella bacterium like this one caused the outbreak of illness. The bacteria move using whiplike structures called flagella.

Talking With
Dr. Cindy Friedman

? How did you get started in science?

When I was young, we always had pets around the house and a lot of books about medicine and science. I wanted to be a veterinarian. In college I decided that I loved animals but didn't want to practice medicine on them. I'd rather keep them as a hobby and devote my career to human medicine.

? Why did you specialize in infectious diseases?

Out of all the subjects I studied in medical school, I liked microbiology the best—learning about different viruses and bacteria. Then, when I did my medical training in New Jersey, we had a lot of patients from Latin America. So I saw quite a few tropical and exotic diseases, which further heightened my interest.

? What do you enjoy about your job?

I really like being able to help more than one patient at a time. We do this by figuring out the risk factors for a disease and how to prevent people from getting it. Sometimes the answer is complicated, like adding chlorine to the water. Sometimes it's simple measures, like washing your hands or cooking your food thoroughly.

Cindy needed to answer questions like these to figure out what caused the illness.

? What clues did you have in the Colorado case?

At first, state investigators thought the bacteria came from some contaminated food. But when they questioned the children, they couldn't identify one place where the children had all eaten.

? What experience did the children share?

The investigators did a second set of interviews and learned that the children had all visited the zoo the week before they got sick. They didn't eat the same food at the zoo. But they all went to a special exhibit at the reptile house.

Questions for Investigation

☐ How did the children get infected?

☐ Did the salmonella come from infected food?

☐ What common place had the children visited?

☐ Why did some children get infected and not others?

☐ How can the zoo prevent future infections?

? Did you think the exhibit might be a new clue?

Yes. It was a clue because reptiles frequently carry the salmonella bacteria without becoming ill. In the special exhibit, there were four baby Komodo dragons, meat-eating lizards from the island of Komodo in Indonesia. They were displayed in a pen filled with mulch, surrounded by a wooden barrier about two feet high. We tested the Komodo dragons and found that one of them had salmonella bacteria. But it wasn't a petting exhibit, so I couldn't understand how the children got infected.

? How did you gather new data?

I questioned the children who became ill and compared their answers with those of children who didn't become ill. I asked about their behavior at the exhibit—where they stood, what they touched, and whether they had anything to eat or drink there. I also asked all the children if they washed their hands after visiting the exhibit. Those who did destroyed the bacteria. It was only the children who didn't wash their hands who became ill.

These images suggest ways to fight harmful bacteria that cause diseases.

Wash your hands often.

Avoid using your fingers and double dipping.

? What was the source of the contamination?

I found that anyone who touched the wooden barrier was much more likely to have gotten sick. Children would go up to the barrier and put their hands on it. Then some of them would put their hands in their mouth or would eat without washing their hands first. Those were the children who became infected with salmonella.

The Komodo dragon is the largest lizard species in existence. Found on Komodo Island in Indonesia, it is nearly extinct.

Keep picnic food cold.

Refrigerate food promptly.

Cook meat thoroughly.

##

After Cindy swabbed the barrier at the zoo, she then tested the sample at the CDC labs.

? What's it like being a disease detective?

It's more the old-fashioned idea of medicine. What I do is examine the patients and listen to the stories they tell—where they've traveled, what they ate, and what they were exposed to. Then I try to figure out what caused their illness.

? How did you test your hypothesis?

We took cultures—swabs from the top of the barrier where the children put their hands. When we tested those cultures in the lab, we found salmonella bacteria.

? What did you conclude about the bacteria?

The infected Komodo dragon left its droppings in the mulch and the animals walked in it. Then they would stand on their hind legs, bracing themselves by putting their front paws on top of the barrier.

? What recommendations did you make?

We didn't want to tell zoos not to have reptile exhibits, because they're a good thing. And children should be able to get close to the animals. But at this particular exhibit, the outbreak could have been prevented with a double barrier system, so that the reptiles and the children couldn't touch the same barrier. And hand-washing is really important. Zoos should have signs instructing people to wash their hands after going to that kind of exhibit. In homes and schools with pet reptiles, hand-washing is important, too.

Writing in Science

Career Link Review the scientific process that Cindy used to solve the case of salmonella infections. What makes her a disease detective? Write a paragraph describing the steps Cindy follows and the skills she uses in her career as an investigator of infectious diseases.

Go Online
PHSchool.com

For: More on this career
Visit: PHSchool.com
Web Code: ceb-1000

A ◆ 3

Chapter Preview

interactive
Textbook

Each transparent ball is a tiny freshwater ▶
organism known as a *Volvox.*

Lab zone™ Chapter **Project**

Mystery Object

It's not always easy to tell whether something is alive. In this chapter, you will learn the characteristics of living things. As you study this chapter, your challenge will be to determine whether or not a mystery object is alive.

Your Goal To study a mystery object for several days to determine whether or not it is alive

To complete the project, you must

- care for your object following your teacher's instructions
- observe your object each day, and record your data
- determine whether your object is alive, and if so, to which domain and kingdom it belongs
- follow the safety guidelines in Appendix A

Plan It! Before you get started, create a list of characteristics that living things share. Think about whether nonliving things also share these characteristics. Also, think about what kind of tests you can carry out to look for signs of life. Create data tables in which to record your observations.

1 What Is Life?

Reading Preview

Key Concepts
- What characteristics do all living things share?
- Where do living things come from?
- What do living things need to survive?

Key Terms
- organism • cell • unicellular
- multicellular • stimulus
- response • development
- spontaneous generation
- controlled experiment
- autotroph • heterotroph
- homeostasis

Target Reading Skill

Using Prior Knowledge Look at the section headings and visuals to see what this section is about. Then write what you already know about living things in a graphic organizer like the one below. As you read, write what you learn.

What You Know
1. Living things grow.
2.

What You Learned
1.
2.

Lab zone Discover **Activity**

Is It Living or Nonliving?

1. Your teacher will give you and a partner a wind-up toy.
2. One of you will look for evidence that the toy is alive and the other will look for evidence that the toy is not alive.
3. Observe the wind-up toy. Record the characteristics of the toy that support your position about whether or not the toy is alive.
4. Share your lists of living and nonliving characteristics with your classmates.

Think It Over
Forming Operational Definitions Based on what you learned from the activity, create a list of characteristics that living things share.

It was an unusually damp summer for towns near Dallas, Texas. Bright yellow "blobs" began to appear everywhere. Looking like the slimy creatures in horror films, the blobs oozed slowly along the ground. Eventually, the glistening jelly-like masses overran people's yards and porches. Terrified homeowners didn't know what the blobs were. Some people thought that they were life forms from another planet.

People around Dallas were worried until biologists, scientists who study living things, put people's minds at ease. The blobs were slime molds—living things usually found on damp, decaying material on a forest floor. The unusually wet weather provided ideal conditions for the slime molds to grow.

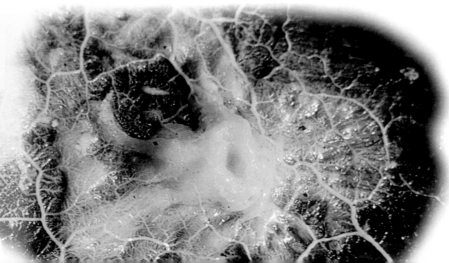

FIGURE 1
Slime Mold
Slime molds similar to these grew all over yards and porches near Dallas, Texas, one summer.

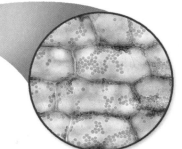

▲ Plant cells

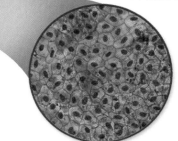

▲ Animal cells

The Characteristics of Living Things

If you were asked to name some living things, or **organisms,** you might name yourself, a pet, and maybe some insects or plants. You would probably not mention a moss growing in a shady spot, the mildew on bathroom tiles, or the slime molds that oozed across lawns. But all of these things are organisms that share important characteristics with all other living things. **All living things have a cellular organization, contain similar chemicals, use energy, respond to their surroundings, grow and develop, and reproduce.**

Cellular Organization All organisms are made of small building blocks called cells. A **cell** is the basic unit of structure and function in an organism. The smallest cells are so tiny that you could fit more than a million of them on the period at the end of this sentence. To see most cells, you need a micro-scope—a tool that uses lenses, like those in eyeglasses, to mag-nify small objects.

Organisms may be composed of only one cell or of many cells. **Unicellular,** or single-celled organisms, include bacteria (bak TIHR ee uh), the most numerous organisms on Earth. A bacterial cell carries out all of the functions necessary for the organism to stay alive.

Multicellular organisms are composed of many cells. In many multicellular organisms, the cells are specialized to do certain tasks. For example, you are made of trillions of cells. Specialized cells in your body, such as muscle and nerve cells, work together to keep you alive. Nerve cells carry messages about your surroundings to your brain. Other nerve cells then carry messages to your muscle cells, making your body move.

FIGURE 2
Cellular Organization
Like all living things, the frog and plant are made of cells. Although the cells of different organisms are not identical, they share important characteristics.
Making Generalizations *In what ways are cells similar?*

Try This **Activity**

React!

In this activity, you will test your responses to three different stimuli.

1. Have a partner clap his or her hands together about ten centimeters in front of your face. Describe how you react.

2. Look at one of your eyes in a mirror. Cover the eye with your hand for a minute. While looking in the mirror, remove your hand. Observe how the size of your pupil changes.

3. Bring a slice of lemon close to your nose and mouth. Describe what happens.

Classifying For each action performed, name the stimulus and the response.

The Chemicals of Life The cells of all living things are composed of chemicals. The most abundant chemical in cells is water. Other chemicals, called carbohydrates (kahr boh HY drayts), are a cell's main energy source. Two other chemicals, proteins (PROH teenz) and lipids, are the building materials of cells, much as wood and bricks are the building materials of houses. Finally, nucleic (noo KLEE ik) acids are the genetic material—the chemical instructions that direct the cell's activities.

Energy Use The cells of organisms use energy to do what living things must do, such as grow and repair injured parts. An organism's cells are always hard at work. For example, as you read this paragraph, not only are your eye and brain cells busy, but most of your other cells are working, too. The cells of your stomach and intestine are digesting food. Your blood cells are moving chemicals around your body. If you've hurt yourself, some of your cells are repairing the damage.

Response to Surroundings If you've ever seen a plant in a sunny window, you may have observed that the plant's stems have bent so that the leaves face the sun. Like a plant bending toward the light, all organisms react to changes in their environment. A change in an organism's surroundings that causes the organism to react is called a **stimulus** (plural *stimuli*). Stimuli include changes in temperature, light, sound, and other factors.

FIGURE 3
Stimulus and Response
All organisms respond to changes in their surroundings. When startled by the opossum, the kitten bares its teeth in response.

An organism reacts to a stimulus with a **response**—an action or change in behavior. For example, has someone ever knocked over a glass of water by accident during dinner, causing you to jump? The sudden spilling of water was the stimulus that caused your startled response.

Growth and Development Another characteristic of living things is that they grow and develop. Growth is the process of becoming larger. **Development** is the process of change that occurs during an organism's life to produce a more complex organism. To grow and develop, organisms use energy to create new cells. Look at Figure 4 to see how a sunflower seed develops as it grows into a sunflower plant.

Reproduction Another characteristic of organisms is the ability to reproduce, or produce offspring that are similar to the parents. Robins lay eggs that develop into young robins that closely resemble their parents. Apples produce seeds that develop into apple trees, which in turn make more seeds. The mildew on your bathroom tiles will produce more mildew if you do not clean it off!

 **Reading Checkpoint** How do growth and development differ?

FIGURE 4
Sunflower Growth and Development
Over time, a tiny sunflower seed grows and develops into a tall sunflower plant. A great deal of energy is needed to produce the cells of a mature sunflower plant.
Comparing and Contrasting *How do the seedlings resemble the sunflower plant? How do they differ?*

▲ **Tiny sunflower seedlings**

▲ **Sunflower seeds**

▲ **A mature sunflower**

FIGURE 5

Redi's Experiment

Francesco Redi designed one of the first controlled experiments. In his experiment, Redi showed that flies do not spontaneously arise from decaying meat. **Controlling Variables** *What is the manipulated variable in this experiment?*

▲ **Maggots on meat**

Uncovered jar   Covered jar

1 Redi placed meat in two identical jars. He left one jar uncovered. He covered the other jar with a cloth that let in air.

2 After a few days, Redi saw maggots (young flies) on the decaying meat in the open jar. There were no maggots on the meat in the covered jar.

3 Redi reasoned that flies had laid eggs on the meat in the open jar. The eggs hatched into maggots. Because flies could not lay eggs on the meat in the covered jar, there were no maggots there. Redi concluded that decaying meat did not produce maggots.

Life Comes From Life

Today, when people observe moths flying out of closets or weeds poking out of cracks in the sidewalk, they know that these organisms are the result of reproduction. **Living things arise from living things through reproduction.**

Four hundred years ago, however, people believed that life could appear from nonliving material. For example, when people saw flies swarming around decaying meat, they concluded that flies could arise from rotting meat. The mistaken idea that living things can arise from nonliving sources is called **spontaneous generation.** It took hundreds of years of experiments to convince people that spontaneous generation does not occur.

Redi's Experiment In the 1600s, an Italian doctor named Francesco Redi helped to disprove spontaneous generation. Redi designed a controlled experiment to show that flies do not arise from decaying meat. In a **controlled experiment**, a scientist carries out two tests that are identical in every respect except for one factor. The one factor that a scientist changes is called the manipulated variable.

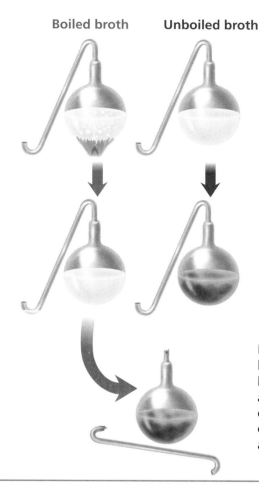

Boiled broth Unboiled broth

1 Pasteur put clear broth into two flasks with curved necks. The necks would let in oxygen but keep out bacteria from the air. Pasteur boiled the broth in one flask to kill any bacteria in the broth. He did not boil the broth in the other flask.

2 In a few days, the unboiled broth became cloudy, showing that new bacteria were growing. The boiled broth remained clear. Pasteur concluded that bacteria do not spontaneously arise from the broth. New bacteria appeared only when living bacteria were already present.

Later, Pasteur took the flask with the broth that had remained clear and broke its curved neck. Bacteria from the air could now enter the flask. In a few days, the broth became cloudy. This evidence confirmed that new bacteria arise only from existing bacteria.

FIGURE 6
Pasteur's Experiment
Louis Pasteur's carefully controlled experiment demonstrated that bacteria arise only from existing bacteria.

▲ **Pasteur in his laboratory**

In Redi's experiment, shown in Figure 5, the manipulated variable was whether or not the jar was covered. Flies were able to enter the uncovered jar and lay their eggs on the meat inside. These eggs hatched into maggots, which developed into new flies. The flies could not enter the covered jar, however. Therefore, no maggots formed on the meat in the covered jar. Through his experiment, Redi was able to conclude that rotting meat does not produce flies.

Pasteur's Experiment Even after Redi's work, many people continued to believe that spontaneous generation could occur. In the mid-1800s, the French chemist Louis Pasteur designed some controlled experiments that finally rejected spontaneous generation. As shown in Figure 6, he demonstrated that new bacteria appeared in broth only when they were produced by existing bacteria. The experiments of Redi and Pasteur helped to convince people that living things do not arise from nonliving material.

Reading Checkpoint **What is a controlled experiment?**

The Needs of Living Things

Though it may seem surprising, flies, bacteria, and all other organisms have the same basic needs as you. **All living things must satisfy their basic needs for food, water, living space, and stable internal conditions.**

Food Recall that organisms need a source of energy to live. They use food as their energy source. Organisms differ in the ways they obtain energy. Some organisms, such as plants, capture the sun's energy and use it to make food. Organisms that make their own food are called **autotrophs** (AW toh trohfs). *Auto-* means "self" and *-troph* means "feeder." Autotrophs use the food they make to carry out their own life functions.

Organisms that cannot make their own food are called **heterotrophs** (HET uh roh trohfs). *Hetero-* means "other." Heterotrophs obtain their energy by feeding on others. Some heterotrophs eat autotrophs and use the energy in the autotroph's stored food. Other heterotrophs consume heterotrophs that eat autotrophs. Therefore, a heterotroph's energy source is also the sun—but in an indirect way. Animals, mushrooms, and slime molds are examples of heterotrophs.

FIGURE 7
Food, Water, and Living Space

This environment meets the needs of the many animals that live there. **Inferring** *How do the trees and other plants meet their needs for food?*

The porcupine, a heterotroph, obtains its energy by feeding on green plants.

Water All living things need water to survive. In fact, most organisms can live for only a few days without water. Organisms need water to obtain chemicals from their surroundings, break down food, grow, move substances within their bodies, and reproduce.

One property of water that is vital to living things is its ability to dissolve more chemicals than any other substance on Earth. In fact, water makes up about 90 percent of the liquid part of your blood. The food that your cells need dissolves in blood and is transported to all parts of your body. Waste from cells dissolves in blood and is carried away. Your body's cells also provide a watery environment in which chemicals are dissolved.

Living Space All organisms need a place to live—a place to get food and water and find shelter. Whether an organism lives in the freezing Antarctic or the scorching desert, its surroundings must provide what it needs to survive.

Because there is a limited amount of space on Earth, some organisms must compete for space. Trees in a forest, for example, compete with other trees for sunlight above ground. Below ground, their roots compete for water and minerals.

The stream fulfills the moose's need for water.

The owl finds a suitable living space in a tree hollow.

FIGURE 8
Homeostasis
Sweating helps your body maintain a steady body temperature. Your body produces sweat during periods of strenuous activity. As the sweat evaporates, it cools your body down.

Stable Internal Conditions Organisms must be able to keep the conditions inside their bodies stable, even when conditions in their surroundings change significantly. For example, your body temperature stays steady despite changes in the air temperature. The maintenance of stable internal conditions is called **homeostasis** (hoh mee oh STAY sis).

Homeostasis keeps internal conditions just right for cells to function. Think about your need for water after a hard workout. When water levels in your body decrease, chemicals in your body send signals to your brain, causing you to feel thirsty.

Other organisms have different mechanisms for maintaining homeostasis. Consider barnacles, which as adults are attached to rocks at the edge of the ocean. At high tide, they are covered by water. At low tide, however, the watery surroundings disappear, and barnacles are exposed to hours of sun and wind. Without a way to keep water in their cells, they would die. Fortunately, a barnacle can close up its hard outer plates, trapping some water inside. In this way, a barnacle can keep its body moist until the next high tide.

 **Reading Checkpoint** What is homeostasis?

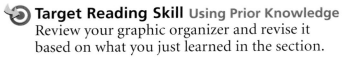

Section 1 Assessment

 **Target Reading Skill** Using Prior Knowledge Review your graphic organizer and revise it based on what you just learned in the section.

Reviewing Key Concepts

1. a. **Reviewing** List the six characteristics of living things.
   b. **Inferring** A bird sitting in a tree flies away as you walk by. Which of the life characteristics explains the bird's behavior?
   c. **Applying Concepts** Explain why the tree, which does not move away, is also considered a living thing.

2. a. **Defining** What was meant by the idea of *spontaneous generation*?
   b. **Explaining** Why is this idea incorrect?
   c. **Summarizing** How did Pasteur's experiment help show that spontaneous generation does not occur?

3. a. **Identifying** What four things do all organisms need to survive?
   b. **Describing** Which need is a fox meeting by feeding on berries?
   c. **Applying Concepts** The arctic fox has thick, dense fur in the winter and much shorter fur in the summer. How does this help the fox maintain homeostasis?

Lab zone At-Home Activity

Observing Life With a family member, observe a living thing, such as a family pet, a houseplant, or a bird outside your window. Record your observations as you study the organism. Prepare a chart that shows how the organism meets the four needs of living things discussed in this section.

Please Pass the Bread!

Problem

What factors are necessary for bread molds to grow?

Skills Focus

observing, controlling variables

Materials

- paper plates
- plastic dropper
- bread without preservatives
- sealable plastic bags
- tap water
- packing tape

Procedure

1. Brainstorm with others to predict which factors might affect the growth of bread mold. Record your ideas.

2. Place two slices of bread of the same size and thickness on separate, clean plates.

3. To test the effect of moisture on bread mold growth, add drops of tap water to one bread slice until the whole slice is moist. Keep the other slice dry. Expose both slices of bread to the air for one hour.

4. Put each slice into its own sealable bag. Press the outside of each bag to remove the air. Seal the bags. Then use packing tape to seal the bags again. Store the bags in a warm, dark place.

5. Copy the data table into your notebook.

6. Every day for at least five days, briefly remove the sealed bags from their storage place. Record whether any mold has grown. Estimate the area of the bread where mold is present. **CAUTION:** *Do not unseal the bags. At the end of the experiment, give the sealed bags to your teacher.*

Analyze and Conclude

1. **Observing** How did the appearance of the two slices of bread change over the course of the experiment?

2. **Inferring** How can you explain any differences in appearance between the two slices?

3. **Controlling Variables** What was the manipulated variable in this experiment? Why was it necessary to control all other variables except this one?

4. **Communicating** Suppose that you lived in Redi's time. A friend tells you that molds just suddenly appear on bread. How would you explain to your friend about Redi's experiment and how it applies to molds and bread?

Design an Experiment

Choose another factor that may affect mold growth, such as temperature or the amount of light. Set up an experiment to test the factor you choose. Remember to keep all conditions the same except for the one you are testing. *Obtain your teacher's permission before carrying out your investigation.*

Data Table				
	Moistened Bread Slice		Unmoistened Bread Slice	
Day	Mold Present?	Area With Mold	Mold Present?	Area With Mold
1				
2				

Classifying Organisms

Reading Preview

Key Concepts
- Why do biologists organize living things into groups?
- What do the levels of classification indicate about the relationship between organisms?
- How are taxonomic keys useful?
- What is the relationship between classification and evolution?

Key Terms
- classification • taxonomy
- binomial nomenclature
- genus • species • evolution

🎯 Target Reading Skill
Asking Questions Before you read, preview the red headings. In a graphic organizer like the one below, ask a *what*, *why*, or *how* question for each heading. As you read, write the answers to your questions.

Classifying Organisms

Question	Answer
Why do scientists classify?	Scientists classify because . . .

Discover Activity

Can You Organize a Junk Drawer?

1. Your teacher will give you some items that you might find in the junk drawer of a desk. Your job is to organize the items.
2. Examine the objects and decide on three groups into which you can sort them.
3. Place each object into one of the groups, based on how the item's features match the characteristics of the group.
4. Compare your grouping system with those of your classmates.

Think It Over
Classifying Which of your classmates' grouping systems seemed most useful? Why?

Suppose you had only ten minutes to run into a supermarket to get what you needed—milk and tomatoes. Could you do it? In most supermarkets this would be an easy task. You'd probably find out where the dairy and produce sections are, and head straight to those areas. Now imagine if you had to shop for these same items in a market where things were randomly placed throughout the store. Where would you begin? You'd have to search through a lot of things before you found what you needed. You could be there for a long time!

FIGURE 9
Classifying Vegetables
Vegetables in the produce section of a supermarket are neatly organized.

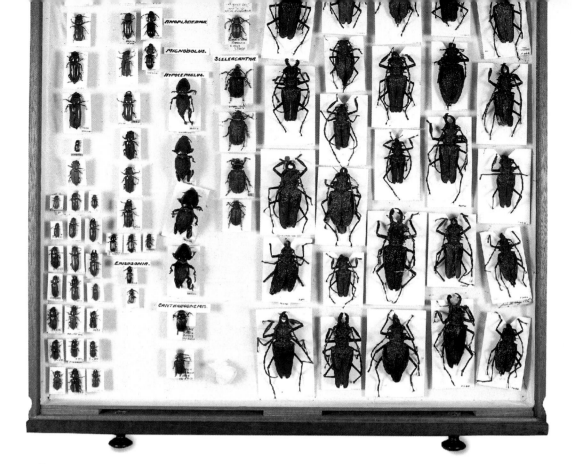

Why Do Scientists Classify?

Just as shopping can be a problem in a disorganized store, finding information about a specific organism can also be a problem. So far, scientists have identified more than one million kinds of organisms on Earth. That's a large number, and it is continually growing as scientists discover new organisms. Imagine how difficult it would be to find information about one particular organism if you had no idea even where to begin. It would be a lot easier if similar organisms were placed into groups.

Organizing living things into groups is exactly what biologists have done. Biologists group organisms based on similarities, just as grocers group milk with dairy products and tomatoes with produce. **Classification** is the process of grouping things based on their similarities.

Biologists use classification to organize living things into groups so that the organisms are easier to study. The scientific study of how living things are classified is called **taxonomy** (tak SAHN uh mee). Taxonomy is useful because once an organism is classified, a scientist knows a lot about that organism. For example, if you know that a crow is classified as a bird, then you know that a crow has wings, feathers, and a beak.

 **Reading Checkpoint** What is the scientific study of how living things are classified called?

FIGURE 10
Classifying Beetles
These beetles belong to a large insect collection in a natural history museum. They have been classified according to characteristics they share. **Observing** *What characteristics may have been used to group these beetles?*

DISCOVERY CHANNEL SCHOOL

Living Things

Video Preview
▶ Video Field Trip
Video Assessment

The Naming System of Linnaeus

Taxonomy also involves naming organisms. In the 1750s, the Swedish naturalist Carolus Linnaeus devised a system of naming organisms that is still used today. Linnaeus placed organisms in groups based on their observable features. Based on his observations, Linnaeus gave each organism a unique, two-part scientific name. This naming system Linnaeus used is called **binomial nomenclature** (by NOH mee ul NOH men klay chur). The word *binomial* means "two names."

Genus and Species The first word in an organism's scientific name is its genus. A **genus** (JEE nus) (plural *genera*) is a classification grouping that contains similar, closely related organisms. For example, pumas, marbled cats, and house cats are all classified in the genus *Felis*. Organisms that are classified in the genus *Felis* share characteristics such as sharp, retractable claws and behaviors such as hunting other animals.

The second word in a scientific name often describes a distinctive feature of an organism, such as where it lives or its appearance. Together, the two words indicate a unique species. A **species** (SPEE sheez) is a group of similar organisms that can mate with each other and produce offspring that can also mate and reproduce.

FIGURE 11
Binomial Nomenclature

These three different species of cats belong to the same genus. Their scientific names share the same first word, *Felis*. The second word of their names describes a feature of the animal.

Felis concolor
(Puma)
Concolor means "the same color" in Latin. Notice that this animal's coat is mostly the same color.

Felis marmorata
(Marbled cat)
Notice the marbled pattern of this animal's coat. *Marmorata* means "marble" in Latin.

Felis domesticus
(House cat)
Domesticus means "of the house" in Latin.

Aristotle and Classification

Many hundreds of years before Linnaeus, a Greek scholar named Aristotle developed a classification system for animals. Aristotle first divided animals into those he considered to have blood and those he did not. This graph shows Aristotle's classification system for "animals with blood."

1. **Reading Graphs** Into how many groups were these animals classified?

2. **Interpreting Data** Which group made up the largest percentage of animals?

3. **Calculating** What percentage of these animals either fly or swim?

4. **Inferring** In Aristotle's classification system, where would a cow be classified? A whale?

5. **Predicting** Would Aristotle's classification system be useful today? Explain.

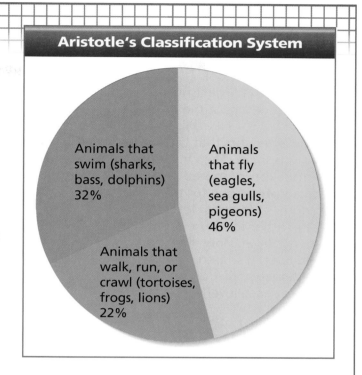

Aristotle's Classification System

Animals that swim (sharks, bass, dolphins) 32%

Animals that fly (eagles, sea gulls, pigeons) 46%

Animals that walk, run, or crawl (tortoises, frogs, lions) 22%

Using Binomial Nomenclature Notice in Figure 11 that a complete scientific name is written in italics. Only the first letter of the first word in a scientific name is capitalized. Notice also that scientific names contain Latin words. Linnaeus used Latin words in his naming system because Latin was the language that scientists used during that time.

Binomial nomenclature makes it easy for scientists to communicate about an organism because everyone uses the same scientific name for the same organism. Using different names for the same organism can get very confusing. For instance, look at the animal in Figure 12. People call it by a variety of names. Depending on where you live, you might call this animal a woodchuck, groundhog, or whistlepig. Fortunately, it has only one scientific name— *Marmota monax*.

Reading Checkpoint How is a scientific name written?

FIGURE 12
Marmota monax
Although there are many common names for this animal, it has only one scientific name, *Marmota monax*.
Making Generalizations *What is the advantage of scientific names?*

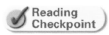

Observing

Test your observational skills using Figure 13. Look carefully at the organisms pictured together at the kingdom level. Make a list of the characteristics that the organisms share. Then make two more lists of shared characteristics—one for the organisms at the class level and the other for those at the genus level. How does the number of shared characteristics on your lists change at each level?

Levels of Classification

The classification system that scientists use today is based on the contributions of Linnaeus. But today's classification system uses a series of many levels to classify organisms.

To help you understand the levels in classification, imagine a room filled with everybody who lives in your state. First, all of the people who live in your town raise their hands. Then, those who live in your neighborhood raise their hands. Then, those who live on your street raise their hands. Finally, those who live in your house raise their hands. Each time, fewer people raise their hands. But you'd be in all of the groups. The most general group you belong to is the state. The most specific group is the house. The more levels you share with others, the more you have in common with them.

The Major Levels of Classification Most biologists today classify organisms into the levels shown in Figure 13. Of course, organisms are not grouped by where they live, but rather by their shared characteristics. First, an organism is placed in a broad group, which in turn is divided into more specific groups.

As Figure 13 shows, a domain is the highest level of organization. Within a domain, there are kingdoms. Within kingdoms, there are phyla (FY luh) (singular *phylum*). Within phyla are classes. Within classes are orders. Within orders are families. Each family contains one or more genera. Finally, each genus contains one or more species. **The more classification levels that two organisms share, the more characteristics they have in common.**

Classifying an Owl Take a closer look at Figure 13 to see how the levels of classification apply to the great horned owl. Look at the top row of the figure. As you can see, a wide variety of other organisms also belong to the same domain as the horned owl.

Next, look at the kingdom, phylum, class, and order levels. Notice that as you move down the levels in the figure, there are fewer kinds of organisms in each group. More importantly, the organisms in each group have more in common with each other. For example, the class Aves includes all birds, while the order Strigiformes includes only owls. Different owls have more in common with each other than they do with other types of birds.

Reading Checkpoint Which is a broader classification level—a kingdom or a family?

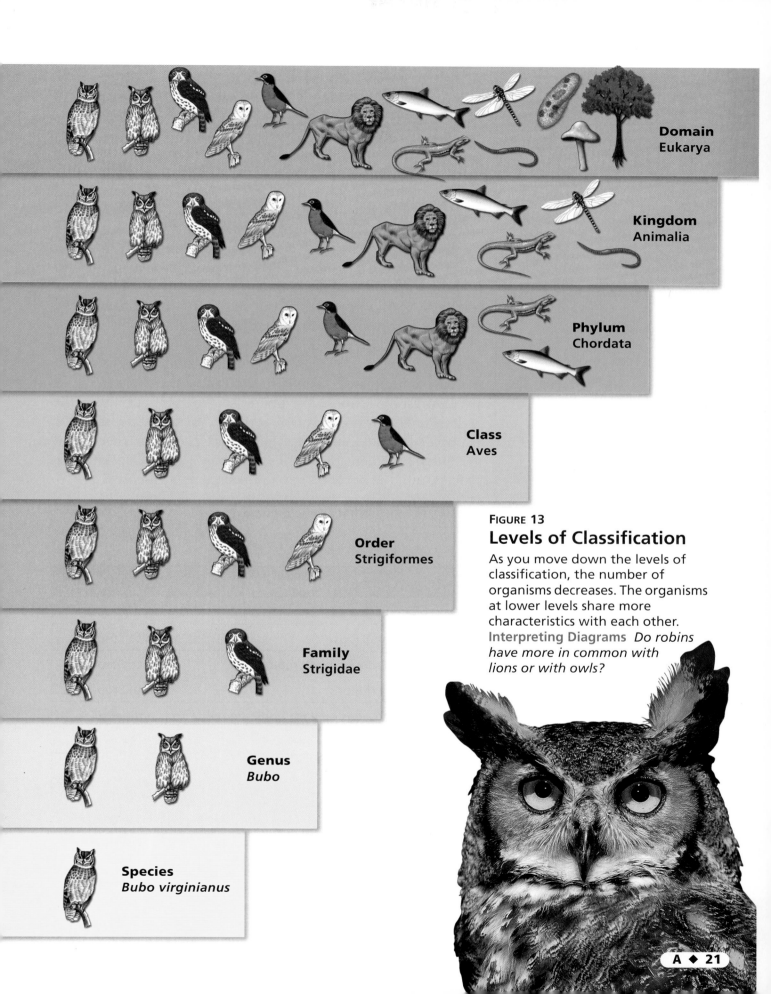

Domain
Eukarya

Kingdom
Animalia

Phylum
Chordata

Class
Aves

Order
Strigiformes

Family
Strigidae

Genus
Bubo

Species
Bubo virginianus

FIGURE 13
Levels of Classification

As you move down the levels of classification, the number of organisms decreases. The organisms at lower levels share more characteristics with each other.
Interpreting Diagrams *Do robins have more in common with lions or with owls?*

Go Online
PHSchool.com

For: More on classifying living things
Visit: PHSchool.com
Web Code: ced-1012

FIGURE 14
Identifying Organisms
You can use a taxonomic key to identify this organism. The six paired statements in this key describe physical characteristics of different organisms.
Drawing Conclusions *What is this creature?*

Taxonomic Keys

Why should you care about taxonomy? Suppose that you are watching television and feel something tickling your foot. Startled, you look down and see a tiny creature crawling across your toes. Although it's only the size of a small melon seed, you don't like the looks of its two claws waving at you. Then, in a flash, it's gone.

How could you find out what the creature was? You could use a field guide. Field guides are books with illustrations that highlight differences between similar-looking organisms. You could also use a taxonomic key. **Taxonomic keys are useful tools for determining the identity of organisms.** A taxonomic key consists of a series of paired statements that describe the physical characteristics of different organisms.

The taxonomic key in Figure 14 can help you identify the mysterious organism. To use the key, start by reading the pair of statements numbered 1a and 1b. Notice that the two statements are contrasting. Choose the one statement that applies to the organism. Follow the direction at the end of that statement. For example, if the organism has eight legs, follow the direction at the end of statement 1a, which says "Go to Step 2." Continue this process until the key leads you to the organism's identity.

 **Reading Checkpoint** **What are field guides?**

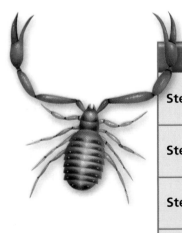

Taxonomic Key			
Step 1	**1a.**	Has 8 legs	Go to Step 2.
	1b.	Has more than 8 legs	Go to Step 3.
Step 2	**2a.**	Has one oval-shaped body region	Go to Step 4.
	2b.	Has two body regions	Go to Step 5.
Step 3	**3a.**	Has one pair of legs on each body segment	Centipede
	3b.	Has two pairs of legs on each body segment	Millipede
Step 4	**4a.**	Is less than 1 millimeter long	Mite
	4b.	Is more than 1 millimeter long	Tick
Step 5	**5a.**	Has clawlike pincers	Go to Step 6.
	5b.	Has no clawlike pincers	Spider
Step 6	**6a.**	Has a long tail with a stinger	Scorpion
	6b.	Has no tail or stinger	Pseudoscorpion

Evolution and Classification

At the time that Linnaeus developed his classification system, people thought that species never change. In 1859, a British naturalist named Charles Darwin published a theory about how species can change over time. Darwin's theory has had a major impact on how species are classified.

Darwin's Theory Darwin collected data for his theory on the Galapagos Islands off the western coast of South America. As he studied the islands' finches, he observed that some species of finches were similar to each other but different from finches living in South America.

Darwin hypothesized that some members of a single species of finch flew from South America to the islands. Once on the islands, the species changed little by little over many generations until it was different from the species remaining in South America. After a while, the birds on the island could no longer mate and reproduce with those on the mainland. They had become a new species. In this way, two groups of a single species can accumulate enough differences over a very long time to become two separate species. This process by which species gradually change over time is called **evolution.**

Classification Today The theory of evolution has changed the way biologists think about classification. Scientists now understand that certain organisms are similar because they share a common ancestor. For example, Darwin hypothesized that the finches on the Galapagos Islands shared a common ancestor with the finches in South America. When organisms share a common ancestor, they share an evolutionary history. Today's system of classification considers the history of a species. **Species with similar evolutionary histories are classified more closely together.**

Determining Evolutionary History How do scientists determine the evolutionary history of a species? One way is to compare the structure of organisms. But today, scientists rely primarily on information about the chemical makeup of the organisms' cells. The more closely two species are related, the more similar the chemicals that make up their cells.

FIGURE 15
Galapagos Finches

These three species of finches that live on the Galapagos Islands may have arisen from a single species. Notice the differences in these birds' appearances, especially their beaks.

The large ground finch cracks open seeds with its strong, wide beak.

The large tree finch uses its grasping beak to trap insects.

The cactus ground finch uses its pointed beak to pierce the outer covering of cactus plants.

FIGURE 16
Classifying Skunks and Weasels
The skunk (bottom) and weasel (right) were once classified in the same family. Based on new chemical information, scientists reclassified skunks and weasels into different families.

New Information Sometimes, by studying the chemical makeup of organisms, scientists discover new information that changes what they had previously thought. For example, skunks and weasels were classified in the same family for 150 years. However, when scientists compared nucleic acids from the cells of skunks and weasels, they found many differences. These differences suggested that the two groups are not as closely related as previously thought. Some scientists proposed changing the classification of skunks. As a result, skunks were reclassified into their own family called Mephitidae, which means "noxious gas" in Latin.

 **Reading Checkpoint** **What kind of information do scientists mainly rely on to determine evolutionary history?**

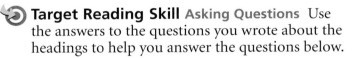

Section 2 Assessment

Target Reading Skill **Asking Questions** Use the answers to the questions you wrote about the headings to help you answer the questions below.

Reviewing Key Concepts

1. a. Reviewing Why do biologists classify?
  b. Inferring Suppose someone tells you that a jaguarundi is classified in the same genus as house cats. What characteristics do you think a jaguarundi might have?
2. a. Listing List in order the levels of classification, beginning with domain.
  b. Applying Concepts Woodchucks are classified in the same family as squirrels, but in a different family than mice. Do woodchucks have more characteristics in common with squirrels or mice? Explain.
3. a. Reviewing What is a taxonomic key?
  b. Applying Concepts Create a taxonomic key that could help identify a piece of fruit as an apple, orange, strawberry, or banana.

4. a. Reviewing What is evolution?
  b. Explaining How is knowing a species' evolutionary history important in its classification?
  c. Predicting You discover a new organism that has a chemical makeup extremely similar to that of chickens. What is likely to be true about the evolutionary histories of your organism and chickens?

Lab zone **At-Home Activity**

Kitchen Classification With a family member, go on a "classification hunt" in the kitchen. Look in your refrigerator, cabinets, and drawers to discover what classification systems your family uses to organize items. Then explain to your family member the importance of classification in biology.

Living Mysteries

Problem

How can you create a taxonomic key to help identify tree leaves?

Skills Focus

observing, classifying, inferring

Materials

- a variety of leaves
- hand lens
- metric ruler

Procedure

1. Your teacher will give you five different tree leaves. Handle the leaves carefully.

2. Use a hand lens to examine each of the leaves. Look for characteristics such as those described in the table. Make a list of five or more identifying characteristics for each leaf.

Leaf Characteristics to Consider	
Characteristic	**Observations**
Overall Shape	Is the leaf needlelike and narrow, or is it flat and wide? For a flat leaf, is it rounded, oblong, heart-shaped, or some other shape?
Simple vs. Compound	Is the leaf a single unit, or is it made up of individual leaflets? If it is made up of leaflets, how are they arranged on the leaf stalk?
Pattern of Veins	Do the leaf's veins run parallel from a central vein, or do they form a branching pattern?
Leaf Edges	Are the edges of the leaf jagged or smooth?
Leaf Texture	Is the leaf's surface fuzzy, shiny, or another texture?

3. Use your observations to create a taxonomic key for the leaves. In creating your taxonomic key, use the characteristics you listed along with any others that you observe. Remember that your taxonomic key should consist of paired statements, similar to the one shown in Figure 14 in this chapter.

4. Exchange your leaves and taxonomic key with a partner. If your partner cannot identify all of the leaves using your key, revise your key as necessary.

Analyze and Conclude

1. **Observing** How are your leaves similar or different from one another?

2. **Classifying** How did you decide which characteristics to use in your taxonomic key?

3. **Inferring** Choose one of your leaves and look back over the list of characteristics you used to classify it. Do you think every single leaf of the same type would share those characteristics? Explain.

4. **Communicating** Explain in your own words why a taxonomic key is helpful. Include in your explanation why it is important that the paired statements in a taxonomic key be contrasting statements.

More to Explore

Suppose you are hiking through the woods and see many flowers of different colors, shapes, and sizes. You decide to create a taxonomic key to help identify the flowers. What characteristics would you include in the key?

Domains and Kingdoms

Reading Preview

Key Concepts
- What characteristics are used to classify organisms?
- How do bacteria and archaea differ?
- What are the kingdoms within the domain Eukarya?

Key Terms
- prokaryote • nucleus
- eukaryote

Target Reading Skill
Comparing and Contrasting As you read, compare and contrast the characteristics of organisms in domains Bacteria, Archaea, and Eukarya, by completing a table like the one below.

Characteristics of Organisms

Domain or Kingdom	Cell Type and Number	Able to Make Food?
Bacteria	Prokaryote; unicellular	
Archaea		
Eukarya: Protists		
Fungi		
Plants		
Animals		

Discover Activity

Which Organism Goes Where?

1. [icons] Your teacher will give you some organisms to observe. Two of the organisms are classified in the same kingdom.
2. Observe the organisms. Decide which organisms might belong in the same kingdom. Write the reasons for your decision. Wash your hands after handling the organisms.
3. Discuss your decision and reasoning with your classmates.

Think It Over
Forming Operational Definitions What characteristics do you think define the kingdom into which you placed the two organisms together?

Suppose you were an apprentice helping Linnaeus classify organisms. You probably would have identified every organism as either a plant or an animal. That's because over 200 years ago, people could not see the tiny organisms that are known to exist today. When microscopes, which make small objects look larger, were invented, a whole new world was revealed. As more and more powerful microscopes were developed, scientists discovered many new organisms and identified important differences among cells.

Today, a three-domain system of classification is commonly used. Shown in Figure 17, the three domains are Bacteria, Archaea, and Eukarya. Within the domains are kingdoms. **Organisms are placed into domains and kingdoms based on their cell type, their ability to make food, and the number of cells in their bodies.**

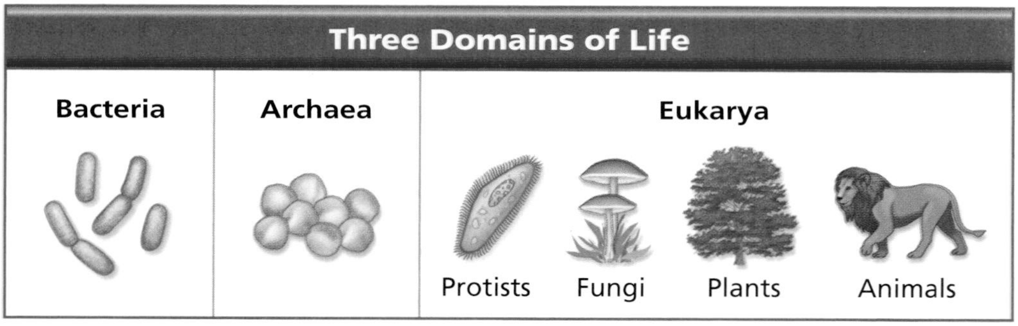

FIGURE 17
In the three-domain system of classification, all known organisms belong to one of three domains—Bacteria, Archaea, or Eukarya.

Three Domains of Life

Bacteria	Archaea	Eukarya
		Protists Fungi Plants Animals

Domain Bacteria

Although you may not know it, members of the domain Bacteria are all around you. You can find them in the yogurt you eat, on every surface you touch, and inside your body, both when you are healthy and sick.

Members of the domain Bacteria are prokaryotes (proh KA ree ohtz). **Prokaryotes** are organisms whose cells lack a nucleus. A **nucleus** (NOO klee us) (plural *nuclei*) is a dense area in a cell that contains nucleic acids—the chemical instructions that direct the cell's activities. In prokaryotes, nucleic acids are not contained within a nucleus.

Some bacteria are autotrophs, while others are heterotrophs. Bacteria may be harmful, such as those that cause strep throat. However, most bacteria are helpful. Some produce vitamins and foods like yogurt, and some recycle essential chemicals, such as nitrogen.

 **What is a nucleus?**

Domain Archaea

Deep in the Pacific Ocean, hot gases and molten rock spew out from a vent in the ocean floor. It is hard to imagine that any living thing could exist in such harsh conditions. Surprisingly, a group of tiny organisms thrives in such places. They are members of the domain Archaea (ahr KEE uh), whose name comes from the Greek word for "ancient."

Archaea can be found in some of the most extreme environments on Earth, including hot springs, very salty water, swamps, and the intestines of cows! Scientists think that the harsh conditions in which archaea live are similar to those of ancient Earth.

Like bacteria, archaea are unicellular prokaryotes. And like bacteria, some archaea are autotrophs while others are heterotrophs. Archaea are classified in their own domain, however, because their chemical makeup differs from that of bacteria. **Although bacteria and archaea are similar in some ways, there are important differences in the structure and chemical makeup of their cells.**

 **Where can archaea be found?**

FIGURE 18
Domain Bacteria
The bristles of a toothbrush (blue) scrub away at a film of bacteria (yellow) on a tooth. The bacteria in the inset are responsible for causing cavities.

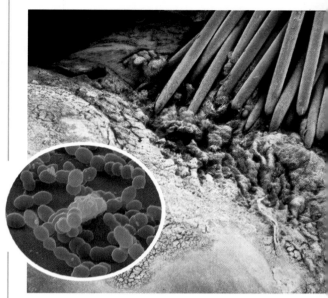

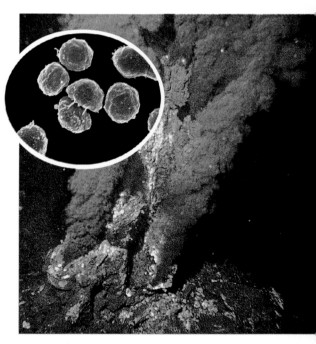

FIGURE 19
Domain Archaea
Heat-loving archaea (inset) thrive in deep-sea vents like these.
Classifying *What characteristics do archaea and bacteria share?*

▲ Protists: Paramecium

▲ Fungi: Mushrooms

FIGURE 20
Domain Eukarya
You can encounter organisms from all four kingdoms of Eukarya on a hike through the woods.
Making Generalizations *What characteristic do all Eukarya share?*

Domain Eukarya

What do seaweeds, mushrooms, tomatoes, and dogs have in common? They are all members of the domain Eukarya. Organisms in this domain are **eukaryotes** (yoo KA ree ohtz)—organisms with cells that contain nuclei. **Scientists classify organisms in the domain Eukarya into one of four kingdoms: protists, fungi, plants, or animals.**

Protists A protist (PROH tist) is any eukaryotic organism that cannot be classified as an animal, plant, or fungus. Because its members are so different from one another, the protist kingdom is sometimes called the "odds and ends" kingdom. For example, some protists are autotrophs, while others are heterotrophs. Most protists are unicellular, but some, such as seaweeds, are large multicellular organisms.

Fungi If you have eaten mushrooms, then you have eaten fungi (FUN jy). Mushrooms, molds, and mildew are all fungi. Most fungi are multicellular eukaryotes. A few, such as the yeast you use for baking, are unicellular eukaryotes. Fungi are found almost everywhere on land, but only a few live in fresh water. All fungi are heterotrophs. Most fungi feed by absorbing nutrients from dead or decaying organisms.

Plants Dandelions on a lawn, mosses in a forest, and peas in a garden are familiar members of the plant kingdom. Plants are all multicellular eukaryotes and most live on land. In addition, plants are autotrophs that make their own food. Plants provide food for most of the heterotrophs on land.

The plant kingdom includes a great variety of organisms. Some plants produce flowers, while others do not. Some plants, such as giant redwood trees, can grow very tall. Others, like mosses, never grow taller than a few centimeters.

Go Online
SciLINKS NSTA

For: Links on kingdoms
Visit: www.SciLinks.org
Web Code: scn-0113

▲ **Plants:** Moss

▲ **Animals:** Salamander

Animals A dog, a flea on the dog's ear, and a cat that the dog chases have much in common because all are animals. All animals are multicellular eukaryotes. In addition, all animals are heterotrophs. Animals have different adaptations that allow them to locate food, capture it, eat it, and digest it. Members of the animal kingdom live in diverse environments throughout Earth. Animals can be found from ocean depths to mountaintops, from hot, scalding deserts to cold, icy landscapes.

 **Reading Checkpoint** Which two kingdoms consist only of heterotrophs?

Section 3 Assessment

Target Reading Skill Comparing and Contrasting Use the information in your table about Bacteria, Archaea, and Eukarya to help you answer the questions below.

Reviewing Key Concepts

1. **a.** Listing What are the three domains into which organisms are classified?
   b. Classifying What information do you need to know to determine the domain to which an organism belongs?
2. **a.** Defining What is a prokaryote?
   b. Classifying Which two domains include only organisms that are prokaryotes?
   c. Comparing and Contrasting How do the members of the two domains of prokaryotes differ?

3. **a.** Reviewing What do the cells of protists, fungi, plants, and animals have in common?
   b. Comparing and Contrasting How are protists and plants similar? How are they different?
   c. Inferring You learn that the Venus flytrap is in the same kingdom as pine trees. What characteristics do these organisms share?

Writing in Science

Detailed Observation Study a photo of an animal. Then write a detailed description of the animal without naming it. Describe the animal so that an artistic friend could paint it in detail without seeing it. Use adjectives that clearly and vividly describe the animal.

The Origin of Life

Reading Preview

Key Concepts
- How was the atmosphere of early Earth different from today's atmosphere?
- How do scientists hypothesize that life arose on early Earth?

Key Term
- fossil

Target Reading Skill
Identifying Supporting Evidence As you read, identify the evidence that supports scientists' hypothesis of how life arose on Earth. Write the evidence in a graphic organizer like the one below.

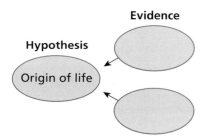

Evidence

Hypothesis

Origin of life

How Can the Composition of Air Change?

1. 🌱 🐭 Your teacher will give you two covered plastic jars. One contains a plant, and one contains an animal.
2. Observe the organisms in each jar. Talk with a partner about how you think each organism affects the composition of the air in its jar.
3. Predict how the amount of oxygen in each jar would change over time if left undisturbed.
4. Return the jars to your teacher.

Think It Over
Inferring Scientists hypothesize that Earth's early atmosphere was different from today's atmosphere. What role might early organisms have played in bringing about those changes?

You stare out the window of your time machine. You have traveled more than 3.5 billion years back in time, to an early point in Earth's history. The landscape is unfamiliar—rugged, with bare, jagged rocks and little soil. You search for a hint of green, but there is none. You see only blacks, browns, and grays. Lightning flashes all around you. You hear the rumble of thunder, howling winds, and waves pounding the shore.

You neither see nor hear any living things. However, you know that this is the time period when scientists hypothesize that early life forms arose on Earth. You decide to explore. To be safe, you put on your oxygen mask. Stepping outside, you wonder what kinds of organisms could ever live in such a place.

The Atmosphere of Early Earth

You were smart to put on your oxygen mask before exploring early Earth! You would not have been able to breathe because there was little oxygen in the air. Scientists think that conditions on early Earth were very different than they are today. **On ancient Earth, nitrogen, water vapor, carbon dioxide, and methane were probably the most abundant gases in the atmosphere.** In contrast, the major gases in the atmosphere today are nitrogen and oxygen.

Life on Early Earth Evidence suggests that the earliest forms of life appeared on Earth some time between 3.5 and 4.0 billion years ago. Because there was no oxygen, you, like most of today's organisms, could not have lived on Earth back then.

No one can ever be sure what the first life forms were like, but scientists have formed hypotheses about them. First, early life forms did not need oxygen to survive. Second, they were probably unicellular organisms. Third, they probably lived in the oceans. The first organisms probably resembled the archaea that live today in extreme environments, such as in polar ice caps, hot springs, and the mud of ocean bottoms.

Modeling Conditions on Early Earth One of the most intriguing questions that scientists face is explaining how early life forms arose. Although Redi and Pasteur showed that living things do not spontaneously arise on today's Earth, scientists reason that the first life forms probably did arise from nonliving materials.

In 1953, a young American graduate student, Stanley Miller, and his advisor, Harold Urey, provided the first clues as to how organisms might have arisen on Earth. They designed an experiment in which they recreated the conditions of early Earth in their laboratory. They placed water (to represent the ocean) and a mixture of the gases thought to compose Earth's early atmosphere into a flask. They were careful to keep oxygen and unicellular organisms out of the mixture. Then, they sent an electric current through the mixture to simulate lightning.

Within a week, the mixture darkened. In the dark fluid, Miller and Urey found some small chemical units that, if joined together, could form proteins—one of the building blocks of life.

 **Reading Checkpoint** What are the major gases in the atmosphere today?

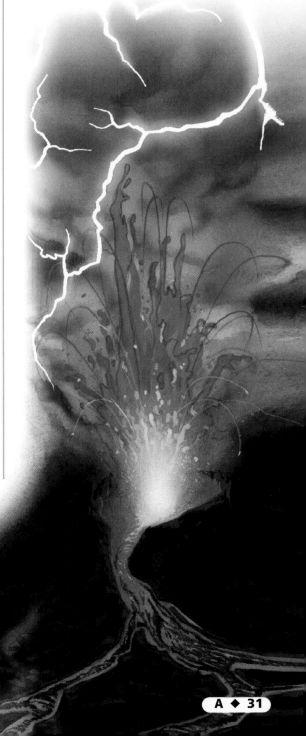

FIGURE 21
Early Earth
The atmosphere of early Earth had little oxygen. There were frequent volcanic eruptions, earthquakes, and violent storms. *Inferring Could modern organisms have survived on ancient Earth? Why or why not?*

The First Cells

In experiments similar to Miller and Urey's, other scientists succeeded in producing chemical units that make up carbohydrates and nucleic acids. The experimental results led scientists to formulate a hypothesis about how life arose on Earth.

Scientists hypothesize that the small chemical units of life formed gradually over millions of years in Earth's waters. Some of these chemical units joined to form the large chemical building blocks found in cells. Eventually, some of these large chemicals joined together and became the forerunners of the first cells.

Support From Fossil Evidence This hypothesis is consistent with fossil evidence. A **fossil** is a trace of an ancient organism that has been preserved in rock or another substance. Scientists have discovered fossils of what appear to have been archaea-like organisms. These ancient fossils have been dated to be between 3.4 and 3.5 billion years old. Therefore, these fossils support the idea that cells may have existed back then.

The first cells could not have needed oxygen to survive. They were probably heterotrophs that used the chemicals in their surroundings for energy. As the cells grew and reproduced, their numbers increased. In turn, the amount of chemicals available to them decreased.

At some point much later, some of the cells may have developed the ability to make their own food. These early ancestors of today's autotrophs had an important effect on the atmosphere. As they made their own food, they produced oxygen as a waste product. As the autotrophs thrived, oxygen accumulated in Earth's atmosphere. Over hundreds of millions of years, the amount of oxygen increased to its current level.

 **Reading Checkpoint** What is a fossil?

FIGURE 22
Fossil Evidence
These cell-like fossils were found in the rugged terrain of western Australia. They are the oldest fossils known—about 3.5 billion years old.

FIGURE 23
Unanswered Questions
Scientists continue to search for clues about the origin of life.
Applying Concepts *What kind of evidence might be found in rocks?*

Unanswered Questions Many scientists today continue to explore the question of how and where life first arose on Earth. Laboratory experiments, like those by Miller and Urey, can never prove how life first appeared on Earth. Such experiments can only test hypotheses about how life forms could have arisen. No one will ever know for certain how and when life first appeared on Earth. However, scientists will continue to ask questions, test their models, and look for experimental and fossil evidence about the origin of life on Earth.

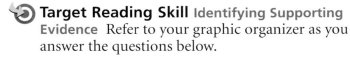

Section 4 Assessment

🎯 **Target Reading Skill** **Identifying Supporting Evidence** Refer to your graphic organizer as you answer the questions below.

Reviewing Key Concepts
1. a. **Naming** Which gases were probably most abundant in Earth's early atmosphere?
   b. **Describing** How did Miller and Urey model the conditions in Earth's early atmosphere?
   c. **Inferring** What can be inferred from the results of Miller and Urey's experiment?
2. a. **Reviewing** What experiments in addition to Miller and Urey's helped scientists hypothesize about how life arose on Earth?
   b. **Sequencing** Place these events in the proper sequence according to the hypothesis about how life arose on Earth: small chemical units form, cells make their own food, the first cells form, oxygen levels increase in the atmosphere, large chemical building blocks form.

c. **Inferring** How is the existence of organisms in hot springs today consistent with the scientific hypothesis of how life forms arose on Earth?

Writing in Science

Advertisement You are in charge of exhibits at a science museum. The museum is building an exhibit that models early Earth. Write an ad for the museum to attract visitors to see the new exhibit. Clearly describe to visitors what they will see and hear.

① What Is Life?

Key Concepts

- All living things have a cellular organization, contain similar chemicals, use energy, respond to their surroundings, grow and develop, and reproduce.

- Living things arise from living things through reproduction.

- All living things must satisfy their basic needs for food, water, living space, and stable internal conditions.

Key Terms

organism	development
cell	spontaneous generation
unicellular	controlled experiment
multicellular	autotroph
stimulus	heterotroph
response	homeostasis

② Classifying Organisms

Key Concepts

- Biologists use classification to organize living things into groups so that the organisms are easier to study.

- The more classification levels that two organisms share, the more characteristics they have in common.

- Taxonomic keys are useful tools for determining the identity of organisms.

- Species with similar evolutionary histories are classified more closely together.

Key Terms

classification
taxonomy
binomial
  nomenclature
genus
species
evolution

③ Domains and Kingdoms

Key Concepts

- Organisms are placed into domains and kingdoms based on their cell type, their ability to make food, and the number of cells in their bodies.

- Although bacteria and archaea are similar in some ways, there are important differences in the structure and chemical makeup of their cells.

- Scientists classify organisms in the domain Eukarya into one of four kingdoms: protists, fungi, plants, or animals.

Key Terms

prokaryote
nucleus
eukaryote

④ The Origin of Life

Key Concepts

- On ancient Earth, nitrogen, water vapor, carbon dioxide, and methane were probably the most abundant gases in the atmosphere.

- Scientists hypothesize that the small chemical units of life formed gradually over millions of years in Earth's waters. Some of these chemical units joined to form the large chemical building blocks found in cells. Eventually, some of these large chemicals joined together and became the forerunners of the first cells.

Key Term

fossil

Review and Assessment

Organizing Information

Concept Mapping Copy the concept map about the needs of organisms onto a separate sheet of paper. Then complete it and add a title. (For more on Concept Mapping, see the Skills Handbook.)

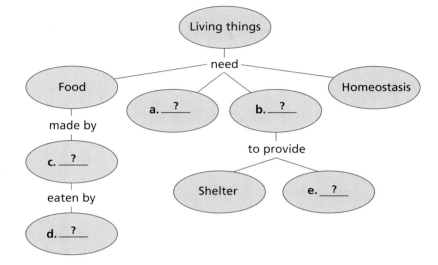

Reviewing Key Terms

Choose the letter of the best answer.

1. The idea that life could spring from nonliving matter is called
   a. development.
   b. spontaneous generation.
   c. homeostasis.
   d. evolution.

2. The scientific study of how living things are classified is called
   a. development.   b. biology.
   c. taxonomy.   d. evolution.

3. A genus is divided into
   a. species.   b. phyla.
   c. families.   d. classes.

4. Which organisms have cells without nuclei?
   a. protists
   b. archaea
   c. plants
   d. fungi

5. Which gas was NOT a large part of Earth's early atmosphere?
   a. methane
   b. nitrogen
   c. oxygen
   d. water vapor

If the statement is true, write *true*. If it is false, change the underlined word or words to make the statement true.

6. Bacteria are <u>unicellular</u> organisms.

7. <u>Heterotrophs</u> can make their own food.

8. Linnaeus devised a system of naming organisms called <u>binomial nomenclature</u>.

9. The gray wolf, *Canis lupus,* and the red wolf, *Canis rufus,* belong to the same <u>species</u>.

10. The cells of a <u>prokaryote</u> lack a nucleus.

Writing in Science

Letter You are an ocean scientist who has just discovered a new organism deep in the ocean. Write a letter to a colleague explaining how the organism should be classified and why.

Living Things

Video Preview
Video Field Trip
▶ **Video Assessment**

Review and Assessment

Checking Concepts

11. Your friend thinks that plants are not alive because they do not move. How would you respond to your friend?

12. Describe how your pet, or a friend's pet, meets its needs as a living thing.

13. What are the advantages of identifying an organism by its scientific name?

14. What does the chemical makeup of the cells of an organism tell scientists about its evolutionary history?

15. What is the major difference between fungi and plants?

16. Describe where Earth's early organisms lived and how they obtained food.

Thinking Critically

17. **Applying Concepts** How do you know that a robot is not alive?

18. **Relating Cause and Effect** When people believed that spontaneous generation occurred, there was a recipe for making mice: Place a dirty shirt and a few wheat grains in an open pot; wait three weeks. List the reasons why this recipe might have worked. How could you demonstrate that spontaneous generation was not responsible for the appearance of mice?

19. **Inferring** Which two of the following organisms are most closely related: *Entamoeba histolytica, Escherichia coli, Entamoeba coli*? Explain your answer.

20. **Classifying** How many domains do the following organisms represent? Kingdoms?

21. **Applying Concepts** If you could travel to a planet with an atmosphere like that of early Earth, would you be able to survive? Explain.

Applying Skills

Refer to the illustrations below to answer Questions 22–25.

A student designed the experiment pictured below to test how light affects the growth of plants.

22. **Controlling Variables** Is this a controlled experiment? If so, identify the manipulated variable. If not, why not?

23. **Developing Hypotheses** What hypothesis might this experiment be testing?

24. **Predicting** Based on what you know about plants, predict how each plant will change in two weeks.

25. **Designing Experiments** Design a controlled experiment to determine whether the amount of water that a plant receives affects its growth.

Lab zone Chapter **Project**

Performance Assessment Prepare a display presenting your conclusion about your mystery object. Describe the observations that helped you to reach your conclusion. Compare your ideas with those of other students. If necessary, defend your work.

Standardized Test Prep

Choose the letter of the best answer.

1. Which of the following statements about cells is *not* true?
   A Cells are the building blocks of living things.
   B Cells carry out the basic life functions of living things.
   C Some organisms are made up of only one cell.
   D Most cells can be seen with the naked eye.

2. Organisms that are autotrophs are classified in which of the following domains?
   F Bacteria
   G Archaea
   H Eukarya
   J all of the above

Use the table below and your knowledge of science to answer Questions 3–4.

Some Types of Trees			
Common Name of Tree	Kingdom	Family	Species
Bird cherry	Plants	Rosaceae	*Prunus avium*
Flowering cherry	Plants	Rosaceae	*Prunus serrula*
Smooth-leaved elm	Plants	Ulmaceae	*Ulmus minor*
Whitebeam	Plants	Rosaceae	*Sorbus aria*

3. In the system of binomial nomenclature, what is the name for the whitebeam tree?
   A Rosaceae
   B *Sorbus aria*
   C *Prunus serrula*
   D *Ulmus minor*

4. Which of the following organisms is most different from the other three?
   F *Prunus avium*
   G *Prunus serrula*
   H *Ulmus minor*
   J *Sorbus aria*

5. Pasteur's experiment in which he boiled broth in some flasks, but not in others, was a controlled experiment because
   A it showed that bacteria do not arise spontaneously.
   B the necks of both flasks were curved.
   C boiling or not boiling the broth was the only variable he changed.
   D the broth in both flasks remained clear.

Constructed Response

6. Name five characteristics that all living things share. Then describe each characteristic or give an example.

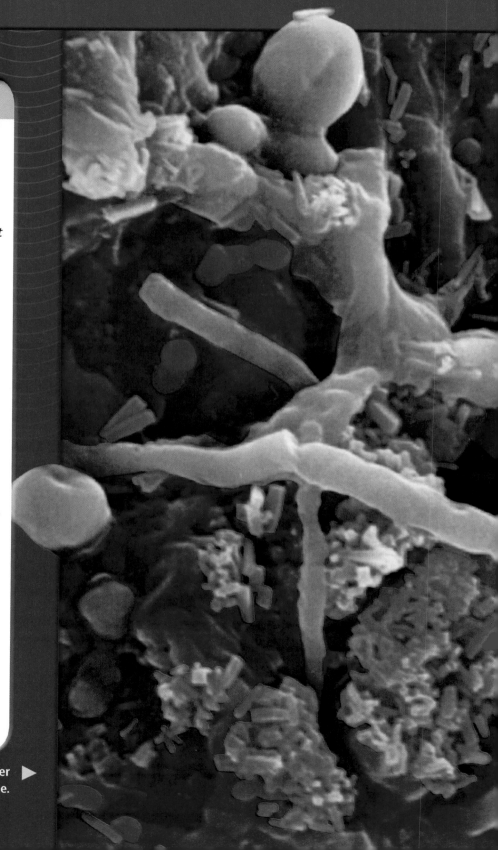

Chapter

2

Viruses and Bacteria

Chapter Preview

Interactive Textbook

Bacteria (blue and purple rods) and other microorganisms lurk in a kitchen sponge. ▶

Lab zone™ **Chapter Project**

Be a Disease Detective

Not too long ago, catching certain viral and bacterial "childhood diseases" was a routine part of growing up. Those diseases included chickenpox, mumps, pertussis (whooping cough), and others. In this project, you will select one childhood disease to investigate.

Your Goal To survey people of different ages to find out what they know about a childhood disease

To complete this project, you must

● select and research one disease to learn more about it

● prepare a questionnaire to survey people about their experience with and knowledge of the disease

● question a total of 30 people in different age groups, and report any patterns that you find

Plan It! With several classmates, make a list of childhood diseases. Research one disease to find out more about it. Think about the kinds of questions you will need to ask in a survey and how you will select the people to survey. Then draft your questionnaire.

Viruses

Reading Preview

Key Concepts
- How do viruses differ from living things?
- What is the basic structure of a virus?
- How do viruses multiply?

Key Terms
- virus • host • parasite
- bacteriophage

Target Reading Skill

Sequencing As you read, make two flowcharts that show how active and hidden viruses multiply. Put the steps in the process in separate boxes in the flowchart in the order in which they occur.

How Active Viruses Multiply

Virus attaches to the surface of a living cell

↓

Virus injects genetic material into cell

↓

FIGURE 1
Virus Shapes
Viruses come in various shapes.

Lab zone · Discover **Activity**

Which Lock Does the Key Fit?
1. Your teacher will give you a key.
2. Study the key closely. Think about what shape the keyhole on its lock must have. On a piece of paper, draw the shape of the keyhole.
3. The lock for your key is contained in the group of locks your teacher will provide. Try to match your key to its lock without inserting the key into the keyhole.

Think It Over
Inferring Suppose that each type of cell had a unique "lock" on its surface. How might a unique lock help protect a cell from invading organisms?

It is a dark and quiet night. An enemy spy slips silently across the border. Invisible to the guards, the spy creeps cautiously along the edge of the road, heading toward the command center. Undetected, the spy sneaks by the center's security system and reaches the door. Breaking into the control room, the spy takes command of the central computer. The enemy is in control.

Moments later the command center's defenses finally activate. Depending on the enemy's strength and cunning, the defenses may squash the invasion before much damage is done. Otherwise the enemy will win and take over the territory.

▼ This robotlike virus, called a bacteriophage, infects bacteria.

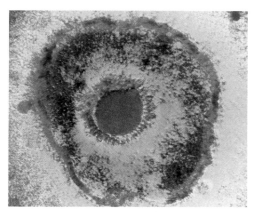

▲ The round chickenpox virus causes an itchy rash on human skin.

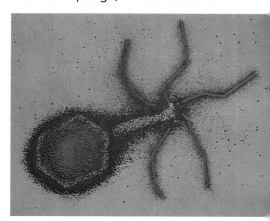

What Is a Virus?

Although this spy story may read like a movie script, it describes similar events that can occur in your body. The spy acts very much like a virus invading an organism. A **virus** is a tiny, non-living particle that enters and then reproduces inside a living cell. No organisms are safe from viruses. From the smallest bacterial cell to the tallest tree, from your pet cat to your younger brother, there is a virus able to invade that organism's cells.

Characteristics of Viruses Most biologists today consider viruses to be nonliving because viruses do not have all the characteristics essential for life. Viruses are not cells and do not use their own energy to grow or to respond to their surroundings. Viruses also cannot make food, take in food, or produce wastes. The only way in which viruses are like organisms is that they are able to multiply. **Although viruses can multiply, they do so differently than organisms. Viruses can multiply only when they are inside a living cell.**

The organism that a virus enters and multiplies inside is called a host. A **host** is an organism that provides a source of energy for a virus or another organism. A virus acts like a **parasite** (PA ruh syt), an organism that lives on or in a host and causes it harm. Almost all viruses destroy the cells in which they multiply.

Virus Shapes As you can see in Figure 1, viruses vary widely in shape. Some viruses are round, while some are rod-shaped. Other viruses are shaped like bricks, threads, or bullets. There are even viruses that have complex, robotlike shapes, such as the bacteriophage in Figure 1. A **bacteriophage** (bak TEER ee oh fayj) is a virus that infects bacteria. In fact, its name means "bacteria eater."

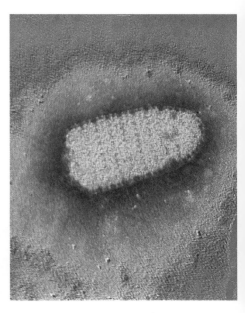

▲ The bullet-shaped rabies virus infects nerve cells in certain animals.

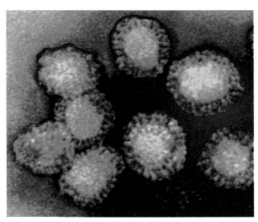

▼ These round viruses are responsible for causing West Nile disease in animals.

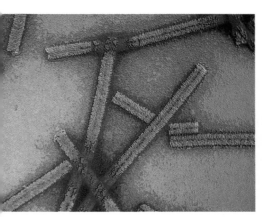

▲ Tube-shaped tobacco mosaic viruses infect tobacco plants.

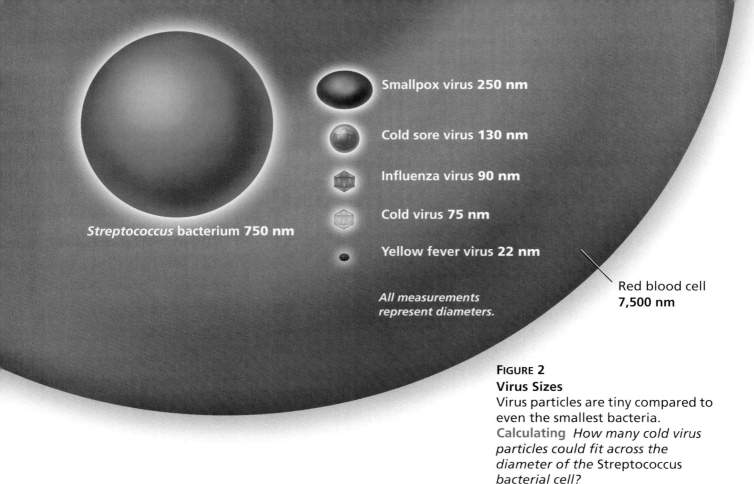

Smallpox virus **250 nm**

Cold sore virus **130 nm**

Influenza virus **90 nm**

Cold virus **75 nm**

Yellow fever virus **22 nm**

Streptococcus bacterium **750 nm**

All measurements represent diameters.

Red blood cell
7,500 nm

FIGURE 2
Virus Sizes
Virus particles are tiny compared to even the smallest bacteria.
Calculating *How many cold virus particles could fit across the diameter of the* Streptococcus *bacterial cell?*

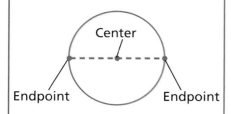

Math Skills

Diameter

The diameter of a circle is a line that passes through the center of the circle and has both of its endpoints on the circle. To find the diameter, draw a line like the one shown below. Then, use a metric ruler to measure the length of the line. For example, the diameter of a penny is about 1.9 mm.

Center

Endpoint   Endpoint

Practice Problem Measure the diameter of a quarter and a CD.

Virus Sizes Just as viruses vary in shape, they also vary in size. Viruses are smaller than cells and cannot be seen with the microscopes you use in school. Viruses are so small that they are measured in units called nanometers (nm). One nanometer is one billionth of a meter (m). The smallest viruses are about 20 nanometers in diameter, while the largest viruses are more than 200 nanometers in diameter. The average virus is quite small when compared with even the smallest cells—those of bacteria.

Naming Viruses Because viruses are not considered organisms, scientists do not use traditional binomial nomenclature to name them. Currently, scientists name viruses in a variety of ways. Some viruses, such as the polio virus, are named after the disease they cause. Other viruses are named for the organisms they infect. The tobacco mosaic virus, for example, infects plants in the tobacco family. Scientists named the West Nile virus after the place in Africa where it was first found. Sometimes, scientists name viruses after people. The Epstein-Barr virus, for example, was named for the two scientists who first identified the virus that causes the disease known as mononucleosis, or mono.

 Reading Checkpoint   Which is larger—a virus or a bacterium?

The Structure of Viruses

Although viruses may look very different from one another, they all have a similar structure. **All viruses have two basic parts: a protein coat that protects the virus and an inner core made of genetic material.** A virus's genetic material contains the instructions for making new viruses. Some viruses are also surrounded by an additional outer membrane, or envelope.

The proteins on the surface of a virus play an important role during the invasion of a host cell. Each virus contains unique surface proteins. The shape of the surface proteins allows the virus to attach to certain cells in the host. Like keys, a virus's proteins fit only into certain "locks," or proteins, on the surface of a host's cells. Figure 3 shows how the lock-and-key action works.

Because the lock-and-key action of a virus is highly specific, a certain virus can attach only to one or a few types of cells. For example, most cold viruses infect cells only in the nose and throat of humans. These cells are the ones with proteins on their surface that complement or "fit" those on the virus. This explains why each virus has very specific host cells that it is able to infect.

 **Reading Checkpoint** **What information does a virus's genetic material contain?**

FIGURE 3
Virus Structure and Infection

All viruses consist of genetic material surrounded by a protein coat. Some viruses, like the ones shown here, are surrounded by an outer membrane envelope. A virus can attach to a cell only if the virus' surface proteins can fit those on the cell.

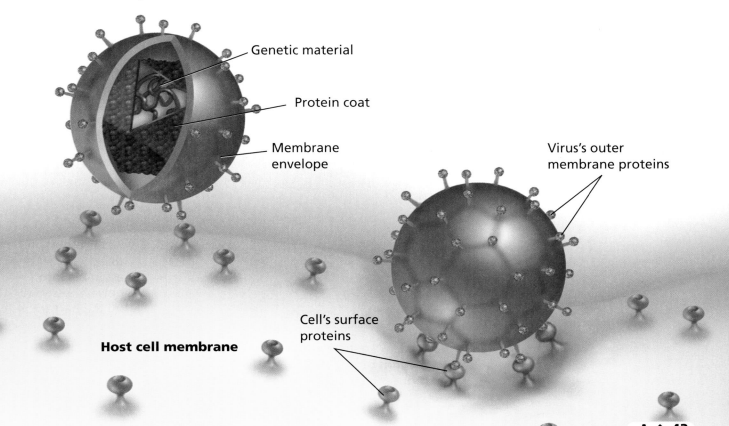

Virus particle

Genetic material

Protein coat

Membrane envelope

Virus's outer membrane proteins

Cell's surface proteins

Host cell membrane

How Viruses Multiply

After a virus attaches to a host cell, it enters the cell. **Once inside a cell, a virus's genetic material takes over many of the cell's functions. It instructs the cell to produce the virus's proteins and genetic material. These proteins and genetic material then assemble into new viruses.** Some viruses take over cell functions immediately. Other viruses wait for a while.

Active Viruses After entering a cell, an active virus immediately goes into action. The virus's genetic material takes over cell functions, and the cell quickly begins to produce the virus's proteins and genetic material. Then these parts assemble into new viruses. Like a photocopy machine left in the "on" position, the invaded cell makes copy after copy of new viruses. When it is full of new viruses, the host cell bursts open, releasing hundreds of new viruses as it dies.

FIGURE 4
Active and Hidden Viruses
Active viruses enter cells and immediately begin to multiply, leading to the quick death of the invaded cells. Hidden viruses "hide" for a while inside host cells before becoming active.

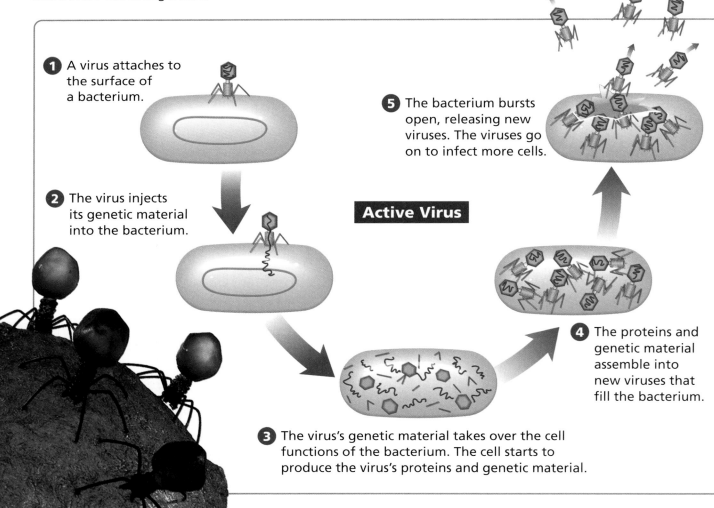

1 A virus attaches to the surface of a bacterium.

2 The virus injects its genetic material into the bacterium.

Active Virus

3 The virus's genetic material takes over the cell functions of the bacterium. The cell starts to produce the virus's proteins and genetic material.

4 The proteins and genetic material assemble into new viruses that fill the bacterium.

5 The bacterium bursts open, releasing new viruses. The viruses go on to infect more cells.

Hidden Viruses Other viruses do not immediately become active. Instead, they "hide" for a while. After a hidden virus enters a host cell, its genetic material becomes part of the cell's genetic material. The virus does not appear to affect the cell's functions and may stay in this inactive state for years. Each time the host cell divides, the virus's genetic material is copied along with the host's genetic material. Then, under certain conditions, the virus's genetic material suddenly becomes active. It takes over the cell's functions in much the same way that active viruses do. Soon, the cell is full of new viruses and bursts open.

The virus that causes cold sores is an example of a hidden virus. It can remain inactive for months or years inside nerve cells in the face. While hidden, the virus causes no symptoms. When it becomes active, the virus causes a swollen, painful sore to form near the mouth. Strong sunlight and stress are two factors that scientists believe may activate a cold sore virus. After an active period, the virus once again "hides" in the nerve cells until it becomes active again.

 **Reading Checkpoint** **Where in a host cell does a hidden virus "hide" while it is inactive?**

Go **O**nline
active art

For: Active and Hidden Viruses activity
Visit: PHSchool.com
Web Code: cep-1021

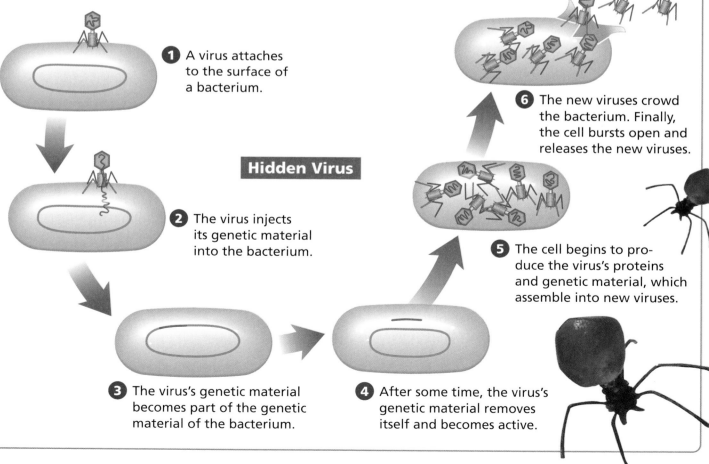

1 A virus attaches to the surface of a bacterium.

2 The virus injects its genetic material into the bacterium.

Hidden Virus

3 The virus's genetic material becomes part of the genetic material of the bacterium.

4 After some time, the virus's genetic material removes itself and becomes active.

5 The cell begins to produce the virus's proteins and genetic material, which assemble into new viruses.

6 The new viruses crowd the bacterium. Finally, the cell bursts open and releases the new viruses.

Viruses and the Living World

If you've ever had a cold sore or been sick with a cold or the flu, you know that viruses can cause disease. However, you might be surprised to learn that viruses can also be put to good use.

Viruses and Disease Some viral diseases, such as colds, are mild—people are sick for a short time but soon recover. Other viral diseases, such as acquired immunodeficiency syndrome, or AIDS, have much more serious effects on the body.

Viruses also cause diseases in organisms other than humans. For example, apple trees infected by the apple mosaic virus may produce less fruit. House pets, such as dogs and cats, can get deadly viral diseases, such as rabies and distemper.

Usefulness of Viruses The news about viruses isn't all bad. In a technique called gene therapy, scientists take advantage of a virus's ability to enter a host cell. They add genetic material to a virus and then use the virus as a "messenger service" to deliver the genetic material to cells that need it.

Gene therapy shows some promise as a medical treatment for disorders such as cystic fibrosis (SIS tik fy BRO sis). People with cystic fibrosis lack the genetic material they need to keep their lungs functioning properly. Gene therapy delivers the needed genetic material to their lung cells.

FIGURE 5
Viruses and Disease
Veterinarians can give pets injections that protect the animals against many viral diseases.

 **Reading Checkpoint** How is a virus's ability to get inside a host cell useful to scientists?

Section 1 Assessment

Target Reading Skill Sequencing Refer to your flowcharts about how viruses multiply as you answer Question 3.

Reviewing Key Concepts

1. **a. Defining** What is a virus?
   b. Comparing and Contrasting How are viruses similar to organisms? How are they different?
   c. Inferring Scientists hypothesize that viruses could not have existed on Earth before organisms appeared. Use what you know about viruses to support this hypothesis.

2. **a. Identifying** What basic structure do all viruses share?
   b. Relating Cause and Effect What role do the proteins in a virus's outer coat play in the invasion of a host cell?

3. **a. Reviewing** Trace the steps by which an active virus multiplies, from when it first enters a host to when the host cell bursts open.
   b. Sequencing List the additional steps that occur when a hidden virus multiplies.
   c. Classifying Do you think that the influenza virus is an active virus or a hidden virus? Explain your reasoning.

Math Practice

Diameter Measure the diameter of a dime. Then, find a round object that you predict might have a diameter that is ten times the size of a dime. Measure the diameter of the object. How close was your prediction?

How Many Viruses Fit on a Pin?

Problem

How can a model help you understand how small viruses are?

Skills Focus

calculating, making models

Materials

- straight pin • long strips of paper • pencil
- meter stick • scissors • tape
- calculator (optional)

Procedure

1. Examine the head of a straight pin. Write a prediction about the number of viruses that could fit on the pinhead. **CAUTION:** *Avoid pushing the pin against anyone's skin.*

2. Assume that the pinhead has a diameter of about 1 mm. If the pinhead were enlarged 10,000 times, then its diameter would measure 10 m. Create a model of the pinhead by cutting and taping together narrow strips of paper to make a strip that is 10 m long. The strip of paper represents the diameter of the enlarged pinhead.

3. Lay the 10-m strip of paper on the floor of your classroom or in the hall. Imagine creating a large circle that had the strip as its diameter. The circle would be the pinhead at the enlarged size. Calculate the area of the enlarged pinhead using this formula:

   Area $= \pi \times$ radius^2

   Remember that you can find the radius by dividing the diameter by 2.

4. A virus particle may measure 200 nm on each side (1 nm equals a billionth of a meter). If the virus were enlarged 10,000 times, each side would measure 0.002 m. Cut out a square 0.002 m by 0.002 m to serve as a model for a virus. (*Hint:* 0.002 m = 2 mm.)

5. Next, find the area in meters of one virus particle at the enlarged size. Remember that the area of a square equals side × side.

6. Now divide the area of the pinhead that you calculated in Step 3 by the area of one virus particle to find out how many viruses could fit on the pinhead.

7. Exchange your work with a partner, and check each other's calculations.

Analyze and Conclude

1. **Calculating** Approximately how many viruses can fit on the head of a pin?

2. **Predicting** How does your calculation compare with the prediction you made? If the two numbers are very different, explain why your prediction may have been inaccurate.

3. **Making Models** What did you learn about the size of viruses by magnifying both the viruses and pinhead to 10,000 times their actual size?

4. **Communicating** In a paragraph, explain why scientists sometimes make and use enlarged models of very small things such as viruses.

More to Explore

Think of another everyday object that you could use to model some other facts about viruses, such as their shapes or how they infect cells. Describe your model and explain why the object would be a good choice.

These papilloma viruses, ▶ which cause warts, are about 50 nm in diameter.

Reading Preview

Key Concepts
- How do the cells of bacteria differ from those of eukaryotes?
- What do bacteria need to survive?
- Under what conditions do bacteria thrive and reproduce?
- What positive roles do bacteria play in people's lives?

Key Terms
- bacteria • cytoplasm
- ribosome • flagellum
- respiration • binary fission
- asexual reproduction
- sexual reproduction
- conjugation • endospore
- pasteurization • decomposer

Target Reading Skill
Building Vocabulary A definition states the meaning of a word or phrase by telling about its most important feature or function. After you read the section, reread the paragraphs that contain definitions of Key Terms. Use all the information you have learned to write a definition of each Key Term in your own words.

Lab zone Discover **Activity**

How Quickly Can Bacteria Multiply?

1. Your teacher will give you some beans and paper cups. Number the cups 1 through 8. Each bean will represent a bacterial cell.
2. Put one bean into cup 1 to represent the first generation of bacteria. Approximately every 20 minutes, a bacterial cell reproduces by dividing into two cells. Put two beans into cup 2 to represent the second generation of bacteria.
3. Calculate how many bacterial cells there would be in the third generation if each cell in cup 2 divided into two cells. Place the correct number of beans in cup 3.
4. Repeat Step 3 five more times. All the cups should now contain beans. How many cells are in the eighth generation? How much time has elapsed since the first generation?

Think It Over

Inferring Based on this activity, explain why the number of bacteria can increase rapidly in a short period of time.

They thrive in your container of yogurt. They lurk in your kitchen sponge. They coat your skin and swarm inside your nose. You cannot escape them because they live almost everywhere—under rocks, in the ocean, and all over your body. In fact, there are more of these organisms in your mouth than there are people on Earth! You don't notice them because they are very small. These organisms are bacteria.

The Bacterial Cell

Although there are billions of bacteria on Earth, they were not discovered until the late 1600s. A Dutch merchant named Anton van Leeuwenhoek (LAY vun hook) found them by accident. Leeuwenhoek made microscopes as a hobby. One day, while using one of his microscopes to look at scrapings from his teeth, he saw some tiny, wormlike organisms in the sample. However, Leeuwenhoek's microscopes were not powerful enough to see any details inside these organisms.

Cell Structures If Leeuwenhoek had owned one of the high-powered microscopes in use today, he would have seen the single-celled organisms known as **bacteria** (singular *bacterium*) in detail. **Bacteria are prokaryotes. The genetic material in their cells is not contained in a nucleus.** In addition to lacking a nucleus, the cells of bacteria also lack many other structures that are found in the cells of eukaryotes.

Most bacterial cells are surrounded by a rigid cell wall that protects the cell. Just inside the cell wall is the cell membrane, which controls what materials pass into and out of the cell. The region inside the cell membrane, called the **cytoplasm** (SY toh plaz um), contains a gel-like material. Located in the cytoplasm are tiny structures called **ribosomes** (RY buh sohmz), chemical factories where proteins are produced. The cell's genetic material, which looks like a tangled string, is also found in the cytoplasm. If you could untangle the genetic material, you would see that it forms a circular shape. The genetic material contains the instructions for all of the cell's functions.

A bacterial cell may also have a **flagellum** (fluh JEL um) (plural *flagella*), a long, whiplike structure that helps a cell to move. A flagellum moves the cell by spinning in place like a propeller. A bacterial cell can have many flagella, one, or none. Most bacteria that do not have flagella cannot move on their own. Instead, they are carried from place to place by the air, water currents, objects, or other methods.

Go Online
PHSchool.com

For: More on bacteria
Visit: PHSchool.com
Web Code: ced-1022

FIGURE 6
Bacterial Cell Structures
This model shows the structures found in a typical bacterial cell.
Relating Diagrams and Photos
What structures does the Salmonella *bacterium in the photograph use to move?*

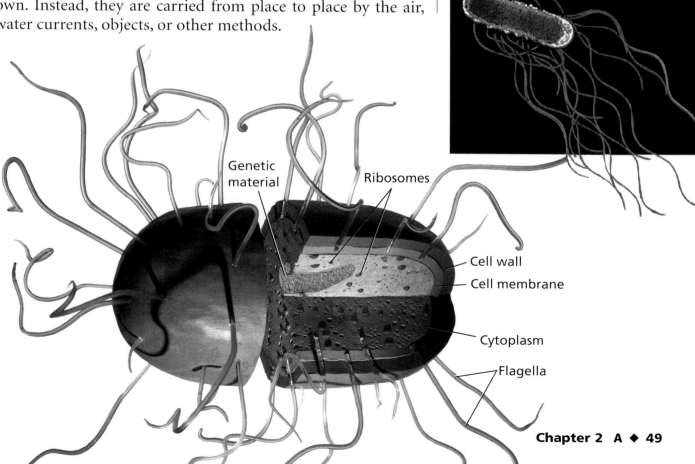

Genetic material

Ribosomes

Cell wall

Cell membrane

Cytoplasm

Flagella

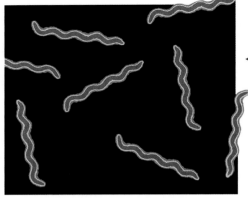

◀ *Borrelia burgdorferi* bacteria, which cause Lyme disease, are spiral-shaped.

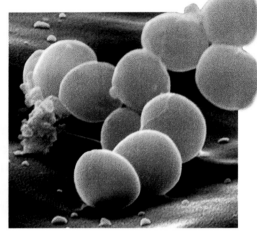

FIGURE 7
Bacterial Cell Shapes
Most bacteria have one of three basic shapes.

Escherichia coli bacteria ▶ have rodlike shapes. These bacteria are found in your intestines.

▲ These *Staphylococcus aureus*, found on human skin, are spherical.

Lab zone ▶ Try This **Activity**

Bacteria for Breakfast
In this activity, you will observe helpful bacteria in a common food.

1. Put on your apron. Add water to plain yogurt to make a thin mixture.
2. With a plastic dropper, place a drop of the mixture on a glass slide.
3. Use another plastic dropper to add one drop of methylene blue dye to the slide. **CAUTION:** *This dye can stain your skin.*
4. 🧤 Put a coverslip on the slide.
5. Observe the slide under both the low- and high-power lenses of a microscope.

Observing Draw a diagram of what you see under high power. Label any cell structures that you see.

Cell Shapes If you were to look at bacteria under a microscope, you would notice that most bacterial cells have one of three basic shapes: spherical, rodlike, or spiral. Figure 7 shows these different shapes. It is the chemical makeup of the cell wall that determines the shape of a bacterial cell. The shape of the cell helps scientists identify the type of bacteria. For example, bacteria that cause strep throat are spherical.

Cell Sizes Bacteria vary greatly in size. The largest known bacterium is about as big as the period at the end of this sentence. An average bacterium, however, is much smaller. For example, strep throat bacteria are about 0.5 to 1 micrometer in diameter. A micrometer is one millionth of a meter.

Obtaining Food and Energy
From the bacteria that live in soil to those that live in the pores of your skin, all bacteria need certain things to survive. **Bacteria must have a source of food and a way of breaking down the food to release its energy.**

Obtaining Food Some bacteria are autotrophs and make their own food. Autotrophic bacteria make food in one of two ways. Some capture and use the sun's energy as plants do. Others, such as bacteria that live deep in mud, do not use the sun's energy. Instead, these bacteria use the energy from chemical substances in their environment to make their food.

Some bacteria are heterotrophs and cannot make their own food. Instead, heterotrophic bacteria must consume other organisms or the food that other organisms make. Heterotrophic bacteria may consume a variety of foods—from milk and meat, which you might also eat, to the decaying leaves on a forest floor.

Respiration Like all organisms, bacteria need a constant supply of energy to carry out their functions. This energy comes from food. The process of breaking down food to release its energy is called **respiration.** Like many other organisms, most bacteria need oxygen to break down their food. But a few kinds of bacteria do not need oxygen for respiration. In fact, those bacteria die if oxygen is present in their surroundings. For them, oxygen is a poison that kills!

✓ **Reading Checkpoint** What are the two ways that autotrophic bacteria can make food?

FIGURE 8
Obtaining Food

Bacteria can obtain food in several ways. **Comparing and Contrasting** *How do autotrophs and heterotrophs differ in the way they obtain food?*

◀ These autotrophic bacteria, which live in hot springs, use chemical energy from their environment to make food.

These heterotrophic ▶ bacteria, found in yogurt, break down the sugars in milk for food.

The autotrophic bacteria ▶ that cause the green, cloudy scum in this pond use the sun's energy to make food.

Reproduction

Under the right conditions, the number of bacteria can increase quite quickly. **When bacteria have plenty of food, the right temperature, and other suitable conditions, they thrive and reproduce frequently.** Under these ideal conditions, some bacteria can reproduce as often as once every 20 minutes. It's a good thing that growing conditions for bacteria are rarely ideal. Otherwise, there would soon be no room on Earth for other organisms!

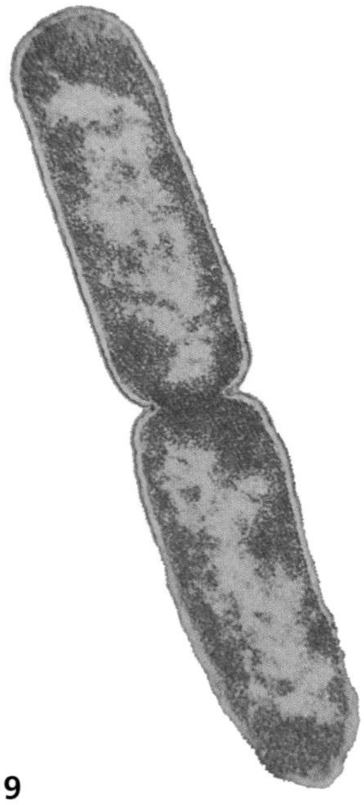

Asexual Reproduction Bacteria reproduce by a process called **binary fission,** in which one cell divides to form two identical cells. Binary fission is a form of asexual reproduction. **Asexual reproduction** is a reproductive process that involves only one parent and produces offspring that are identical to the parent. During binary fission, a cell first duplicates its genetic material and then divides into two separate cells. Each new cell gets its own complete copy of the parent cell's genetic material as well as some of the parent's ribosomes and cytoplasm.

Sexual Reproduction Some bacteria may at times undergo a simple form of sexual reproduction. **Sexual reproduction** involves two parents who combine their genetic material to produce a new organism, which differs from both parents. During a process called **conjugation** (kahn juh GAY shun), one bacterium transfers some of its genetic material into another bacterium through a thin, threadlike bridge that joins the two cells. After the transfer, the cells separate. Conjugation, shown in Figure 10, results in bacteria with new combinations of genetic material. When these bacteria divide by binary fission, the new genetic material passes to the new cells. Conjugation does not increase the number of bacteria. However, it does result in new bacteria that are genetically different from the parent cells.

FIGURE 9
Asexual Reproduction
Bacteria such as *Escherichia coli* reproduce by binary fission. Each new cell is identical to the parent cell.

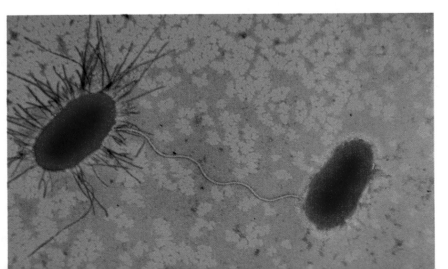

FIGURE 10
Sexual Reproduction
During conjugation, one bacterium transfers some of its genetic material into another bacterium.
Observing *What structure allows the cells to transfer genetic material?*

Population Explosion

Suppose a bacterium reproduces by binary fission every 20 minutes. The new cells survive and reproduce at the same rate. This graph shows how the bacterial population would grow from a single bacterium.

1. **Reading Graphs** What variable is being plotted on the horizontal axis? What is being plotted on the vertical axis?

2. **Interpreting Data** According to the graph, how many cells are there after 20 minutes? 1 hour? 2 hours?

3. **Drawing Conclusions** Describe the pattern you see in the way the bacterial population increases over 2 hours.

4. **Predicting** Do you think the bacterial population would continue to grow at the same rate? Why or why not?

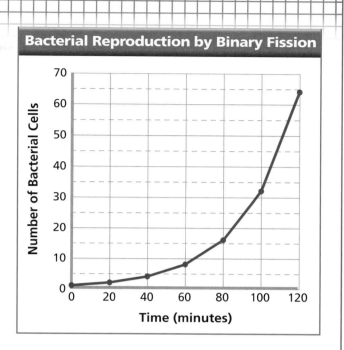

Bacterial Reproduction by Binary Fission

Endospore Formation Sometimes, conditions in the environment become unfavorable for the growth of bacteria. For example, food sources can disappear, water can dry up, or the temperature can fall or rise dramatically. Some bacteria can survive harsh conditions by forming endospores like those in Figure 11. An **endospore** is a small, rounded, thick-walled, resting cell that forms inside a bacterial cell. It contains the cell's genetic material and some of its cytoplasm.

Because endospores can resist freezing, heating, and drying, they can survive for many years. For example, the bacteria that cause botulism, *Clostridium botulinum*, produce heat-resistant endospores that can survive in improperly canned foods. Endospores are also light—a breeze can lift and carry them to new places. If an endospore lands in a place where conditions are suitable, it opens up. Then the bacterium can begin to grow and multiply.

 Under what conditions do endospores form?

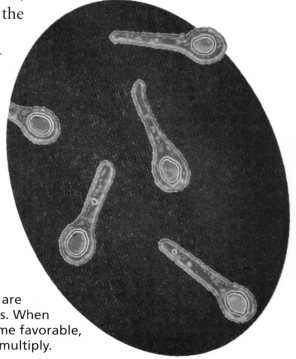

FIGURE 11
Endospore Formation
The red circles within these bacteria are endospores that can survive for years. When conditions in the environment become favorable, the bacteria can begin to grow and multiply.

The Role of Bacteria in Nature

When you hear the word *bacteria*, you may think about getting sick. After all, strep throat, many ear infections, and other diseases are caused by bacteria. However, most bacteria are either harmless or helpful to people. In fact, in many ways, people depend on bacteria. **Bacteria are involved in oxygen and food production, environmental recycling and cleanup, and in health maintenance and medicine production.**

Oxygen Production Would it surprise you to learn that the air you breathe depends in part on bacteria? As autotrophic bacteria use the sun's energy to produce food, they also release oxygen into the air. As you learned in Chapter 1, there was little oxygen in Earth's atmosphere billions of years ago. Scientists think that autotrophic bacteria were responsible for first adding oxygen to Earth's atmosphere. Today, the distant offspring of those bacteria help keep oxygen levels in the air stable.

Science and **History**

Bacteria and Foods of the World

Ancient cultures lacked refrigeration and other modern methods of preventing food spoilage. People in these cultures developed ways of using bacteria to preserve foods. You may enjoy some of these foods today.

2300 B.C. Cheese
Ancient Egyptians made cheese from milk. Cheese-making begins when bacteria feed on the sugars in milk. The milk separates into solid curds and liquid whey. The curds are processed into cheeses, which keep longer than milk.

1000 B.C. Pickled Vegetables
The Chinese salted vegetables and packed them in containers. Naturally occurring bacteria fed on the vegetables and produced a sour taste. The salt pulled water out of the vegetables and left them crisp. These vegetables were part of the food rations given to workers who built the Great Wall of China.

500 B.C. Dried Meat
People who lived in the regions around the Mediterranean Sea chopped meat, seasoned it with salt and spices, rolled it, and hung it to dry. Bacteria in the drying meat gave unique flavors to the food. The rolled meat would keep for weeks in cool places.

2500 B.C.	1500 B.C.	500 B.C.

Food Production Do you like cheese, sauerkraut, or pickles? The activities of helpful bacteria produce all of these foods and more. For example, bacteria that grow in apple cider change the cider to vinegar. Bacteria that grow in milk produce dairy products such as buttermilk, yogurt, sour cream, and cheeses.

However, some bacteria cause food to spoil when they break down the food's chemicals. Spoiled food usually smells or tastes foul and can make you very sick. Refrigerating and heating foods are two ways to slow down food spoilage. Another method, called pasteurization, is most often used to treat beverages such as milk and juice. During **pasteurization,** the food is heated to a temperature that is high enough to kill most harmful bacteria without changing the taste of the food. As you might have guessed, this process was named after Louis Pasteur, its inventor.

Writing in Science

Research and Write Find out more about one of these ancient food-production methods and the culture that developed it. Write a report about the importance of the food to the culture.

A.D. 500
Soy Sauce
People in China crushed soybeans into mixtures of wheat, salt, bacteria, and other microorganisms. The microorganisms fed on the proteins in the wheat and soybeans. The salt pulled water out of the mixture. The protein-rich soy paste that remained was used to flavor foods. The soy sauce you may use today is made in a similar manner.

A.D. 1500
Chocolate Beverage
People in the West Indies mixed beans from the cocoa plant with bacteria and other microorganisms and then dried and roasted them. The roasted beans were then brewed to produce a beverage with a chocolate flavor. The drink was served cold with honey, spices, and vanilla.

A.D. 1850
Sourdough Bread
Gold prospectors in California ate sourdough bread. The *Lactobacillus sanfrancisco* bacteria gave the bread its sour taste. Each day before baking, cooks would set aside some dough that contained the bacteria to use in the next day's bread.

A.D. 500   A.D. 1500   A.D. 2500

FIGURE 12
Environmental Recycling
Decomposing bacteria are at work recycling the chemicals in these leaves. **Predicting** *What might a forest be like if there were no decomposing bacteria in the soil?*

Environmental Recycling If you recycle glass or plastic, then you have something in common with some heterotrophic bacteria. These bacteria, which live in the soil, are **decomposers**—organisms that break down large chemicals in dead organisms into small chemicals.

Decomposers are "nature's recyclers." They return basic chemicals to the environment for other living things to reuse. For example, the leaves of many trees die in autumn and drop to the ground. Decomposing bacteria spend the next months breaking down the chemicals in the dead leaves. The broken-down chemicals mix with the soil and can then be absorbed by the roots of nearby plants.

Another type of recycling bacteria, called nitrogen-fixing bacteria, help plants survive. Nitrogen-fixing bacteria live in the soil and in swellings on the roots of certain plants, such as peanut, pea, and soybean. These helpful bacteria convert nitrogen gas from the air into nitrogen products that plants need to grow. On their own, plants cannot use nitrogen present in the air. Therefore, nitrogen-fixing bacteria are vital to the plants' survival.

Environmental Cleanup Some bacteria help to clean up Earth's land and water. Can you imagine having a bowl of oil for dinner instead of soup? Well, some bacteria prefer the oil. They convert the poisonous chemicals in oil into harmless substances. Scientists have put these bacteria to work cleaning up oil spills in oceans and gasoline leaks in the soil under gas stations.

 **Reading Checkpoint** What role do bacterial decomposers play in the environment?

FIGURE 13
Environmental Cleanup
Scientists use bacteria such as these *Ochrobactrum anthropi* to help clean up oil spills.

Health and Medicine Did you know that many of the bacteria living in your body actually keep you healthy? In your digestive system, for example, your intestines teem with bacteria. Some help you digest your food. Some make vitamins that your body needs. Others compete for space with disease-causing organisms, preventing the harmful bacteria from attaching to your intestines and making you sick.

Scientists have put some bacteria to work making medicines and other substances. The first medicine-producing bacteria were made in the 1970s. By manipulating the bacteria's genetic material, scientists engineered bacteria to produce human insulin. Although healthy people can make their own insulin, those with some types of diabetes cannot. Many people with diabetes need to take insulin daily. Thanks to bacteria's fast rate of reproduction, large numbers of insulin-making bacteria can be grown in huge vats. The human insulin they produce is then purified and made into medicine.

FIGURE 14
Bacteria and Digestion
Bacteria living naturally in your intestines help you digest food.

Section 2 Assessment

Target Reading Skill Building Vocabulary
Use your definitions to help answer the questions below.

Reviewing Key Concepts

1. a. Reviewing Where is the genetic material located in a bacterial cell?
   b. Summarizing What is the role of each of these structures in a bacterial cell: cell wall, cell membrane, ribosomes, flagellum?
2. a. Listing What are the three ways in which bacteria obtain food?
   b. Describing How do bacteria obtain energy to carry out their functions?
   c. Inferring You have just discovered a new bacterium that lives inside sealed cans of food. How do you think these bacteria obtain food and energy?
3. a. Defining What is binary fission?
   b. Explaining Under what conditions do bacteria thrive and reproduce frequently by binary fission?

   c. Inferring Why might bacteria that undergo conjugation be better able to survive when conditions become less than ideal?
4. a. Listing A friend states that all bacteria are harmful to people. List three reasons why this statement is inaccurate.
   b. Applying Concepts In what ways might bacteria contribute to the success of a garden in which pea plants are growing?

Lab zone At-Home **Activity**

Edible Bacteria With a family member, look around your kitchen for foods that are made using bacteria. Read the food labels to see if bacteria is mentioned in the food's production. Discuss with your family member the helpful roles that bacteria play in people's lives.

Comparing Disinfectants

Problem

How well do disinfectants control the growth of bacteria?

Skills Focus

observing, controlling variables

Materials

- clock
- wax pencil
- 2 plastic droppers
- transparent tape
- 2 household disinfectants
- 3 plastic petri dishes with sterile nutrient agar

Procedure

1. Copy the data table into your notebook.

2. Work with a partner. Obtain 3 petri dishes containing sterile nutrient agar. Without opening them, use a wax pencil to label the bottoms A, B, and C. Write your initials on each plate.

3. Wash your hands thoroughly with soap, and then run a fingertip across the surface of your worktable. Your partner should hold open the cover of petri dish A, while you run that fingertip gently across the agar in a zig-zag motion. Close the dish immediately.

4. Repeat Step 3 for dishes B and C.

5. Use a plastic dropper to transfer 2 drops of one disinfectant to the center of petri dish A. Open the cover just long enough to add the disinfectant to the dish. Close the cover immediately. Record the name of the disinfectant in your data table. **CAUTION:** *Do not inhale vapors from the disinfectant.*

6. Repeat Step 5 for dish B but add 2 drops of the other disinfectant. **CAUTION:** *Do not mix any disinfectants together.*

7. Do not add any disinfectant to dish C.

8. Tape down the covers of all 3 petri dishes so that they will remain tightly closed. Allow the 3 dishes to sit upright on your work surface for at least 5 minutes. **CAUTION:** *Do not open the petri dishes again. Wash your hands with soap and water.*

9. As directed by your teacher, store the petri dishes in a warm, dark place where they can remain for at least 3 days. Remove them only to make a brief examination each day.

10. After one day, observe the contents of each dish without removing the covers. Estimate the percentage of the agar surface that shows any changes. Record your observations. Return the dishes to their storage place when you have finished making your observations. Wash your hands with soap.

Data Table				
Petri Dish	Disinfectant	Day 1	Day 2	Day 3
A				
B				
C				

11. Repeat Step 10 after the second day and again after the third day.

12. After you and your partner have made your last observations, return the petri dishes to your teacher unopened.

Analyze and Conclude

1. **Observing** How did the appearance of dish C change during the lab?

2. **Comparing and Contrasting** How did the appearance of dishes A and B compare with dish C?

3. **Drawing Conclusions** How did the appearance of dishes A and B compare with each other? What can you conclude about the two disinfectants from your observations?

4. **Controlling Variables** Why was it important to set aside one petri dish that did not contain any disinfectant?

5. **Communicating** Based on the results of this lab, what recommendation would you make to your family about the use of disinfectants? Explain where in the house these products would be needed most and why.

Design an Experiment

Go to a store and look at soap products that claim to be "antibacterial" soaps. How do their ingredients differ from other soaps? Design an experiment to test how well these products control the growth of bacteria. *Obtain your teacher's permission before carrying out your investigation.*

Viruses, Bacteria, and Your Health

Reading Preview

Key Concepts
- How do infectious diseases spread?
- What treatments are effective for bacterial and viral diseases?
- How can you protect yourself against infectious diseases?

Key Terms
- infectious disease
- toxin
- antibiotic
- antibiotic resistance
- vaccine

Target Reading Skill

Using Prior Knowledge Look at the section headings and visuals to see what this section is about. Then write what you already know about diseases caused by viruses and bacteria in a graphic organizer like the one below. As you read, write what you learn.

What You Know
1. You can catch a cold from somebody who has one.
2.

What You Learned
1.
2.

Lab zone Discover **Activity**

How Can You Become "Infected"?

1. Put on goggles and plastic gloves. Your teacher will give you a plastic dropper and a plastic cup half filled with a liquid. Do not taste, smell, or touch the liquid.
2. Your teacher will signal the start of a "talking" period. Choose a classmate to talk with briefly. As you talk, exchange a dropperful of the liquid in your cup with your classmate.
3. At your teacher's signal, talk to another classmate. Exchange a dropperful of liquid.
4. Repeat Step 3 two more times.
5. Your teacher will add a few drops of a liquid to each student's cup. If your fluid turns pink, it indicates that you have "contracted a disease" from one of your classmates. Wash your hands when you have finished the activity.

Think It Over

Predicting How many more rounds would it take for everyone in your class to "become infected"? Why do you think some diseases can spread quickly through a population?

One day you're feeling fine. The next day, you're achy, sneezy, and can hardly get out of bed. You've caught a cold—or more accurately, a cold has caught you!

How Infectious Diseases Spread

Have you ever wondered how you "catch" a cold, strep throat, or the chickenpox? These and many other diseases are called **infectious diseases**—illnesses that pass from one organism to another. **Infectious diseases can spread through contact with an infected person, a contaminated object, an infected animal, or an environmental source.** Once contact occurs, disease-causing agents, such as viruses and bacteria, may enter a person through breaks in the skin, or they may be inhaled or swallowed. Others may enter the body through the moist linings of the eyes, ears, nose, mouth, or other body openings.

Contact With an Infected Person Direct contact such as touching, hugging, or kissing an infected person can spread some infectious diseases. For example, kissing an infected person can transmit cold sores. Contact can also occur indirectly. A common form of indirect contact is inhaling the tiny drops of moisture that an infected person sneezes or coughs into the air. These drops of moisture may contain disease-causing organisms, such as flu or cold viruses.

Contact With a Contaminated Object Certain viruses and bacteria can survive for a while outside a person's body. They can be spread via objects such as eating utensils. For example, drinking from a cup used by an infected person can spread diseases such as strep throat and mononucleosis. If you touch an object that an infected person has sneezed or coughed on, you may transfer some viruses or bacteria to yourself if you then touch your mouth or eyes. You may also get sick if you drink water or eat food that an infected person has contaminated.

Contact With an Infected Animal Animal bites can transmit some serious infectious diseases to humans. For example, the deadly disease rabies can be transferred through the bite of an infected dog, raccoon, or some other animals. Tick bites can transmit the bacteria that cause Lyme disease. Mosquito bites can spread the virus that causes encephalitis, a serious disease in which the brain tissues swell.

Contact With Environmental Sources Certain viruses and bacteria live naturally in food, soil, and water. These places can be environmental sources of disease. For example, poultry, eggs, and meat often contain salmonella bacteria. Eating foods that contain these bacteria can lead to one type of food poisoning. Cooking the foods thoroughly kills the bacteria. *Clostridium tetani,* a soil-dwelling bacterium, can enter a person's body through a wound. It produces a **toxin,** or poison, that causes the deadly disease tetanus.

 **Reading Checkpoint** **What is one way you can prevent the spread of infectious diseases?**

FIGURE 15
How Infectious Diseases Spread
Infectious diseases spread by contact with infected or contaminated sources.

▲ Sneezing releases disease-causing organisms into the air.

Sharing of ▶ contaminated objects can transfer organisms.

The bite of a ▶ *Culex nigripalpus* mosquito can transmit the virus that causes encephalitis.

▲ Raw eggs may contain salmonella bacteria that cause food poisoning.

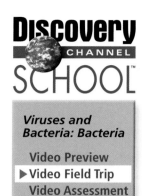

Treating Infectious Diseases

There are thousands of infectious diseases, many of which are caused by bacteria and viruses. Others are caused by protists and fungi, which you will learn about in Chapter 3.

It's likely that at one point or another, you will come in contact with an infectious disease. Once you start to have symptoms of an infectious disease, your attention probably quickly turns to helping yourself feel better.

Bacterial Diseases **Fortunately, many bacterial diseases can be cured with medications known as antibiotics.** An **antibiotic** is a chemical that can kill bacteria without harming a person's cells. Antibiotics are made naturally by some bacteria and fungi. Today, antibiotics such as penicillin are made in large quantities in factories. Penicillin works by weakening the cell walls of some bacteria and causing the cells to burst.

FIGURE 16
Common Bacterial Diseases

Many common infectious diseases are caused by bacteria. Understanding how such diseases spread is useful in knowing how to prevent them.
Classifying *Which of these bacterial diseases are spread by contact with an infected person?*

LYME DISEASE

Symptoms:	Rash at site of tick bite; chills; fever; body aches; joint swelling
How It Spreads:	Bite of an infected deer tick
Treatment:	Antibiotic
Prevention:	Tuck pants into socks; wear a long-sleeved shirt.

▼ Tuberculosis bacteria

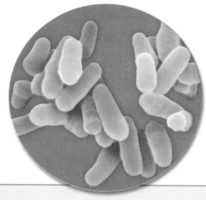

▲ **Lyme disease tick**

TUBERCULOSIS (TB)

Symptoms:	Fatigue; mild fever; weight loss; night sweats; cough
How It Spreads:	Inhaling droplets
Treatment:	Antibiotic
Prevention:	Avoid contact with people with an active infection; vaccine (for those at high risk)

If you have ever had a strep throat infection, you know that the infection makes swallowing feel like your throat is full of barbed wire. But soon after you begin taking the antibiotic that your doctor prescribes, your throat feels better. The antibiotic quickly kills the bacteria that cause strep throat.

Unfortunately, antibiotics are less effective today than they once were. Over the years, many bacteria have become resistant to antibiotics. **Antibiotic resistance** results when some bacteria are able to survive in the presence of an antibiotic.

The recent increase in tuberculosis cases demonstrates the impact of antibiotic resistance. As patients began to take antibiotics to treat tuberculosis in the 1940s, the number of tuberculosis cases dropped significantly. Unfortunately, there were always a few tuberculosis bacteria that were resistant to the antibiotics. As resistant bacteria survive and reproduce, the number of resistant bacteria increases. The number of tuberculosis cases has increased over the last 20 years. Today, antibiotic resistance is a serious problem and some bacterial diseases are becoming very difficult to treat.

Go Online

SciLINKS NSTA

For: Links on infectious diseases
Visit: www.SciLinks.org
Web Code: scn-0123

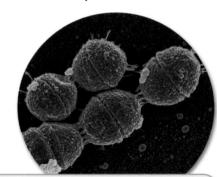

▼ **Strep throat bacteria**

TETANUS (Lockjaw)

Symptoms:	Stiff jaw and neck muscles; spasms; difficulty swallowing
How It Spreads:	Deep puncture wound
Treatment:	Antibiotic; opening and cleaning the wound
Prevention:	Vaccine

STREP THROAT

Symptoms:	Fever; sore throat; swollen glands
How It Spreads:	Inhaling droplets; contact with a contaminated object
Treatment:	Antibiotic
Prevention:	Avoid contact with infected people; do not share utensils, cups, or other objects.

FOOD POISONING

Symptoms:	Vomiting; cramps; diarrhea; fever
How It Spreads:	Eating foods containing the bacteria
Treatment:	Antitoxin medicines
Prevention:	Properly cook and store foods; avoid foods in rusted and swollen cans.

Viral Diseases Unlike with bacterial diseases, there are currently no medications that can cure viral infections. However, many over-the-counter medications can help relieve symptoms of a viral infection. These medications are available without a prescription. While over-the-counter medications can make you feel better, they can also delay your recovery if you resume your normal routine while you are still sick. They can also hide symptoms that would normally prompt you to go to a doctor.

The best treatment for viral infections is often bed rest. Resting, drinking lots of fluids, and eating well-balanced meals may be all you can do while you recover from a viral disease.

 **Reading Checkpoint** What are over-the-counter medications?

Common Viral Diseases
Although there is currently no cure for viral diseases, there are ways to treat the symptoms and prevent their transmission.

INFLUENZA (Flu)

Symptoms:	High fever; sore throat; headache; cough
How It Spreads:	Contact with contaminated objects; inhaling droplets
Treatment:	Bed rest; fluids
Prevention:	Vaccine (mainly for the high-risk ill, elderly, and young)

HEPATITIS C

Symptoms:	Oftentimes no symptoms; jaundice (yellowing of the eyes and skin); fatigue
How It Spreads:	Contact with the blood of an infected person
Treatment:	Drugs to slow viral multiplication
Prevention:	Avoid contact with infected blood.

CHICKENPOX

Symptoms:	Fever; red, itchy rash
How It Spreads:	Contact with the rash; inhaling droplets
Treatment:	Antiviral drug (for adults)
Prevention:	Vaccine

ACQUIRED IMMUNO-DEFICIENCY SYNDROME (AIDS)

Symptoms:	Weight loss; chronic fatigue; fever; diarrhea; frequent infections
How It Spreads:	Sexual contact; contact with blood; pregnancy, birth, and breastfeeding
Treatment:	Drugs to slow viral multiplication
Prevention:	Avoid contact with infected body fluids.

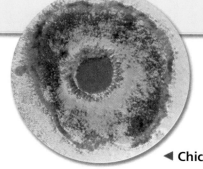
◀ Chickenpox virus

Preventing Infectious Diseases

Of course, you would probably rather not get sick in the first place. **Vaccines are important tools that help prevent the spread of infectious diseases.** A **vaccine** is a substance introduced into the body to stimulate the production of chemicals that destroy specific viruses or bacteria. A vaccine may be made from dead or altered viruses or bacteria. Because they are dead or altered, the viruses or bacteria in the vaccine do not cause disease. Instead, they activate the body's natural defenses. In effect, the vaccine puts the body "on alert." If that virus or bacterium ever invades the body, it is destroyed before it can cause disease. You may have been vaccinated against diseases such as polio, measles, tetanus, and chickenpox.

Another important way to protect against infectious diseases is to keep your body healthy. You need to eat nutritious food, as well as get enough sleep, fluids, and exercise. You can also protect yourself by washing your hands often and by not sharing eating or drinking utensils. Storing food properly, keeping kitchen equipment and surfaces clean, and cooking meats well can prevent food poisoning.

Unfortunately, despite your best efforts, you'll probably get infectious diseases, such as colds, from time to time. When you do get ill, get plenty of rest and follow your doctor's recommendations. Also, it's very important to try not to infect others.

FIGURE 18
Preventing Infectious Diseases
Hand washing is a simple yet effective way to prevent the spread of many infectious diseases. **Applying Concepts** *How else can you prevent the spread of infectious diseases?*

 **Reading Checkpoint** **Why don't vaccines cause disease themselves?**

Section 3 Assessment

Target Reading Skill **Using Prior Knowledge** Review your graphic organizer and revise it based on what you just learned in the section.

Reviewing Key Concepts

1. a. Defining What is an infectious disease?
   b. Describing What are the four ways infectious diseases can spread?
   c. Developing Hypotheses Twenty people became sick after attending a strawberry festival. Describe a scenario that could explain how the people got sick.
2. a. Reviewing What is the best treatment for bacterial diseases? For viral diseases?
   b. Relating Cause and Effect Use what you know about how antibiotics work to explain why they are ineffective against viral diseases.

3. a. Reviewing What is a vaccine?
   b. Explaining How are vaccines important in keeping your body healthy?
   c. Predicting Suppose two people catch the flu. One person has been vaccinated against the flu while the other has not. Who will recover more quickly? Why?

Writing in Science

Public Service Announcement Write a public service announcement for a radio show that teaches young children how to stay healthy and avoid diseases such as the flu. Include a list of do's and don'ts and other helpful advice.

Antibiotic Resistance— An Alarming Trend

Penicillin, the first antibiotic, became available for use in 1943. Soon antibiotics became known as the "wonder drugs." Over the years, they have reduced the occurrence of many bacterial diseases and saved millions of lives. But each time an antibiotic is used, a few resistant bacteria may survive. They pass on their resistance to the next generation of bacteria. As more patients take antibiotics, the number of resistant bacteria increases.

In 1987, penicillin killed more than 99.9 percent of a type of ear infection bacteria. By 2000, about 30 percent of these bacteria were resistant to penicillin. Diseases such as tuberculosis are on the rise due in part to growing antibiotic resistance.

The Issues

What Can Doctors Do?

Each year, more than 20 billion dollars worth of antibiotics are sold to drugstores and hospitals worldwide. More than half of antibiotic prescriptions are unnecessary. They include those written for colds and other viral illnesses, which antibiotics are ineffective against. If doctors could better identify the cause of an infection, they could avoid prescribing unnecessary antibiotics.

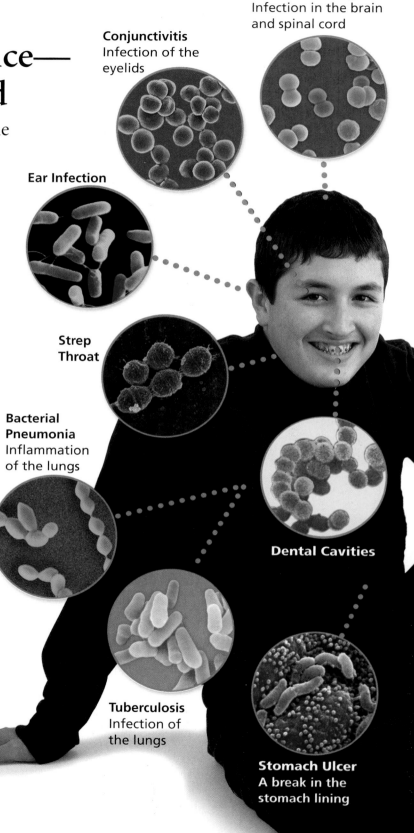

Conjunctivitis Infection of the eyelids

Bacterial Meningitis Infection in the brain and spinal cord

Ear Infection

Strep Throat

Bacterial Pneumonia Inflammation of the lungs

Dental Cavities

Tuberculosis Infection of the lungs

Stomach Ulcer A break in the stomach lining

What Can Patients Do?

If a doctor prescribes a ten-day course of antibiotics, the patient should take all of the prescription to make sure that all the bacteria have been killed. If a patient stops taking the antibiotic, resistant bacteria will survive and reproduce. Then, a second or third antibiotic may be necessary. Patients also need to learn that some illnesses are best treated with rest and not with antibiotics.

Limiting Nonmedical Uses of Antibiotics

About half of the antibiotics used each year are not given to people. Instead, the drugs are fed to food animals, such as cattle and poultry, to prevent illness and increase growth. Reducing this type of use would limit the amount of the drugs in food animals and in the people who eat them. But these actions might increase the risk of disease in animals and lead to higher meat prices.

Finding New Antibiotics

Scientists are trying to identify new antibiotics. By using new and different antibiotics, scientists hope that bacteria will not develop resistance as quickly. Scientists are also researching other ways to fight bacteria.

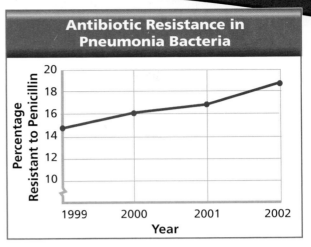

The percentage of resistant bacteria has increased steadily over the years.

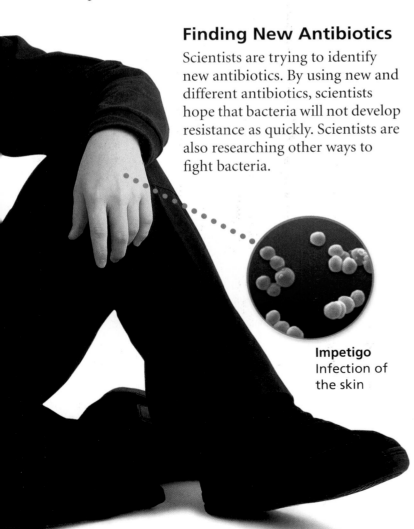

Impetigo
Infection of the skin

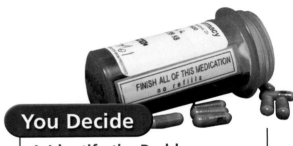

You Decide

1. Identify the Problem
How can the use of antibiotics make these medicines less effective?

2. Analyze the Options
List all the ways to fight the development of antibiotic resistance in bacteria. Mention any costs or drawbacks.

3. Find a Solution
Make a persuasive poster about one way to deal with antibiotic resistance. Support your viewpoint with sound reasons.

For: More on bacterial resistance
Visit: PHSchool.com
Web Code: ceh-1020

1 Viruses

Key Concepts

- Although viruses can multiply, they do so differently than organisms. Viruses can multiply only when they are inside a living cell.

- All viruses have two basic parts: an outer coat that protects the virus and an inner core made of genetic material.

- Once inside a cell, a virus's genetic material takes over many of the cell's functions. The genetic material instructs the cell to produce the virus's proteins and genetic material. These proteins and genetic material then assemble into new viruses.

Key Terms

virus
host
parasite
bacteriophage

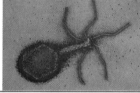

2 Bacteria

Key Concepts

- Bacteria are prokaryotes. The genetic material in their cells is not contained in a nucleus.

- Bacteria must have a source of food and a way of breaking down the food to release its energy.

- When bacteria have plenty of food, the right temperature, and other suitable conditions, they thrive and reproduce frequently.

- Bacteria are involved in oxygen and food production, environmental recycling and cleanup, and in health maintenance and medicine production.

Key Terms

bacteria	asexual reproduction
cytoplasm	sexual reproduction
ribosome	conjugation
flagellum	endospore
respiration	pasteurization
binary fission	decomposer

3 Viruses, Bacteria, and Your Health

Key Concepts

- Infectious diseases can spread through contact with an infected person, a contaminated object, an infected animal, or an environmental source.

- Fortunately, many bacterial diseases can be cured with medications known as antibiotics.

- Unlike with bacterial diseases, there are currently no medications that can cure viral infections.

- Vaccines are important tools that help prevent the spread of infectious diseases.

Key Terms

infectious disease
toxin
antibiotic
antibiotic resistance
vaccine

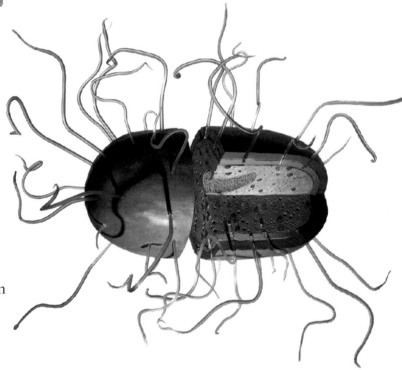

Review and Assessment

Go Online
PHSchool.com

For: Self-Assessment
Visit: PHSchool.com
Web Code: cea-1020

Organizing Information

Comparing and Contrasting Copy the Venn diagram comparing viruses and bacteria onto a separate sheet of paper. Then complete it and add a title. (For more information on Comparing and Contrasting, see the Skills Handbook.)

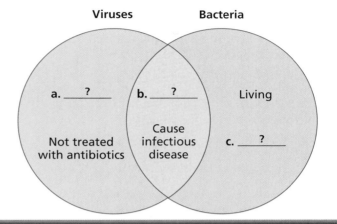

Viruses   Bacteria

a. ___?___   b. ___?___   Living

Not treated with antibiotics   Cause infectious disease   c. ___?___

Reviewing Key Terms

Choose the letter of the best answer.

1. Bacteriophages are viruses that attack and destroy
   a. other viruses. b. bacteria.
   c. plants. d. humans.

2. Which part of a virus determines which host cells it can infect?
   a. nucleus
   b. ribosomes
   c. flagellum
   d. surface proteins

3. Viruses multiply
   a. by conjugation.
   b. by binary fission.
   c. by taking over a cell's functions.
   d. both asexually and sexually.

4. Most bacteria are surrounded by a rigid protective structure called the
   a. cell wall.
   b. cell membrane.
   c. protein coat.
   d. flagellum.

5. Which of the following help prevent the spread of infectious diseases?
   a. toxins
   b. vaccines
   c. parasites
   d. endospores

If the statement is true, write *true*. If it is false, change the underlined word or words to make the statement true.

6. <u>Active viruses</u> enter a cell and immediately begin to multiply.

7. During <u>conjugation</u>, one bacterium transfers genetic material to another bacterial cell.

8. <u>Binary fission</u> is the process of breaking down food to release energy.

9. Bacteria form <u>endospores</u> to survive unfavorable conditions in their surroundings.

10. A <u>vaccine</u> is a chemical that can kill bacteria without harming a person's cells.

Writing in Science

Debate Suppose you are preparing for a debate about whether bacteria are beneficial or harmful. Select one side of the argument and write a paragraph defending your position. Be sure to give an example to support your argument.

Discovery CHANNEL SCHOOL

Viruses and Bacteria: Bacteria
Video Preview
Video Field Trip
▶ Video Assessment

Review and Assessment

Checking Concepts

11. List three ways that viruses differ from cells.

12. Explain why a certain virus will attach to only one or a few types of cells.

13. Describe how a hidden virus multiplies.

14. What are the parts of a bacterial cell? Explain the role of each part.

15. Describe how bacteria reproduce.

16. How do the bacteria that live in your intestines help you?

17. Explain how antibiotics kill bacteria.

18. How do vaccines prevent the spread of some infectious diseases?

Thinking Critically

19. **Classifying** Classify the bacteria in each photo according to their shape.

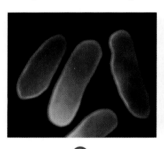 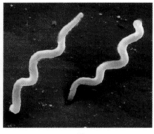

A   **B**

20. **Comparing and Contrasting** Describe the similarities and differences between active and hidden viruses.

21. **Problem Solving** Bacteria will grow in the laboratory on a gelatin-like substance called agar. Viruses will not grow on agar. If you needed to grow viruses in the laboratory, what kind of substance would you have to use? Explain your reasoning.

22. **Predicting** A friend has been prescribed a ten-day course of antibiotics for a bacterial infection. Your friend feels much better after three days and decides to stop taking the medication. What do you think might happen and why?

Math Practice

23. **Diameter** How much greater is the diameter of a penny than the diameter of a dime?

Applying Skills

Use the graph to answer Questions 24–27.

The graph shows how the number of bacteria that grow on a food source changes over time.

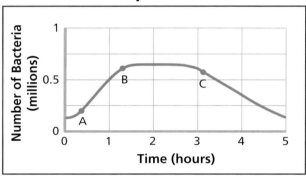

A Bacterial Population Over Time

24. **Reading Graphs** What do the numbers on the vertical axis represent?

25. **Interpreting Data** Explain what is happening between points A and B.

26. **Developing Hypotheses** Develop a hypothesis to explain why the number of bacteria appears to stay constant between points B and C.

27. **Designing Experiments** How could you test the hypothesis you developed in Question 26? What would your results show?

Lab zone Chapter **Project**

Performance Assessment Present your project to your class. Explain why you chose the questions and survey group that you did. Use graphs or other visual displays to highlight any patterns that you found. Be sure to support your conclusions with data.

Standardized Test Prep

Choose the letter of the best answer.

1. If you know that an organism is a prokaryote, you know that
   A its cell does not contain a nucleus.
   B its cell does not contain ribosomes.
   C the organism is a heterotroph.
   D the organism cannot move on its own.

2. Which of these statements about the sizes of bacteria and viruses is true?
   F Viruses can be seen with a hand lens but bacteria cannot.
   G Both bacteria and viruses can be seen with a hand lens.
   H Bacteria can be seen with a light microscope but viruses cannot.
   J Neither bacteria nor viruses can be seen with a light microscope.

3. What will most likely happen after the virus in the diagram attaches to the bacterial cell?

   A The virus will inject its proteins into the bacterial cell.
   B The virus will inject its genetic material into the bacterial cell.
   C The bacterial cell will inject its proteins into the virus.
   D The bacterial cell will inject its genetic material into the virus.

4. Which of the following statements about viruses is *not* true?
   F Viruses can multiply only inside a living cell.
   G Viruses have genetic material.
   H Virus particles are smaller than bacterial cells.
   J Diseases caused by viruses can be cured by antibiotics.

5. Paola grew a new culture of bacteria and measured the population's growth over time. The number of bacteria increased sharply over the first few hours but then tapered off. Which of the following statements about these observations is true?
   A The initial conditions for bacterial growth were favorable.
   B The number of bacteria increased as the bacteria reproduced asexually.
   C After a period of time, the bacteria started to run out of food, space, and other resources.
   D all of the above

Constructed Response

6. Compare and contrast viruses and bacteria with respect to their sizes, structures, and methods of reproduction.

Chapter 3

Protists and Fungi

Chapter Preview

interactive Textbook

These colorful starfish stinkhorn ▶ mushrooms smell like rotting meat.

Lab zone™ Chapter **Project**

A Mushroom Farm

The fungi you're most familiar with are probably mushrooms. In some ways, mushrooms resemble plants, often growing near plants or even on them like small umbrellas. But mushrooms are very different from plants in some important ways. In this chapter project, you'll learn about these differences.

Your Goal To determine the conditions needed for mushrooms to grow

To complete this project, you must

● choose one variable and design a way to test how it affects mushroom growth

● make daily observations and record them in a data table

● prepare a poster that describes the results of your experiment

● follow the safety guidelines in Appendix A

Plan It! List possible hypotheses about the way variables such as light or moisture could affect the growth of mushrooms. Choose one variable and write out a plan for testing that variable. After your teacher approves your plan, start growing your mushrooms!

Protists

Reading Preview

Key Concept
- What are the characteristics of animal-like, plantlike, and funguslike protists?

Key Terms
- protist • protozoan
- pseudopod
- contractile vacuole • cilia
- symbiosis • mutualism
- algae • pigment • spore

⟳ Target Reading Skill
Outlining As you read, make an outline about protists that you can use for review. Use the red section headings for the main topics and the blue headings for the subtopics.

Protists
I. What is a protist?
II. Animal-like protists
A. Protozoans with pseudopods
B.
C.

Lab zone Discover **Activity**

What Lives in a Drop of Pond Water?
1. Use a plastic dropper to place a drop of pond water on a microscope slide.
2. Put the slide under your microscope's low-power lens. Focus on the objects you see.
3. Find at least three different objects that you think might be organisms. Observe them for a few minutes.
4. Draw the three organisms in your notebook. Below each sketch, describe the movements or behaviors of the organism. Wash your hands thoroughly when you have finished.

Think It Over
Observing What characteristics did you observe that made you think that each organism was alive?

Look at the objects in Figure 1. What do they look like to you? Jewels? Beads? Stained glass ornaments? You might be surprised to learn that these beautiful, delicate structures are the walls of unicellular organisms called diatoms. Diatoms live in both fresh water and salt water and are an important food source for many marine organisms. They have been called the "jewels of the sea."

FIGURE 1
Diatoms
These glasslike organisms are classified as protists.

▲ These shells are the remains of unicellular, animal-like protists called foraminifera.

FIGURE 2
Protists
Protists include animal-like, plantlike, and funguslike organisms.
Comparing and Contrasting *In what ways do protists differ from one another?*

▲ This red alga is a multicellular, plantlike protist found on ocean floors.

What Is a Protist?

Diatoms are only one of the vast varieties of protists. **Protists** are eukaryotes that cannot be classified as animals, plants, or fungi. Because protists are so different from one another, you can think of them as the "odds and ends" kingdom. However, protists do share some characteristics. In addition to being eukaryotes, all protists live in moist surroundings.

The word that best describes protists is *diversity*. For example, most protists are unicellular, but some are multicellular. Some are heterotrophs, some are autotrophs, and others are both. Some protists cannot move, while others zoom around their moist surroundings.

Because of the great variety of protists, scientists have proposed several ways of grouping these organisms. One useful way of grouping protists is to divide them into three categories, based on characteristics they share with organisms in other kingdoms: animal-like protists, plantlike protists, and funguslike protists.

 **Reading Checkpoint** **In what kind of environment do all protists live?**

Animal-Like Protists

What image pops into your head when you think of an animal? A tiger chasing its prey? A snake slithering onto a rock? Most people immediately associate animals with movement. In fact, movement is often involved with an important characteristic of animals—obtaining food. All animals are heterotrophs that must obtain food by eating other organisms.

Like animals, animal-like protists are heterotrophs, and most are able to move from place to place to obtain food. But unlike animals, animal-like protists, or **protozoans** (proh tuh ZOH unz), are unicellular. Protozoans can be classified into four groups, based on the way they move and live.

▲ The yellow slime mold oozing off the leaf is a funguslike protist.

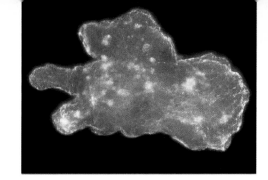

FIGURE 3
Amoeba
Amoebas are sarcodines that live in either water or soil. They feed on bacteria and smaller protists.

Pseudopod
An amoeba uses pseudopods to move and feed. Pseudopods form when cytoplasm flows toward one location and the rest of the amoeba follows.

Food Vacuole
When the ends of two pseudopods fuse, they form a food vacuole. Food is broken down inside the food vacuole in the cytoplasm.

Cytoplasm

Nucleus
The nucleus controls the cell's functions and is involved in reproduction. Amoebas usually reproduce by binary fission.

Contractile Vacuole
The contractile vacuole collects excess water from the cytoplasm and expels it from the cell.

Cell Membrane
Because the cell membrane is very thin and flexible, an amoeba's shape changes constantly.

Go Online
active art

For: Amoeba and Paramecium activity
Visit: PHSchool.com
Web Code: cep-1031

Protozoans With Pseudopods The amoeba in Figure 3 belongs to the group of protozoans called sarcodines. Sarcodines move and feed by forming **pseudopods** (SOO duh pahdz)—temporary bulges of the cell. The word *pseudopod* means "false foot." Pseudopods form when cytoplasm flows toward one location and the rest of the organism follows. Pseudopods enable sarcodines to move. For example, amoebas use pseudopods to move away from bright light. Sarcodines also use pseudopods to trap food. The organism extends a pseudopod on each side of the food particle. The two pseudopods then join together, trapping the particle inside.

Protozoans that live in fresh water, such as amoebas, have a problem. Small particles, like those of water, pass easily through the cell membrane into the cytoplasm. If excess water were to build up inside the cell, the amoeba would burst. Fortunately, amoebas have a **contractile vacuole** (kun TRAK til VAK yoo ohl), a structure that collects the extra water and then expels it from the cell.

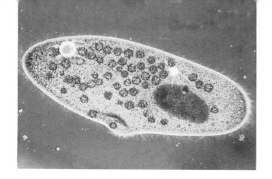

FIGURE 4
Paramecium
Paramecia are ciliates that live mostly in fresh water. Like amoebas, paramecia feed on bacteria and smaller protists.

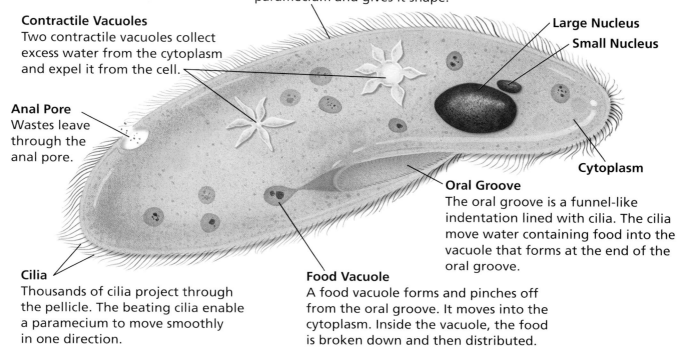

Pellicle
A stiff but flexible covering, called the pellicle, surrounds a paramecium and gives it shape.

Contractile Vacuoles
Two contractile vacuoles collect excess water from the cytoplasm and expel it from the cell.

Anal Pore
Wastes leave through the anal pore.

Large Nucleus
Small Nucleus

Cytoplasm

Oral Groove
The oral groove is a funnel-like indentation lined with cilia. The cilia move water containing food into the vacuole that forms at the end of the oral groove.

Cilia
Thousands of cilia project through the pellicle. The beating cilia enable a paramecium to move smoothly in one direction.

Food Vacuole
A food vacuole forms and pinches off from the oral groove. It moves into the cytoplasm. Inside the vacuole, the food is broken down and then distributed.

Protozoans With Cilia The second group of animal-like protists are the ciliates. Ciliates have structures called **cilia** (SIL ee uh), which are hairlike projections from cells that move with a wavelike motion. Ciliates use their cilia to move and obtain food. Cilia act something like tiny oars to move a ciliate. Their movement sweeps food into the organism.

The cells of ciliates, like the paramecium in Figure 4, are complex. Notice that the paramecium has two contractile vacuoles that expel water from the cell. It also has more than one nucleus. The large nucleus controls the everyday tasks of the cell. The small nucleus functions in reproduction.

Paramecia usually reproduce asexually by binary fission. Sometimes, however, paramecia reproduce by conjugation. This occurs when two paramecia join together and exchange some of their genetic material.

 **What are cilia?**

FIGURE 5
Giardia
When people drink from freshwater streams and lakes, they can get hiker's disease. *Giardia intestinalis* (inset) is the protozoan responsible for this disease. **Inferring** *Why is it important for hikers to filter stream water?*

Protozoans With Flagella The third group of protozoans are flagellates (FLAJ uh lits), protists that use long, whiplike flagella to move. A flagellate may have one or more flagella.

Some of these protozoans live inside the bodies of other organisms. For example, one type of flagellate lives in the intestines of termites. There, they digest the wood that the termites eat, producing sugars for themselves and for the termites. In turn, the termites protect the protozoans. The interaction between these two species is an example of **symbiosis** (sim bee OH sis)—a close relationship in which at least one of the species benefits. When both partners benefit from living together, the relationship is a type of symbiosis called **mutualism.**

Sometimes, however, a protozoan harms its host. For example, *Giardia* is a parasite in humans. Wild animals, such as beavers, deposit *Giardia* in freshwater streams, rivers, and lakes. When a person drinks water containing *Giardia*, these protozoans attach to the person's intestine, where they feed and reproduce. The person develops a serious intestinal condition commonly called hiker's disease.

Protozoans That Are Parasites The fourth type of protozoans are characterized more by the way they live than by the way they move. They are all parasites that feed on the cells and body fluids of their hosts. These protozoans move in a variety of ways. Some have flagella, and some depend on hosts for transport. One even produces a layer of slime that allows it to slide from place to place!

Many of these parasites have more than one host. For example, *Plasmodium* is a protozoan that causes malaria, a disease of the blood. Two hosts are involved in *Plasmodium's* life cycle—humans and a species of mosquitoes found in tropical areas. The disease spreads when a healthy mosquito bites a person with malaria, becomes infected, and then bites a healthy person. Symptoms of malaria include high fevers that alternate with severe chills. These symptoms can last for weeks, then disappear, only to reappear a few months later.

 **What is symbiosis?**

FIGURE 6
Malaria Mosquito
Anopheles mosquitoes can carry the parasitic protozoan *Plasmodium*, which causes malaria in people.

Plantlike Protists

Plantlike protists, which are commonly called **algae** (AL jee), are extremely diverse. **Like plants, algae are autotrophs.** Most are able to use the sun's energy to make their own food.

Algae play a significant role in many environments. For example, algae that live near the surface of ponds, lakes, and oceans are an important food source for other organisms in the water. In addition, much of the oxygen in Earth's atmosphere is made by these algae.

Algae vary greatly in size. Some algae are unicellular, while others are multicellular. Still others are groups of unicellular organisms that live together in colonies. Colonies can contain from a few cells up to thousands of cells. In a colony, most cells carry out all functions. But, some cells may become specialized to perform certain functions, such as reproduction.

Algae exist in a wide variety of colors because they contain many types of **pigments**—chemicals that produce color. Depending on their pigments, algae can be green, yellow, red, brown, orange, or even black.

Diatoms Diatoms are unicellular protists with beautiful glasslike cell walls. Some float near the surface of lakes or oceans. Others attach to objects such as rocks in shallow water. Diatoms are a food source for heterotrophs in the water. Many diatoms can move by oozing chemicals out of slits in their cell walls. They then glide in the slime.

When diatoms die, their cell walls collect on the bottoms of oceans and lakes. Over time, they form layers of a coarse substance called diatomaceous (dy uh tuh MAY shus) earth. Diatomaceous earth makes a good polishing agent and is used in household scouring products. It is even used as an insecticide—the diatoms' sharp cell walls puncture the bodies of insects.

Dinoflagellates Dinoflagellates (dy noh FLAJ uh lits) are unicellular algae surrounded by stiff plates that look like a suit of armor. Because they have different amounts of green, orange, and other pigments, dinoflagellates exist in a variety of colors.

All dinoflagellates have two flagella held in grooves between their plates. When the flagella beat, the dinoflagellates twirl like toy tops as they move through the water. Many glow in the dark. They light up the ocean's surface when disturbed by a passing boat or swimmer.

Lab zone Try This Activity

Watching Protists

In this activity you will watch the interaction between paramecium, an animal-like protist, and *Chlorella*, a plantlike protist.

1. Use a plastic dropper to place 1 drop of paramecium culture on a microscope slide. Add some cotton fibers to slow down the paramecia.

2. Use the microscope's low-power objective to find some paramecia.

3. Add 1 drop of *Chlorella* to the paramecium culture on your slide.

4. Switch to high power and locate a paramecium. Observe what happens. Then wash your hands.

Inferring What evidence do you have that paramecia are heterotrophs? That *Chlorella* are autotrophs?

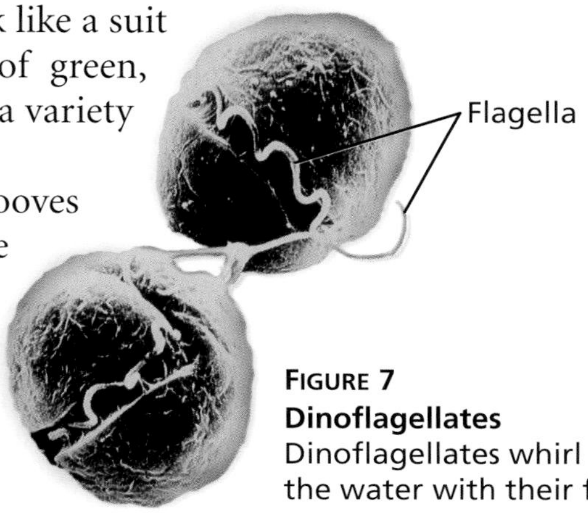

Flagella

FIGURE 7
Dinoflagellates
Dinoflagellates whirl through the water with their flagella.

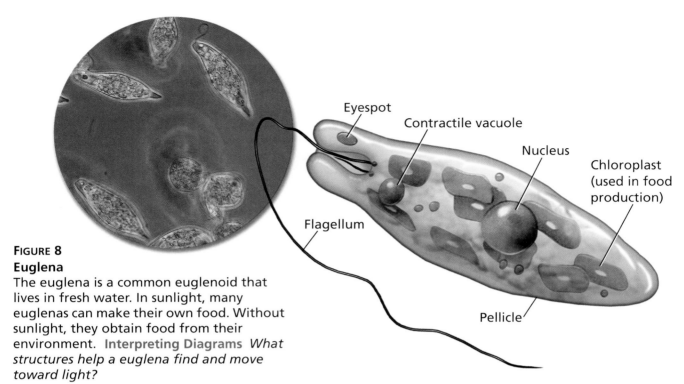

FIGURE 8
Euglena
The euglena is a common euglenoid that lives in fresh water. In sunlight, many euglenas can make their own food. Without sunlight, they obtain food from their environment. **Interpreting Diagrams** *What structures help a euglena find and move toward light?*

Labels on diagram: Eyespot, Contractile vacuole, Nucleus, Chloroplast (used in food production), Flagellum, Pellicle

Euglenoids Euglenoids (yoo GLEE noydz) are green, unicellular algae that are found mostly in fresh water. Unlike other algae, euglenoids have one animal-like characteristic—they can be heterotrophs under certain conditions. When sunlight is available, most euglenoids are autotrophs that produce their own food. However, when sunlight is not available, euglenoids will act like heterotrophs by obtaining food from their environment. Some euglenoids live entirely as heterotrophs.

In Figure 8, you see a euglena, which is a common euglenoid. Notice the long, whiplike flagellum that helps the organism move. Locate the eyespot near the flagellum. Although the eyespot is not really an eye, it contains pigments. These pigments are sensitive to light and help the euglena recognize the direction of a light source. You can imagine how important this response is to an organism that needs light to make food.

Red Algae Almost all red algae are multicellular seaweeds. Divers have found red algae growing more than 260 meters below the ocean's surface. Their red pigments are especially good at absorbing the small amount of light that is able to reach deep ocean waters.

People use red algae in a variety of ways. Carrageenan (ka ruh JEE nun) and agar, substances extracted from red algae, are used in products such as ice cream and hair conditioner. For people in many Asian cultures, red algae is a nutrient-rich food that is eaten fresh, dried, or toasted.

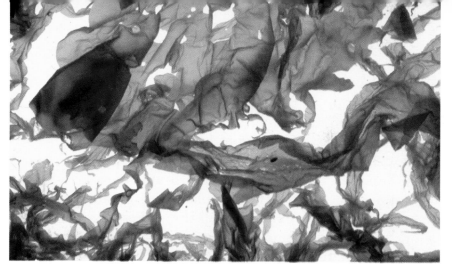

FIGURE 9
Green Algae
Green algae range in size from unicellular organisms to multicellular seaweeds. This multicellular sea lettuce, *Ulva*, lives in oceans.

Green Algae Green algae, which contain green pigments, are quite diverse. Most green algae are unicellular. Some, however, form colonies, and a few are multicellular. Most green algae live in either fresh water or salt water. The few that live on land are found on rocks, in the crevices of tree bark, or in moist soils.

Green algae are actually very closely related to plants that live on land. Green algae and plants contain the same type of green pigment and share other important similarities. In fact, some scientists think that green algae belong in the plant kingdom.

Brown Algae Many of the organisms that are commonly called seaweeds are brown algae. In addition to their brown pigment, brown algae also contain green, yellow, and orange pigments. As you can see in Figure 10, a typical brown alga has many plantlike structures. Holdfasts anchor the alga to rocks. Stalks support the blades, which are the leaflike structures of the alga. Many brown algae also have gas-filled sacs called bladders that allow the algae to float upright in the water.

Brown algae flourish in cool, rocky waters. Brown algae called rockweed live along the Atlantic coast of North America. Giant kelps, which can grow as long as 100 meters, live in some Pacific coastal waters. The giant kelps form large underwater "forests" where many organisms, including sea otters and abalone, live.

Some people eat brown algae. In addition, substances called algins are extracted from brown algae and used as thickeners in puddings and other foods.

 **Reading Checkpoint** What color pigments can brown algae contain?

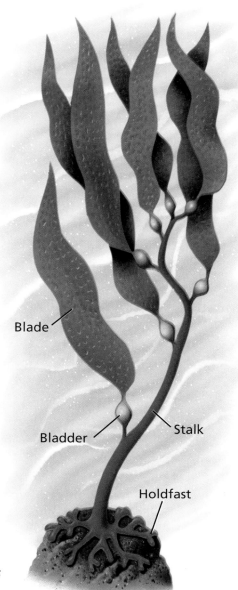

FIGURE 10
Brown Algae
Giant kelps are brown algae that have many plantlike structures.
Interpreting Diagrams *What plant structures do the kelp's holdfasts and blades resemble?*

Blade

Bladder

Stalk

Holdfast

Funguslike Protists

The third group of protists are the funguslike protists. Recall from Chapter 1 that fungi include organisms such as mushrooms and yeast. Until you learn more about fungi in Section 3, you can think of fungi as the "sort of like" organisms. Fungi are "sort of like" animals because they are heterotrophs. They are "sort of like" plants because their cells have cell walls. In addition, most fungi use spores to reproduce. A **spore** is a tiny cell that is able to grow into a new organism.

Like fungi, funguslike protists are heterotrophs, have cell walls, and use spores to reproduce. All funguslike protists are able to move at some point in their lives. The three types of funguslike protists are slime molds, water molds, and downy mildews.

Slime Molds Slime molds are often brilliantly colored. They live on forest floors and other moist, shady places. They ooze along the surfaces of decaying materials, feeding on bacteria and other microorganisms. Some slime molds are so small that you need a microscope to see them. Others may cover an area of several meters!

Slime molds begin their life cycle as tiny, individual amoeba-like cells. The cells use pseudopods to feed and creep around. Later, the cells grow bigger or join together to form a giant, jellylike mass. In some species, the giant mass is multicellular and forms when food is scarce. In others, the giant mass is actually a giant cell with many nuclei.

The mass oozes along as a single unit. When environmental conditions become harsh, spore-producing structures grow out of the mass and release spores. Eventually the spores develop into a new generation of slime molds.

FIGURE 11
Slime Molds
The chocolate tube slime mold first forms a tapioca-like mass (top). When conditions become harsh, the mass grows spore-producing stalks (right). The stalks, or "chocolate tubes," are covered with millions of brown spores.

Water Molds and Downy Mildews Most water molds and downy mildews live in water or moist places. These organisms often grow as tiny threads that look like fuzz. Figure 12 shows a fish attacked by a water mold and a leaf covered by downy mildew.

Water molds and downy mildews attack many food crops, such as potatoes, corn, and grapes. A water mold impacted history when it destroyed the Irish potato crops in 1845 and 1846. The loss of these crops led to a famine. More than one million people in Ireland died, and many others moved to the United States and other countries.

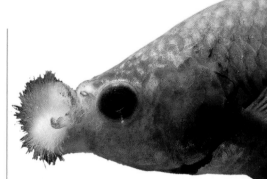

▲ **Water mold on fish**

▼ **Downy mildew on grape leaf**

 **Reading Checkpoint** In what environments are water molds found?

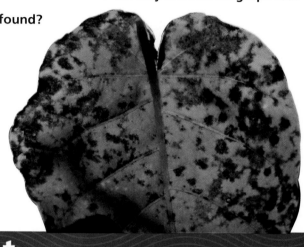

FIGURE 12
Water Molds and Downy Mildews
Many water molds are decomposers of dead aquatic organisms. Others are parasites of fish and other animals. Downy mildews are parasites of many food crops.

Section 1 Assessment

Target Reading Skill Outlining Use your outline about protists to help you answer the questions below.

Reviewing Key Concepts

1. **a.** Listing List the four types of animal-like protists. How does each type move or live?
   b. Comparing and Contrasting How are these four types of protists similar to animals? How are they different?
   c. Classifying You observe an animal-like protist under the microscope. It has no hairlike or whiplike structures. It moves by forming temporary bulges of cytoplasm. How would you classify this protist?
2. **a.** Reviewing In what way are diatoms, dinoflagellates, and other plantlike protists similar to plants?
   b. Making Generalizations Why is sunlight important to plantlike protists?
   c. Making Judgments Would you classify euglena as an animal-like protist or as a plantlike protist? Explain.
3. **a.** Listing What are the three types of funguslike protists?
   b. Describing In what ways are funguslike protists similar to fungi?

Lab zone **At-Home Activity**

Algae Scavenger Hunt Look around your house with a family member to find products that contain substances made from algae. Look at both food and nonfood items. Before you begin, tell your family member that substances such as diatomaceous earth, algin, and carrageenan are products that come from algae. Make a list of the products and the algae-based ingredient they contain. Share your list with the class.

Algal Blooms

Reading Preview

Key Concept
- What are the causes and effects of saltwater and freshwater algal blooms?

Key Terms
- algal bloom
- red tide
- eutrophication

Target Reading Skill
Comparing and Contrasting As you read, compare and contrast the two types of algal blooms in a table like the one below.

Algal Blooms

Properties	Saltwater Blooms	Freshwater Blooms
Causes	Increase in nutrients or temperature	
Effects		

Discover Activity

How Can Algal Growth Affect Pond Life?

1. Pour water into a plastic petri dish until the dish is half full. The petri dish will represent a pond.
2. Sprinkle a spoonful of green paper punches into the water to represent green algae growing in a pond.
3. Sprinkle two more spoonfuls of paper punches into the water to represent one cycle of algae reproduction.
4. Sprinkle four more spoonfuls of paper punches into the water to represent the next reproduction cycle of the algae.

Think It Over

Predicting How might algae growing near the surface affect organisms living deep in a pond?

Over a five week period one year, the bodies of 14 humpback whales washed up along beaches on Cape Cod, Massachusetts. The whales showed no outward signs of sickness. Their stomachs were full of food. Their bodies contained plenty of blubber to insulate them from changes in water temperature. What caused such seemingly healthy animals to die?

When biologists examined the dead whales' tissues, they identified the cause of the puzzling deaths. The whales' cells contained a deadly toxin produced by a dinoflagellate called *Alexandrium tamarense*. The population of these algae had grown rapidly in the ocean waters through which the whales were migrating. When the whales fed on the toxin-producing algae or on fishes that had eaten the algae, the toxins reached a deadly level and killed the whales.

Algae are common in oceans, lakes, and ponds. They float near the surface of the waters and use sunlight to make food. The rapid growth of a population of algae is called an **algal bloom.** Algal blooms can occur in both saltwater and freshwater environments. **In general, algal blooms occur when nutrients increase in the water.**

◀ **A humpback whale**

Saltwater Blooms

In Figure 13, you see an algal bloom in ocean water. Saltwater algal blooms are commonly called **red tides** because the algae that grow rapidly often contain red pigments and turn the color of the water red. But red tides do not always look red. Some red tides are brown, green, or even colorless, depending on the species of algae that blooms. Dinoflagellates and diatoms are two algae that frequently bloom in red tides.

Causes of Red Tides Scientists are not sure why some populations of saltwater algae increase rapidly at times. But red tides occur most often when there is an increase in nutrients in the water. Some red tides occur regularly in certain seasons. For example, the cold bottom layers of the ocean contain a lot of nutrients. When this cold water mixes with the surface waters, more nutrients become available to surface organisms. With greater concentrations of nutrients present in the surface waters, blooms of algae occur. Increases in ocean temperature due to climate changes also affect the occurrence of red tides.

Effects of Red Tides **Red tides are dangerous when the toxins that the algae produce become concentrated in the bodies of organisms that consume the algae.** Shellfish, such as clams and mussels, feed on large numbers of the algae and store the toxins in their cells. Fishes may also feed on the algae and store the toxins. When people or other large organisms eat these shellfish and fishes, it may lead to severe illness or even death. Public health officials close beaches in areas of red tides to prevent people from fishing or gathering shellfish.

FIGURE 13
Red Tide
Rapid algae growth has caused a red tide in this small bay off the coast of California. Blooms of toxic dinoflagellates such as *Gymnodinium* (inset) can have serious consequences.
Relating Cause and Effect *What organisms are affected by red tides?*

For: Links on algae
Visit: www.SciLinks.org
Web Code: scn-0132

 **Reading Checkpoint** **What determines the color of saltwater blooms?**

Freshwater Blooms

Have you ever seen a pond or lake that looked as if it was coated with a layer of green paint or scum? The green layer usually consists of huge numbers of green algae.

Lakes and ponds undergo natural processes of change over time. **Eutrophication**(yoo troh fih KAY shun) is a process in which nutrients, such as nitrogen and phosphorus, build up in a lake or pond over time, causing an increase in algae growth.

Causes of Eutrophication Certain natural events and human activities can increase the rate of eutrophication. For example, when farmers and homeowners spread fertilizers on fields and lawns, some of the nutrients can run off into nearby lakes and ponds. Sewage treatment plants can leak wastewater into the soil. The nutrients in the wastewater make their way from the soil into water that leads into lakes and ponds. These events cause a rapid increase in algae growth. If the nutrient sources can be eliminated and the nutrients used up, eutrophication slows to its natural rate.

Effects of Eutrophication Eutrophication triggers a series of events with serious consequences. First, the layer of algae prevents sunlight from reaching plants and other algae beneath the surface. Those organisms die and sink to the bottom. Then decomposers, such as bacteria, which break down the bodies of the dead organisms, increase in number. Soon the bacteria use up the oxygen in the water. Without oxygen, fishes and other organisms in the water die. About the only organisms that survive are the algae on the surface.

FIGURE 14
Eutrophication
The thick layer of algae on the surface of a pond can threaten other organisms in the water.

 Reading Checkpoint **What natural process of change occurs over time in a pond or a lake?**

Section 2 Assessment

Target Reading Skill Comparing and Contrasting Use the information in your table about algal blooms to help you answer the questions below.

Reviewing Key Concepts

1. a. **Defining** What is an algal bloom?
   b. **Comparing and Contrasting** What might cause an algal bloom to occur in an ocean? In a lake? How would the algal bloom affect organisms living in each?
   c. **Predicting** Would it be easier to control saltwater or freshwater blooms? Explain.

Writing in Science

News Report Something strange has happened to the local pond. It is covered with green scum and dead fish are floating on the surface. You have interviewed scientists about possible causes. Write a news report explaining to the public what has happened.

An Explosion of Life

Problem

How does the amount of fertilizer affect algae growth?

Skills Focus

controlling variables, drawing conclusions, predicting

Materials

- 4 glass jars with lids
- marking pen
- aged tap water
- aquarium water
- graduated cylinder
- liquid fertilizer

Procedure

1. Read through the steps in the procedure. Then write a prediction describing what you think will happen in each of the four jars.

2. Copy the data table into your notebook. Be sure to allow enough lines to make entries for a two-week period.

3. Label four jars A, B, C, and D. Fill each jar half full with aged tap water.

4. Add aquarium water to each jar until the jar is three-fourths full.

5. Add 3 mL of liquid fertilizer to jar B, 6 mL to jar C, and 12 mL to jar D. Do not add any fertilizer to jar A. Loosely screw the lid on each jar. Place all the jars in a sunny location where they will receive the same amount of direct sunlight.

6. Observe the jars every day for two weeks. Compare the color of the water in the four jars. Record your observations.

Analyze and Conclude

1. **Observing** How did the color in the four jars compare at the end of the two-week period? Did your observations match your prediction?

2. **Controlling Variables** What was the purpose of jar A? Explain.

3. **Drawing Conclusions** How can you account for any color differences among the four jars? What process and organisms were responsible for causing that color change?

4. **Predicting** Predict what would have happened if you placed the four jars in a dark location instead of in sunlight. Explain your prediction.

5. **Communicating** Write a warning label to be placed on a bag of fertilizer. On the label, explain what might happen to fish and other organisms if the fertilizer gets into a body of fresh water. Also, outline steps consumers can take to prevent these problems.

Design an Experiment

Some detergents contain phosphates, which are also found in many kinds of fertilizer. Design an experiment to compare how regular detergent and low-phosphate detergent affect the growth of algae. *Obtain your teacher's permission before carrying out your investigation.*

Data Table			
	Observations		
Day	Jar A (no fertilizer)	Jar B (3 mL of fertilizer)	Jar C (6 mL of fertilizer)	Jar D (12 mL of fertilizer)
Day 1				
Day 2				

Reading Preview

Key Concepts
- What characteristics do fungi share?
- How do fungi reproduce?
- What roles do fungi play in nature?

Key Terms
- fungi • hyphae
- fruiting body • budding
- lichen

Target Reading Skill

Asking Questions Before you read, preview the red headings. In a graphic organizer like the one below, ask a *what* or *how* question for each heading. As you read, write answers to your questions.

Fungi

Question	Answer
What are fungi?	Fungi are . . .

Discover Activity

Do All Molds Look Alike?

1. Your teacher will give you two sealed, clear plastic bags—one containing moldy bread and another containing moldy fruit. **CAUTION:** *Do not open the sealed bags at any time.*
2. In your notebook, describe what you see.
3. Next, use a hand lens to examine each mold. Sketch each mold in your notebook and list its characteristics.
4. Return the sealed bags to your teacher. Wash your hands.

Think It Over
Observing How are the molds similar? How do they differ?

Unnoticed, a speck of dust lands on a cricket's back. But this is no ordinary dust—it is alive! Tiny glistening threads emerge from the dust and begin to grow into the cricket's moist body. As they grow, the threads release chemicals that slowly dissolve the cricket's tissues. Within a few days, the cricket's body is little more than a hollow shell filled with a tangle of the deadly threads. Then the threads begin to grow up and out of the dead cricket. They produce long stalks with knobs at their tips. When one of the knobs breaks open, it will release thousands of dustlike specks, which the wind can carry to new victims.

What Are Fungi?

The strange cricket-killing organism is a member of the fungi kingdom. Although you may not have heard of a cricket-killing fungus before, you are probably familiar with other kinds of fungi. For example, the molds that grow on stale bread and the mushrooms that sprout in yards are all fungi.

A bush cricket attacked by a killer fungus. ▶

Most **fungi** share several important characteristics. **Fungi are eukaryotes that have cell walls, are heterotrophs that feed by absorbing their food, and use spores to reproduce.** In addition, fungi need moist, warm places in which to grow. They thrive on moist foods, damp tree barks, lawns coated with dew, damp forest floors, and even wet bathroom tiles.

Cell Structure Fungi range in size from tiny unicellular yeasts to large multicellular fungi. The largest known organism on Earth is actually an underground fungus that covers an area as large as a thousand football fields!

The cells of all fungi are surrounded by cell walls. Except for the simplest fungi, such as unicellular yeasts, the cells of most fungi are arranged in structures called hyphae. **Hyphae** (HY fee) (singular hypha) are the branching, thread-like tubes that make up the bodies of multicellular fungi. The hyphae of some fungi are continuous threads of cytoplasm that contain many nuclei. Substances move quickly and freely through the hyphae.

What a fungus looks like depends on how its hyphae are arranged. In some fungi, the threadlike hyphae are loosely tangled. Fuzzy-looking molds that grow on old foods have loosely tangled hyphae. In other fungi, hyphae are packed tightly together. For example, the stalks and caps of the mushrooms shown in Figure 15 are made of hyphae packed so tightly that they appear solid. Underground, however, a mushroom's hyphae form a loose, threadlike maze in the soil.

Protists and Fungi

Video Preview
▶ Video Field Trip
Video Assessment

✓ Reading Checkpoint **What do the bodies of multicellular fungi consist of?**

FIGURE 15
Structure of a Mushroom
The hyphae in the stalk and cap of a mushroom are packed tightly to form very firm structures. Underground hyphae, are arranged loosely.
Inferring *What function might the underground hyphae perform?*

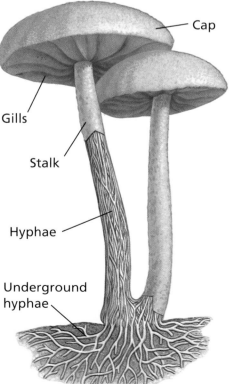

Cap

Gills

Stalk

Hyphae

Underground hyphae

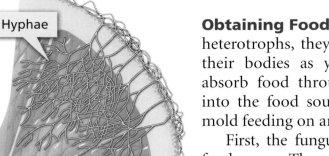

FIGURE 16
How Fungi Obtain Food
The mold *Penicillium* often grows on old fruits such as oranges. Notice that some hyphae grow deep inside the orange.

Hyphae

Obtaining Food Although fungi are heterotrophs, they do not take food into their bodies as you do. Instead, fungi absorb food through hyphae that grow into the food source. Figure 16 shows a mold feeding on an orange.

First, the fungus grows hyphae into a food source. Then digestive chemicals ooze from the hyphae into the food. The chemicals break down the food into small substances that can be absorbed by the hyphae.

As an analogy, imagine sinking your fingers down into a chocolate cake and dripping digestive chemicals out of your fingertips. Then imagine your fingers absorbing the digested cake particles!

Some fungi feed on dead organisms. Other fungi are parasites that break down the chemicals in living organisms.

Reproduction in Fungi

Like it or not, fungi are everywhere. The way they reproduce guarantees their survival and spread. **Fungi usually reproduce by making spores. The lightweight spores are surrounded by a protective covering and can be carried easily through air or water to new sites.** Fungi produce millions of spores, more than can ever survive. Only a few spores will fall where conditions are right for them to grow.

Fungi produce spores in reproductive structures called **fruiting bodies.** The appearances of fruiting bodies vary from one type of fungus to another. For some fungi, such as mushrooms and puffballs, the part of the fungus that you see is the fruiting body. In other fungi, such as bread molds, the fruiting bodies are tiny, stalklike hyphae that grow upward from the rest of the hyphae. A knoblike spore case at the tip of each stalk contains the spores.

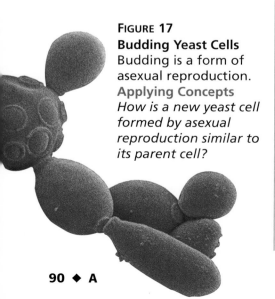

FIGURE 17
Budding Yeast Cells
Budding is a form of asexual reproduction.
Applying Concepts
How is a new yeast cell formed by asexual reproduction similar to its parent cell?

Asexual Reproduction Most fungi reproduce both asexually and sexually. When there is adequate moisture and food, the fungi make spores asexually. Cells at the tips of their hyphae divide to form spores. The spores grow into fungi that are genetically identical to the parent.

Unicellular yeast cells undergo a form of asexual reproduction called **budding.** In budding, no spores are produced. Instead, a small yeast cell grows from the body of a parent cell somewhat similar to the way a bud forms on a tree branch. The new cell then breaks away and lives on its own.

Sexual Reproduction Most fungi can also reproduce sexually, especially when growing conditions become unfavorable. In sexual reproduction, the hyphae of two fungi grow together and genetic material is exchanged. Eventually, a new reproductive structure grows from the joined hyphae and produces spores. The spores develop into fungi that differ genetically from either parent.

Classification of Fungi Figure 18 shows three major groups of fungi. The groups are named for the appearance of their reproductive structures. Additional groups include water species that produce spores with flagella and those that form tight associations with plant roots.

 **Reading Checkpoint** What is budding?

FIGURE 18
Classification of Fungi

Three major groups of fungi include sac fungi, club fungi, and zygote fungi.
Comparing and Contrasting How do the spore-producing structures of sac fungi and club fungi compare?

Sac Fungi ▶
Sac fungi produce spores in structures that look like long sacs, such as those at the tips of these hyphae. This group is the largest group of fungi and includes yeasts, morels, truffles, and some fungi that cause plant diseases. Sac fungi also include fungi that make up lichens.

Club Fungi ▲
Club fungi produce spores in microscopic structures that look like clubs. This group includes mushrooms, bracket fungi, and rusts. Club fungi also include puffballs such as these, one of which is releasing its spores. The most poisonous fungi are club fungi.

Zygote Fungi ▲
Zygote fungi produce very resistant spores that can survive harsh environmental conditions. This group contains many common fruit and bread molds, such as this *Rhizopus*, and molds that attack and kill insects.

FIGURE 19
Truffles
Pigs are often used to hunt for truffles, a highly prized delicacy. Truffles (inset) are the round fruiting bodies of fungi that grow underground among the roots of certain trees. Some truffles are quite rare and can sell for several thousand dollars per kilogram!

The Role of Fungi in Nature

Fungi affect humans and other organisms in many ways. **Fungi play important roles as decomposers and recyclers on Earth. Many fungi provide foods for people. Some fungi cause disease while others fight disease. Still other fungi live in symbiosis with other organisms.**

Environmental Recycling Like bacteria, many fungi are decomposers—organisms that break down the chemicals in dead organisms. For example, many fungi live in the soil and break down the chemicals in dead plant matter. This process returns important nutrients to the soil. Without fungi and bacteria, Earth would be buried under dead plants and animals!

Food and Fungi When you eat a slice of bread, you benefit from the work of yeast. Bakers add yeast to bread dough to make it rise. Yeast cells use the sugar in the dough for food and produce carbon dioxide gas as they feed. The gas forms bubbles, which cause the dough to rise. You see these bubbles as holes in a slice of bread. Without yeast, bread would be flat and solid. Yeast is also used to make wine from grapes. Yeast cells feed on the sugar in the grapes and produce carbon dioxide and alcohol.

Other fungi are also important sources of foods. Molds are used in the production of foods. The blue streaks in blue cheese, for example, are actually growths of the mold *Penicillium roqueforti*. People enjoy eating mushrooms in salads and soups and on pizza. Because some mushrooms are extremely poisonous, however, you should never pick or eat wild mushrooms.

Disease-Fighting Fungi In 1928, a Scottish biologist named Alexander Fleming was examining petri dishes in which he was growing bacteria. To his surprise, Fleming noticed a spot of a bluish-green mold growing in one dish. Curiously, no bacteria were growing near the mold. Fleming hypothesized that the mold, a fungus named *Penicillium*, produced a substance that killed the bacteria near it.

Fleming's work contributed to the development of the first antibiotic, penicillin. It has saved the lives of millions of people with bacterial infections. Since the discovery of penicillin, many additional antibiotics have been isolated from both fungi and bacteria.

Disease-Causing Fungi Many fungi are parasites that cause serious diseases in plants. The sac fungus that causes Dutch elm disease is responsible for killing millions of elm trees in North America and Europe. Corn smut and wheat rust are two club fungi that cause diseases in important food crops. Fungal plant diseases also affect other crops, including rice, cotton, and soybeans, resulting in huge crop losses every year.

Some fungi cause diseases in humans. Athlete's foot fungus causes an itchy irritation in the damp places between toes. Ringworm, another fungal disease, causes an itchy, circular rash on the skin. Because the fungi that cause these diseases produce spores at the site of infection, the diseases can spread easily from person to person. Both diseases can be treated with antifungal medications.

 **Reading Checkpoint** What is one way fungi help fight diseases?

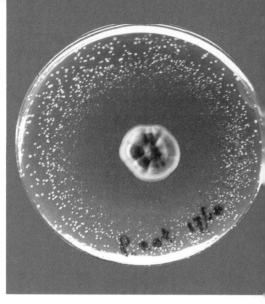

FIGURE 20
Penicillin
A *Penicillium* mold grows in the center of this petri dish. The mold produces the antibiotic penicillin, which prevents the tiny white colonies of bacteria from growing in the area around it.

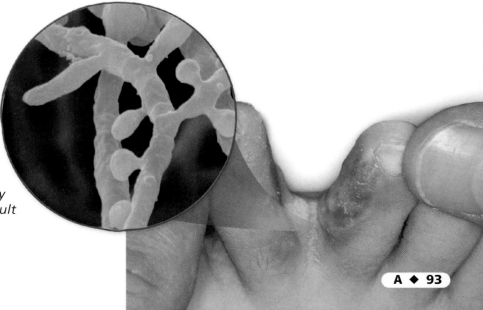

FIGURE 21
Athlete's Foot
Athlete's foot is a disease caused by the fungus *Trichophyton mentagrophytes* (inset). The fungus thrives in the damp places between toes. **Relating Cause and Effect** *Why is the spread of fungal diseases difficult to control?*

Fungi and Trees

A biologist conducted an experiment to see how root-associated fungi affect the growth of four different tree species. Each species was divided into two groups—trees grown with root-associated fungi and trees grown without the fungi.

1. **Reading Graphs** How did the biologist measure tree growth?

2. **Interpreting Data** For each species, which group of trees showed more growth?

3. **Calculating** What is the average height difference between sour orange trees that grew with root-associated fungi and those that grew without fungi? What is the height difference between avocado trees with and without the fungi?

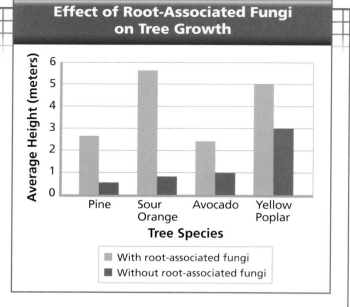

Effect of Root-Associated Fungi on Tree Growth

(Bar graph: Average Height (meters) vs. Tree Species — Pine, Sour Orange, Avocado, Yellow Poplar)

■ With root-associated fungi
■ Without root-associated fungi

4. **Drawing Conclusions** Based on this experiment, how do root-associated fungi affect tree growth?

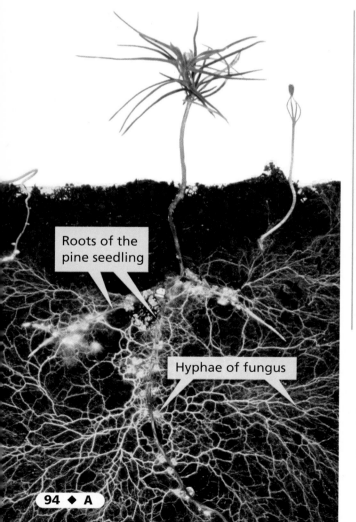

Roots of the pine seedling

Hyphae of fungus

Fungus–Plant Root Associations Some fungi help plants grow larger and healthier when their hyphae grow into, or on, the plant's roots. The hyphae spread out underground and absorb water and nutrients from the soil for the plant. With more water and nutrients, the plant grows larger than it would have grown without its fungal partner. The plant is not the only partner that benefits. The fungi get to feed on the extra food that the plant makes and stores. You can see the partnership between a fungus and a pine seedling in Figure 22.

Most plants have fungal partners. Many plants are so dependent on the fungi that they cannot survive without them. For example, orchid seeds cannot develop without their fungal partners.

 **Reading Checkpoint** How do fungi help plants grow?

FIGURE 22
Fungus–Plant Root Associations
An extensive system of fungal hyphae has grown in association with the roots of the pine seedling in the middle.
Classifying *What type of symbiosis do these two organisms exhibit?*

FIGURE 23
Lichens
The British soldier lichen consists of a fungus and an alga. The inset shows how entwined the alga is among the fungus's hyphae.

Alga

Fungus

Lichens A **lichen** (LY kun) consists of a fungus and either algae or autotrophic bacteria that live together in a mutualistic relationship. You have probably seen some familiar lichens—irregular, flat, crusty patches that grow on tree barks or rocks. The fungus benefits from the food produced by the algae or bacteria. The algae or bacteria, in turn, obtain shelter, water, and minerals from the fungus.

Lichens are often called "pioneer" organisms because they are the first organisms to appear on the bare rocks in an area after a volcanic eruption, fire, or rock slide has occurred. Over time, the lichens break down the rock into soil in which other organisms can grow. Lichens are also useful as indicators of air pollution. Many species of lichens are very sensitive to pollutants and die when pollution levels rise. By monitoring the growth of lichens, scientists can assess the air quality in an area.

Go Online
SciLINKS NSTA

For: Links on fungi
Visit: www.SciLinks.org
Web Code: scn-0133

 **Reading Checkpoint**   **What two organisms make up a lichen?**

Section 3 Assessment

🎯 **Target Reading Skill** Asking Questions Use the answers to the questions you wrote about the headings to help you answer the questions below.

Reviewing Key Concepts

1. **a. Listing** List three characteristics that a bread mold shares with a mushroom.
   b. Comparing and Contrasting How are the cells of a bread mold arranged? How are the cells of a mushroom arranged?
   c. Summarizing How does the cell structure of a fungus help it obtain food?
2. **a. Reviewing** What role do spores play in the reproduction of fungi?
   b. Sequencing Outline the steps by which fungi produce spores by sexual reproduction.
   c. Inferring Why is it advantageous to a fungus to produce millions of spores?

3. **a. Identifying** Name six roles that fungi play in nature.
   b. Predicting Suppose all the fungi in a forest disappeared. What do you think the forest would be like without fungi?

Writing in Science

Wanted Poster Design a "Wanted" poster for a mold that has been ruining food in your kitchen. Present the mold as a "criminal of the kitchen." Include detailed descriptions of the mold's physical characteristics, what it needs to grow, how it grows, and any other details that will help your family identify this mold. Propose ways to prevent new molds from growing in your kitchen.

What's for Lunch?

Problem

How does the presence of sugar or salt affect the activity of yeast?

Skills Focus

measuring, inferring, drawing conclusions

Materials

- 5 small plastic narrow-necked bottles
- 5 round balloons • 5 plastic straws
- dry powdered yeast • sugar • salt
- warm water (40°–45°C) • marking pen
- beaker • graduated cylinder • metric ruler
- string

Procedure

1. Copy the data table into your notebook. Then read over the entire procedure to see how you will test the activity of the yeast cells in bottles A through E. Write a prediction about what will happen in each bottle.

2. Gently stretch each of the balloons so that they will inflate easily.

3. Using the marking pen, label the bottles A, B, C, D, and E.

4. Use a beaker to fill each bottle with the same amount of warm water. **CAUTION:** *Glass is fragile. Handle the beaker gently to avoid breakage. Do not touch broken glass.*

5. Put 25 mL of salt into bottle B.

6. Put 25 mL of sugar into bottles C and E.

7. Put 50 mL of sugar into bottle D.

8. Put 6 mL of powdered yeast into bottle A, and stir the mixture with a clean straw. Remove the straw and discard it.

9. Immediately place a balloon over the opening of bottle A. Make sure that the balloon opening fits very tightly around the neck of the bottle.

10. Repeat Steps 8 and 9 for bottle B, bottle C, and bottle D.

Data Table			Circumference			
Bottle	Prediction	Observations	10 min	20 min	30 min	40 min
A (Yeast alone)						
B (Yeast and 25 mL of salt)						
C (Yeast and 25 mL of sugar)						
D (Yeast and 50 mL of sugar)						
E (No yeast and 25 mL of sugar)						

11. Place a balloon over bottle E without adding yeast to the bottle.

12. Place the five bottles in a warm spot away from drafts. Every ten minutes for 40 minutes, measure the circumference of each balloon by placing a string around the balloon at its widest point. Include your measurements in the data table.

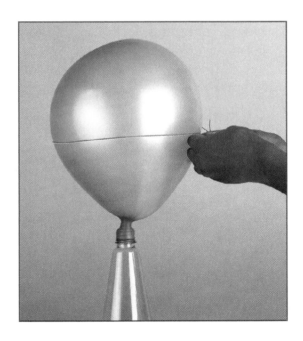

Analyze and Conclude

1. **Measuring** Which balloons changed in size during this lab? How did they change?

2. **Inferring** Explain why the balloon changed size in some bottles and not in others. What caused that change in size?

3. **Interpreting Data** What did the results from bottle C show, compared with the results from bottle D? Why was it important to include bottle E in this investigation?

4. **Drawing Conclusions** Do yeast use salt or sugar as a food source? How do you know?

5. **Communicating** In a paragraph, summarize what you learned about yeast from this investigation. Be sure to support each of your conclusions with the evidence you gathered.

Design an Experiment

Develop a hypothesis about whether temperature affects the activity of yeast cells. Then design an experiment to test your hypothesis. *Obtain your teacher's permission before carrying out your investigation.*

For: Data sharing
Visit: PHSchool.com
Web Code: ced-1033

① Protists

Key Concepts

- Like animals, animal-like protists are heterotrophs, and most are able to move from place to place to obtain food.
- Like plants, algae are autotrophs.
- Like fungi, funguslike protists are heterotrophs, have cell walls, and use spores to reproduce.

Key Terms

protist
protozoan
pseudopod
contractile vacuole
cilia
symbiosis
mutualism
algae
pigment
spore

② Algal Blooms

Key Concepts

- In general, algal blooms occur when nutrients increase in the water.
- Red tides are dangerous when the toxins that the algae produce become concentrated in the bodies of organisms that consume the algae.
- Eutrophication triggers a series of events with serious consequences.

Key Terms

algal bloom
red tide
eutrophication

③ Fungi

Key Concepts

- Fungi are eukaryotes that have cell walls, are heterotrophs that feed by absorbing their food, and use spores to reproduce.
- Fungi usually reproduce by making spores. The lightweight spores are surrounded by a protective covering and can be carried easily through air or water to new sites.
- Fungi play important roles as decomposers and recyclers on Earth. Many fungi provide foods for people. Some fungi cause disease while others fight disease. Still other fungi live in symbiosis with other organisms.

Key Terms

fungi
hyphae
fruiting body
budding
lichen

Review and Assessment

Organizing Information

Sequencing Copy the flowchart about changes in a lake onto a separate sheet of paper. Then complete it and add a title. (For more on Sequencing, see the Skills Handbook.)

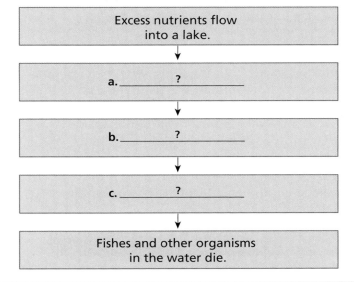

Excess nutrients flow into a lake.

↓

a. _____ ?

↓

b. _____ ?

↓

c. _____ ?

↓

Fishes and other organisms in the water die.

Reviewing Key Terms

Choose the letter of the best answer.

1. Which of the following characteristics describes all protists?
   a. They are unicellular.
   b. They can be seen with the unaided eye.
   c. Their cells have nuclei.
   d. They are unable to move on their own.

2. A protist structure that collects water and expels it from the cell is called a
   a. pseudopod.
   b. contractile vacuole.
   c. cilia.
   d. spore.

3. The interaction between two species in which at least one of the species benefits is called
   a. eutrophication.   b. hyphae.
   c. symbiosis.   d. budding.

4. An overpopulation of saltwater algae is called a(n)
   a. pigment.   b. lichen.
   c. red tide.   d. eutrophication.

5. A lichen is a symbiotic association between
   a. fungi and plant roots.
   b. algae and fungi.
   c. algae and bacteria.
   d. protozoans and algae.

If the statement is true, write *true*. If it is false, change the underlined word or words to make the statement true.

6. Ciliates use <u>flagella</u> to move.
7. Plantlike protists are called <u>protozoans</u>.
8. <u>Eutrophication</u> is the process by which nutrients in a lake build up over time.
9. Most fungi are made up of threadlike structures called <u>spores</u>.
10. Fungi produce spores in structures called <u>fruiting bodies</u>.

Writing in Science

Informational Pamphlet Create a pamphlet to teach young children about fungi. Explain where fungi live, how they feed, and the roles they play. Include illustrations as well.

Discovery CHANNEL **SCHOOL**

Protists and Fungi

Video Preview
Video Field Trip
▶ **Video Assessment**

Review and Assessment

Checking Concepts

11. Describe the process by which an amoeba obtains its food.
12. Describe the differences among algae in terms of their sizes.
13. Compare how animal-like, plantlike, and funguslike protists obtain food.
14. What are algal blooms? What problems can they cause in Earth's waters?
15. How does sexual reproduction occur in fungi?
16. Explain how the two organisms that make up a lichen both benefit from their symbiotic relationship.

Thinking Critically

17. **Comparing and Contrasting** Identify the organisms below. Describe the method by which each obtains food. What structures are involved?

18. **Predicting** If all algae suddenly disappeared from Earth's waters, what would happen to living things on Earth? Explain your answer.
19. **Making Judgments** You see an advertisement for a new, powerful fungicide guaranteed to kill most fungi on contact. What should people take into consideration before choosing to buy this fungicide?
20. **Relating Cause and Effect** You see some green scumlike material growing on the walls of your freshwater aquarium at home. List some possible reasons why this growth has occurred.
21. **Problem Solving** What are some actions that homeowners can take to discourage the growth of mold in their basements? Explain why these actions might help solve the problem.

Applying Skills

Use the graph to answer Questions 22–25.

When yeast is added to bread dough, the yeast cells produce carbon dioxide, which causes the dough to rise. The graph below shows how temperature affects the amount of carbon dioxide that is produced.

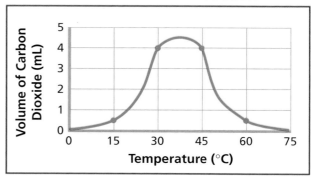

Temperature and Carbon Dioxide Production

22. **Interpreting Data** Based on the graph, at what temperature does yeast produce the most carbon dioxide?
23. **Inferring** Use the graph to explain why yeast is dissolved in warm water, rather than in cold water, when it is used to make bread.
24. **Predicting** Based on the graph, would you expect bread dough to rise if it were placed in a refrigerator (which is kept at about 2° to 5°C)? Explain.
25. **Drawing Conclusions** Explain how temperature affects the amount of carbon dioxide that the yeast cells produce.

Lab zone Chapter **Project**

Performance Assessment Create a poster that summarizes your experiment for the class. In your poster, include your hypothesis and describe the conditions that produced the best mushroom growth. Use diagrams and graphs to display your results. Did the project raise any new questions about mushrooms for you? If so, how could you answer those questions?

Standardized Test Prep

Choose the letter of the best answer.

1. Roberto fills a petri dish with pond water containing a mixture of protozoans and algae. He covers half the dish with aluminum foil and places it on a sunny windowsill. Predict what Roberto might observe after several days.
   A The protozoans and algae would be evenly distributed throughout the dish.
   B The protozoans and algae would be found only in the covered half of the petri dish.
   C More algae would be found in the uncovered half of the dish.
   D The protozoans can now make their own food.

2. Which of the following statements about fungus reproduction is true?
   F Fungi reproduce sexually by budding.
   G Fungi reproduce by making spores.
   H Fungi reproduce asexually when two hyphae join together and exchange genetic material.
   J Fungi do not reproduce sexually.

3. Which of the following statements about a paramecium is correct?
   A It has two contractile vacuoles that remove excess water from the cytoplasm.
   B It uses cilia to move.
   C It has two nuclei.
   D all of the above

4. Which structure tells you that the euglena shown below is an autotroph?

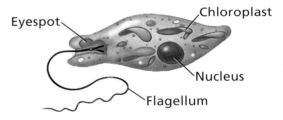

   F eyespot
   G flagellum
   H nucleus
   J chloroplast

5. Which of the following is true of algal blooms?
   A They occur only in fresh water.
   B They occur only in salt water
   C They occur when nutrients in the water increase.
   D They are caused by animal-like protists.

Constructed Response

6. During a hike in a state park, you notice some mushrooms growing on a log. Describe how the mushrooms use the log as a food source. Include information on what mushroom structures play a role in the process and the sequence of events that occur.

Chapter 4

Introduction to Plants

interactive Textbook

Ferns and other plants grow along a woodland stream. ▶

Lab zone™ Chapter **Project**

Design and Build an Interactive Exhibit

Cotton, medicines, and paper are just some of the products that come from plants. Which plants are the sources of these products, and how are the products made? In this project, you will build an exhibit to teach young children how a plant becomes a useful product.

Your Goal To build an interactive exhibit showing how a particular plant is transformed into a useful product

To complete this project successfully, you must

● choose one plant product and research where it comes from

● design an interactive exhibit that shows how the product is made

● build your exhibit and ask some children to critique it

● use the children's feedback to redesign your exhibit

● follow the safety guidelines in Appendix A

Plan It! Think of a creative way to teach children about the plant product you chose. Then sketch out your exhibit design and obtain your teacher's approval to build it. Also, identify a few children who can provide you with useful feedback.

The Plant Kingdom

Reading Preview

Key Concepts
- What characteristics do all plants share?
- What do plants need to live successfully on land?
- How do nonvascular plants and vascular plants differ?
- What are the different stages of a plant's life cycle?

Key Terms
- photosynthesis • tissue
- chloroplast • vacuole
- cuticle • vascular tissue
- fertilization • zygote
- nonvascular plant
- vascular plant • chlorophyll
- sporophyte • gametophyte

Target Reading Skill
Building Vocabulary A definition states the meaning of a word or phrase by telling about its most important feature or function. After you read the section, reread the paragraphs that contain definitions of Key Terms. Use all the information you have learned to write a definition of each Key Term in your own words.

Lab zone • Discover **Activity**

What Do Leaves Reveal About Plants?

1. Your teacher will give you two leaves from plants that grow in two very different environments: a desert and an area with average rainfall.
2. Carefully observe the color, size, shape, and texture of the leaves. Touch the surfaces of each leaf. Examine each leaf with a hand lens. Record your observations in your notebook.
3. When you have finished, wash your hands thoroughly with soap and water.

Think It Over
Inferring Use your observations to determine which plant lives in the desert and which does not. Give at least one reason to support your inference.

There are some very strange plants in the world. There are plants that trap animals, plants that bloom only once every thirty years, and plants with flowers that smell like rotting meat. You probably don't see such unusual plants every day. But you probably do see plants every day. You encounter plants whenever you see moss on a tree trunk, run across a lawn, or pick ripe tomatoes from a garden. And all plants, both the unfamiliar and the familiar, have a lot in common.

What Is a Plant?

Members of the plant kingdom share several characteristics. **Nearly all plants are autotrophs, organisms that produce their own food. All plants are eukaryotes that contain many cells. In addition, all plant cells are surrounded by cell walls.**

Plants Are Autotrophs You can think of a typical plant as a sun-powered, food-making factory. Sunlight provides the energy for this food-making process, called **photosynthesis.** During photosynthesis, a plant uses carbon dioxide gas and water to make food and oxygen. You will learn more about photosynthesis in Section 2.

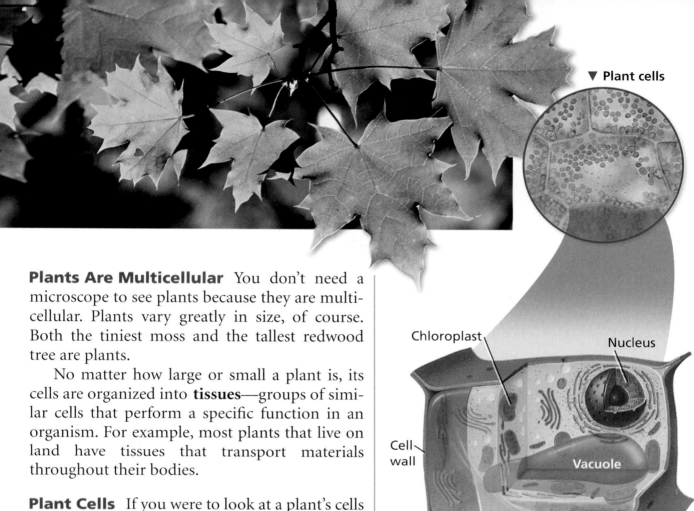

Plants Are Multicellular You don't need a microscope to see plants because they are multicellular. Plants vary greatly in size, of course. Both the tiniest moss and the tallest redwood tree are plants.

No matter how large or small a plant is, its cells are organized into **tissues**—groups of similar cells that perform a specific function in an organism. For example, most plants that live on land have tissues that transport materials throughout their bodies.

Plant Cells If you were to look at a plant's cells under a microscope, you would see that plants are eukaryotes. But unlike the cells of some other eukaryotes, a plant's cells are enclosed by a cell wall. The cell wall surrounds the cell membrane and separates the cell from the environment. Plant cell walls contain cellulose, a material that makes the walls rigid. Cell walls are what makes apples and carrots crunchy. Because their cell walls are rigid, plant cells look like small boxes.

Plant cells also contain many other structures, as shown in Figure 1. **Chloroplasts** (KLAWR uh plasts), which look something like green jelly beans, are the structures in which food is made. The Greek word *chloro* means "green." A **vacuole** is a large storage sac that can expand and shrink like a balloon. The vacuole stores many substances, including water, wastes, and food. A plant wilts when too much water has left its vacuoles.

Chloroplast

Nucleus

Cell wall

Vacuole

Cell membrane

▲ Single plant cell

FIGURE 1

Plant Cell Structures

Like all plants, this maple tree is multicellular. Plants have eukaryotic cells that are enclosed by a cell wall. *Relating Diagrams and Photos Which cell structures can you see in the inset photograph of plant cells?*

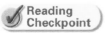 **Reading Checkpoint** **What is the function of the vacuole in a plant cell?**

Go **Online**
active art

For: Plant Cell Structures activity
Visit: PHSchool.com
Web Code: cep-1041

Chapter 4 A ◆ 105

Adaptations for Living on Land

Most plants live on land. How is living on land different from living in water? Imagine multicellular algae floating in the ocean. The algae obtain water and other materials directly from the water around them. Their bodies are held up toward the sunlight by the water. The water also aids in reproduction, allowing sperm cells to swim to egg cells.

Now imagine plants living on land. What adaptations would help them meet their needs without water all around them? **For plants to survive on land, they must have ways to obtain water and other nutrients from their surroundings, retain water, transport materials in their bodies, support their bodies, and reproduce.**

Obtaining Water and Other Nutrients Recall that all organisms need water to survive. Obtaining water is easy for algae because water surrounds them. To live on land, though, plants need adaptations for obtaining water from the soil. Plants must also have ways of obtaining other nutrients from the soil.

Retaining Water Plants must have ways of holding onto the water they obtain. Otherwise, they could easily dry out due to evaporation. When there is more water in plant cells than in the air, the water leaves the plant and enters the air. One adaptation that helps a plant reduce water loss is a waxy, waterproof layer called the **cuticle** that covers the leaves of most plants.

FIGURE 2
Retaining Water
Plants have adaptations that help them retain water. The shiny, waterproof cuticle on this leaf slows down evaporation.

Math | Analyzing Data

Water Loss in Plants

The graph shows how much water a certain plant loses during the hours shown.

1. **Reading Graphs** What variable is plotted along each axis?

2. **Interpreting Data** According to the graph, during what part of the day did the plant lose the most water? The least water?

3. **Drawing Conclusions** What could account for the pattern of water loss shown?

4. **Predicting** How would you expect the graph to look from 10 P.M. to 8 A.M.? Explain your reasoning.

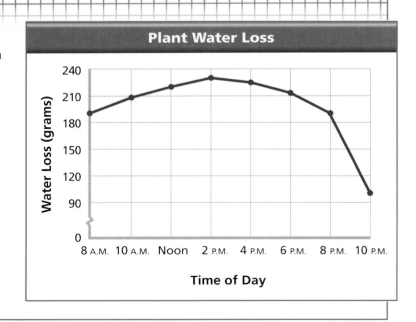

Plant Water Loss

Water Loss (grams) vs. Time of Day

FIGURE 3
Transport and Support
For this tall coconut palm to survive, it must transport water, minerals, and food over long distances. It must also support its body so its leaves are exposed to sunlight.
Relating Cause and Effect *What structures allow plants to transport materials?*

Water and minerals

Food

Transporting Materials A plant needs to transport water, minerals, food, and other materials from one part of its body to another. In general, water and minerals are taken up by the bottom part of the plant, while food is made in the top part. But all of the plant's cells need water, minerals, and food.

In small plants, materials can simply move from one cell to the next. But larger plants need a more efficient way to transport materials farther, from one part of the plant to another. These plants have transporting tissue called vascular tissue. **Vascular tissue** is a system of tubelike structures inside a plant through which water, minerals, and food move.

Support A plant on land must support its own body. It's easier for small, low-growing plants to support themselves. But for larger plants to survive, the plant's food-making parts must be exposed to as much sunlight as possible. Rigid cell walls and vascular tissue strengthen and support the large bodies of these plants.

Reproduction All plants undergo sexual reproduction that involves fertilization. **Fertilization** occurs when a sperm cell unites with an egg cell. The fertilized egg is called a **zygote.** For algae and some plants, fertilization can only occur if there is water in the environment. This is because the sperm cells of these plants swim through the water to the egg cells. Other plants, however, have an adaptation that makes it possible for fertilization to occur in dry environments. You will learn more about this adaptation in Chapter 5.

Reading Checkpoint Why do plants need adaptations to prevent water loss?

FIGURE 4
Plant Classification

The hundreds of thousands of plants that exist today can be classified as either nonvascular plants or vascular plants. Nonvascular plants are small and live in moist environments. Vascular plants can grow tall and live in diverse habitats. **Classifying** *What are the three groups of vascular plants?*

Nonvascular Plants

Nonvascular Plants

Nonvascular plants do not have true vascular tissue for support or transport. They grow low to the ground.

◀ Mosses grow in damp, shady places.

Liverworts grow on moist soil and rocks. ▶

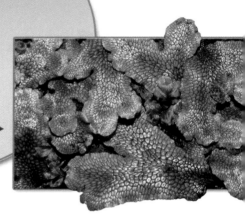

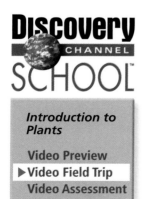

Introduction to Plants

Video Preview
▶ Video Field Trip
Video Assessment

Classification of Plants

Scientists informally group plants into two major groups— nonvascular plants and vascular plants.

Nonvascular Plants Plants that lack a well-developed system of tubes for transporting water and other materials are known as **nonvascular plants.** Nonvascular plants are low-growing and do not have roots for absorbing water from the ground. Instead, they obtain water and materials directly from their surroundings. The materials then simply pass from one cell to the next. This means that materials do not travel very far or very quickly. This slow method of transport helps explain why most nonvascular plants live in damp, shady places.

Most nonvascular plants have only thin cell walls to provide support. This is one reason why these plants cannot grow more than a few centimeters tall.

Vascular Plants Plants with true vascular tissue are called **vascular plants.** Vascular plants are better suited to life in dry areas than are nonvascular plants. Their well-developed vascular tissue solves the problem of transport, moving materials quickly and efficiently throughout the plant's body.

Vascular tissue also provides strength, stability, and support to a plant. Thus, vascular plants are able to grow quite tall.

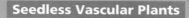

Vascular Plants

Seedless Vascular Plants

Seedless vascular plants reproduce by making spores.

◄ The staghorn fern produces spores at the tips of its antler-shaped leaves. This fern clings to the bark of trees in tropical areas.

Gymnosperms

Gymnosperms are vascular plants that reproduce by seeds. They do not form flowers or fruits.

◄ Ginkgo trees produce fleshy seeds that resemble fruits but are not. The seeds smell like vomit!

▲ The bristlecone pine can live for more than 4,000 years.

Angiosperms

Angiosperms are vascular plants that flower, and produce seeds that are surrounded by fruit.

The beavertail cactus produces brilliantly colored flowers. ▼

Wheat has been an important food crop for thousands of years. The grains, or fruits, are ground to make flour. ►

Rock containing two plant fossils ▶

FIGURE 5
Ancient and Modern Plants
Fossils of ancient plants help scientists understand the origin of plants. These fossils are of two plants that lived about 300 million years ago. Notice the similarities between the fossils and modern-day ferns (top right) and horsetails (above).

Origin of Plants Which organisms were the ancestors of today's plants? In search of answers, biologists studied fossils, the traces of ancient life forms preserved in rock and other substances. The oldest plant fossils are about 400 million years old. The fossils show that even at that early date, plants already had many adaptations for life on land, including vascular tissue.

Better clues to the origin of plants came from comparing the chemicals in modern plants to those in other organisms. In particular, biologists studied a green pigment called **chlorophyll** (KLAWR uh fil), found in the chloroplasts of plants, algae, and some bacteria. Land plants and green algae contain the same forms of chlorophyll. This evidence led biologists to infer that ancient green algae were the ancestors of today's land plants. Further comparisons of genetic material clearly showed that plants and green algae are very closely related. In fact, some scientists think that green algae should be classified in the plant kingdom.

 **Reading Checkpoint** What is chlorophyll?

Complex Life Cycles

Plants have complex life cycles that include two different stages, the sporophyte stage and the gametophyte stage. In the **sporophyte** (SPOH ruh fyt) stage, the plant produces spores, tiny cells that can grow into new organisms. A spore develops into the plant's other stage, called the gametophyte. In the **gametophyte** (guh MEE tuh fyt) stage, the plant produces two kinds of sex cells: sperm cells and egg cells.

Figure 6 shows a typical plant life cycle. A sperm cell and egg cell join to form a zygote. The zygote then develops into a sporophyte. The sporophyte produces spores, which develop into the gametophyte. Then the gametophyte produces sperm cells and egg cells, and the cycle starts again. The sporophyte of a plant usually looks quite different from the gametophyte.

 **Reading Checkpoint** During which stage does a plant produce spores?

FIGURE 6
Plant Life Cycle

Plants have complex life cycles that consist of two stages—the sporophyte stage and the gametophyte stage. **Interpreting Diagrams** *During which stage are sperm and egg cells produced?*

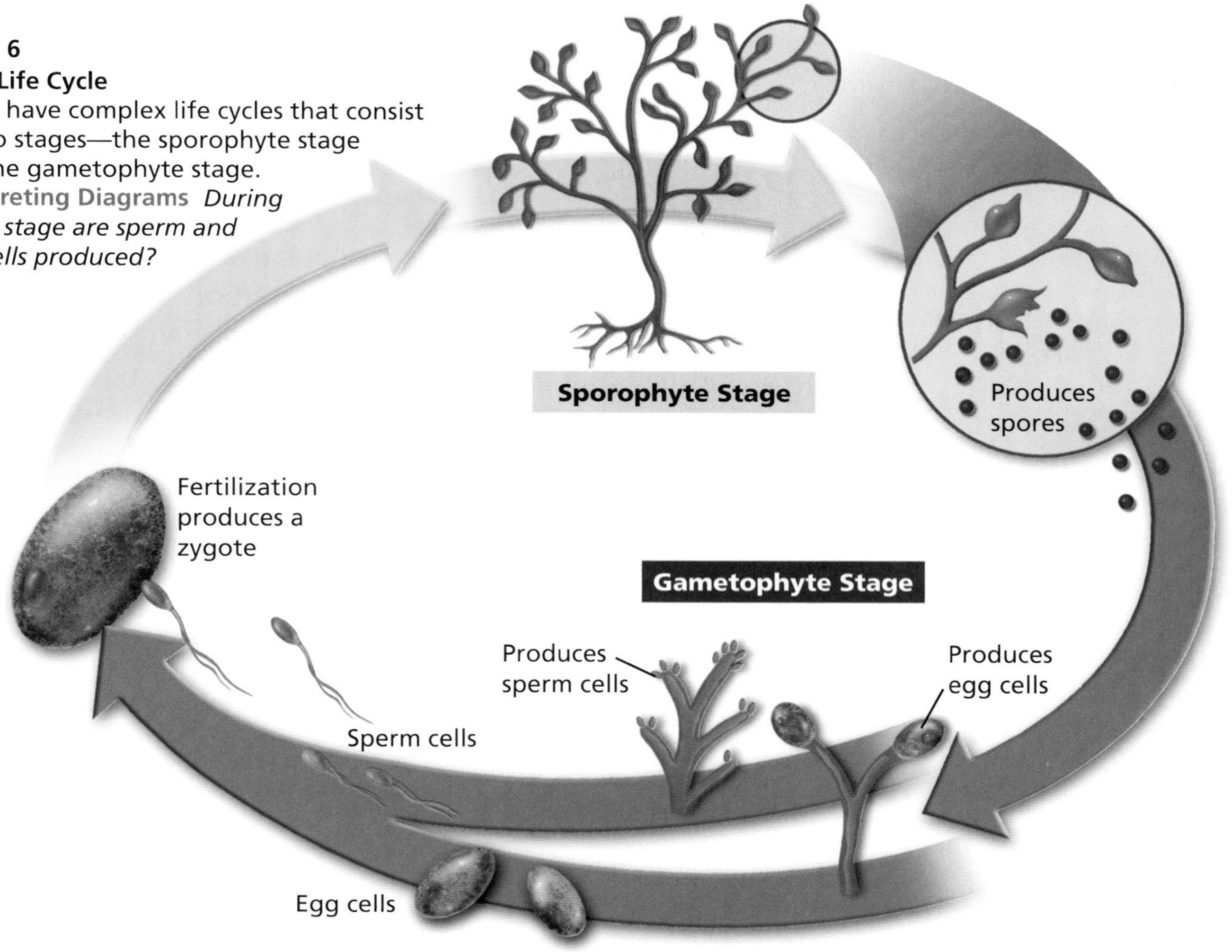

Sporophyte Stage

Produces spores

Fertilization produces a zygote

Gametophyte Stage

Produces sperm cells

Produces egg cells

Sperm cells

Egg cells

Section 1 Assessment

🎯 **Target Reading Skill** Building Vocabulary
Use your sentences to help you answer the questions below.

Reviewing Key Concepts

1. a. Listing List three characteristics of plants.
   b. Comparing and Contrasting Describe three ways that plant cells differ from the cells of some other eukaryotes.
   c. Predicting How might a plant cell be affected if it lacked chloroplasts?
2. a. Identifying What are five adaptations that plants need to survive on land?
   b. Inferring Why is a cuticle a useful adaptation in plants but not in algae?
3. a. Reviewing How do vascular plants differ from nonvascular plants?

   b. Explaining Explain why vascular plants are better suited to life in dry areas.
   c. Classifying Would you expect a tall desert plant to be a vascular plant? Explain.
4. a. Describing What are the two major stages of a plant's life cycle?
   b. Sequencing Describe in order the major events in the life cycle of a plant, starting with a zygote.

Writing in Science

Video Script You are narrating a video called *Living on Land*, which is written from the perspective of a plant. Write a one-page script for your narration. Be sure to discuss the challenges that life on land poses for plants and how they meet their needs.

Technology and Society
• Tech & Design •

Paper

What do a dollar bill, your report card, and a comic book have in common? They are all printed on paper, of course! But where does paper come from? As shown here, paper is made through a process that typically starts with wood from trees. The papermaking process was first invented in China about 2,000 years ago. Today, paper mills around the world rely on powerful machines to produce huge quantities of paper.

① Trees are grown and harvested.
Paper is produced mostly from trees that are grown for this specific purpose.

② Logs are de-barked.
The de-barker removes the bark from the logs.

③ Wood chips are made.
The chipper chops the wood into small pieces.

④ Pulp is formed.
Heat and chemicals break down the chips into fibers called pulp.

The Benefits of Paper

Paper benefits society in so many ways. Many everyday items are made out of paper—tissues, paper cups, and cardboard packaging. Perhaps most important, paper is used as a portable, inexpensive way to print words and images. Throughout time, paper has allowed people to express their thoughts, record history, and share knowledge. In addition, the paper industry employs many people, and generates income for the economy.

Paper and the Environment

Paper has negative impacts on the environment. Each step in the papermaking process requires energy and produces wastes. Some of these wastes, such as dioxins, are toxic. Dioxins form when water is used to flush chemicals from the paper. Paper products also make up a lot of the garbage in landfills. Because of the environmental costs, engineers are working to create a new type of "paper" called electronic paper, or e-paper. Someday soon, you might use flexible, ultra-thin, digital screens instead of paper.

5 **Water is added.**
Water is added to the pulp to form slush. The slush is then sprayed onto wide screens. The water begins to drain off.

6 **Water is removed.**
The paper is squeezed through several presses to remove the excess water.

7 **Paper is dried.**
Heated rollers dry the paper, making it flat and smooth.

Weigh the Impact

1. Identify the Need
How does society rely on paper? How would your life be different if paper had never been invented?

2. Research
Use the Internet to investigate e-paper, a new technology that may replace traditional paper. List some potential uses of e-paper.

3. Write
Write a paragraph or two comparing e-paper and regular paper. Be sure to include the pros and cons of both technologies based on your research.

For: More on paper
Visit: PHSchool.com
Web Code: ceh-1040

Photosynthesis and Light

Reading Preview

Key Concepts
- What happens when light strikes a green leaf?
- How do scientists summarize the process of photosynthesis?

Key Terms
- transmission • reflection
- absorption • accessory pigment

Target Reading Skill

Previewing Visuals Preview Figure 9. Then write two questions that you have about the diagram in a graphic organizer like the one below. As you read, answer your questions.

The Photosynthesis Process

Q.	How is sunlight involved in photosynthesis?
A.	
Q.	

Discover **Activity**

What Colors Make Up Sunlight?

1. Glue a piece of white paper onto the inside bottom of a shoe box.
2. Place the box on its side near a window or outside in a sunny area.
3. Hold a mirror in front of the open side of the box. Adjust the mirror until it reflects sunlight onto the paper in the box. **CAUTION:** *Do not direct the sunlight into your eyes.*
4. Place a prism between the mirror and the box. Adjust the location of the prism so that sunlight passes through the prism.
5. Describe what you see on the paper in the box.

Think It Over
Observing What did you learn about light from this activity?

The year was 1883. T. W. Engelmann, a German biologist, was at work in his laboratory. He peered into the microscope at some algae on a slide. The microscope had a prism located between the light source and the algae. As Engelmann watched the algae, he saw gas bubbles forming in the water around some of the cells. Curiously, no gas bubbles formed around other cells. Although Engelmann did not know it at the time, his experiment provided a clue about how light is involved in photosynthesis. To understand what Engelmann observed, you need to know more about the nature of light.

FIGURE 7
The Visible Spectrum
When white light passes through a prism, you can see that it is made up of the colors of the rainbow.

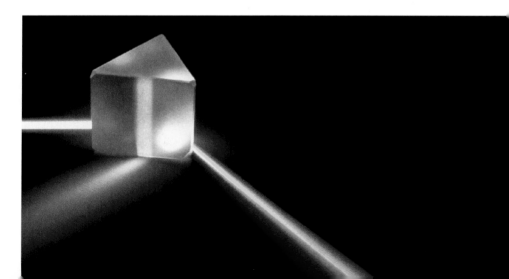

Green light is reflected by the leaf. You see the leaf as green.

Yellow light is reflected by the lemon. You see the lemon as yellow.

FIGURE 8
When Light Strikes Objects
When white light strikes the lemon and the leaf, different colors of light are reflected by the two objects. Because of the reflected light, we see the lemon as yellow and the leaf as green.
Inferring *What happens to the colors of light that are not reflected off the lemon and the leaf?*

The Nature of Light

The sun is the source of energy on Earth. If you take a walk outside on a sunny day, you feel the sun's energy as it warms your skin. You see the energy in the form of light on objects around you. The light that you see is called white light. But when white light passes through a prism like the one in Figure 7, you can see that it is made up of the colors of the rainbow. Scientists refer to these colors—red, orange, yellow, green, blue, and violet—as the visible spectrum.

When Light Strikes Objects In addition to prisms, white light strikes many other objects. Some objects such as glass and other transparent materials allow light to pass through them. This process is called **transmission.** When light hits a shiny surface such as a mirror, the light bounces back. This process is called **reflection.** When dark objects, such as street pavements, take in light, it is called **absorption.**

Most objects, however, reflect some colors of the visible spectrum while they absorb other colors. When white light strikes the lemon in Figure 8, the lemon absorbs most of the light's colors. However, the lemon reflects yellow light. The lemon looks yellow because your eyes see the reflected color.

Plants and Light Like yellow lemons and most other objects, plants absorb some colors of the visible spectrum and reflect others. **When light strikes the green leaves of a plant, most of the green part of the spectrum is reflected. Most of the other colors of light are absorbed.**

Plant Pigments When light strikes a leaf, it is absorbed by pigments found in the leaf's cells. Chlorophyll, the most abundant pigment in leaves, absorbs most of the blue and red light. Most of the green light, on the other hand, is reflected rather than absorbed. This explains why chlorophyll appears green in color, and why leaves usually appear green.

Other pigments, called **accessory pigments,** are also found in leaves. These pigments, which include orange and yellow pigments, absorb different colors of light than chlorophyll does. Most accessory pigments are not visible in plants because they are masked by chlorophyll.

Reading Checkpoint **What is the most abundant pigment in leaves?**

Science and **History**

Unraveling the Mysteries of Photosynthesis

What do plants need to make their own food? What substances do plants produce in the process of photosynthesis? Over time, the work of many scientists has provided answers to these questions.

1771
Joseph Priestley
When Joseph Priestley, an English scientist, placed a burning candle in a covered jar, the flame went out. When he placed both a plant and a candle in a covered jar, the candle kept burning. Priestley concluded that the plant released something into the air that kept the candle burning. Today, we know that plants produce oxygen, a product of photosynthesis.

1779
Jan Ingenhousz
Jan Ingenhousz, a Dutch scientist, placed branches with leaves in water. In sunlight, the leaves produced oxygen bubbles. In the dark, the leaves produced no oxygen. Ingenhousz concluded that plants need sunlight to produce oxygen, a product of photosynthesis.

1643
Jean-Baptiste Van Helmont
A Dutch scientist, Jean-Baptiste Van Helmont, planted a willow tree in a tub of soil. After five years of adding only water, the tree gained 74 kilograms. Van Helmont concluded that trees need only water to grow. Today, we know that water is one of the raw materials of photosynthesis.

1650	1700	1750

The Photosynthesis Process

When light strikes a plant's leaves, it sets in motion the process known as photosynthesis. You can think of photosynthesis as a two-part process. First, the plant captures energy from the sun. Then, it uses that energy to produce food.

Capturing Energy Because light is one form of energy, a substance that absorbs light absorbs energy. Just as a car requires the energy in gasoline to move, plants require energy in the form of light to power photosynthesis. Photosynthesis begins when light strikes the chlorophyll in a plant's chloroplasts. The light energy that is absorbed powers the next stage of the photosynthesis process.

Writing in Science

Research and Write Find out more about one of the scientists discussed in this timeline. Write a dialogue you might have had with the scientist. Discuss how the scientist's work contributed to our current understanding of photosynthesis.

1883
T. W. Engelmann
Building on the work of Jan Ingenhousz, T. W. Engelmann studied how different colors of light affect photosynthesis in green algae. He found that cells bathed in blue and red light had the fastest rates of photosynthesis. Today, scientists know that the chlorophyll in green algae and plants absorbs mostly blue and red light.

1948
Melvin Calvin
The American scientist Melvin Calvin traced the chemical path that the carbon from carbon dioxide follows during photosynthesis. By doing this, Calvin learned about the complex chemical reactions of photosynthesis.

1864
Julius Sachs
A German biologist, Julius Sachs, observed living leaf cells under a microscope. As he watched, he tested the cells for the presence of carbohydrates. Sachs discovered that plants produce carbohydrates during photosynthesis.

1850   1900   1950

For: The Photosynthesis Process
activity
Visit: PHSchool.com
Web Code: cep-1042

The Chemistry of Photosynthesis Light energy is just one of the things that plants need to carry out photosynthesis. Just as you need flour and eggs to make cookies, a plant also needs raw materials to make its own food. Plants use carbon dioxide gas and water as raw materials for photosynthesis.

During this stage of photosynthesis, plants use the energy absorbed by chlorophyll to power a series of complex chemical reactions. In these reactions, carbon dioxide from the air and water from the soil combine to produce sugar, a type of carbohydrate. Another product, oxygen gas, is also produced. The events of photosynthesis are pictured in Figure 9.

FIGURE 9
The Photosynthesis Process

In photosynthesis, the energy in sunlight is used to make sugar and oxygen from carbon dioxide and water. **Classifying** *Which substances are the raw materials of photosynthesis? Which are the products?*

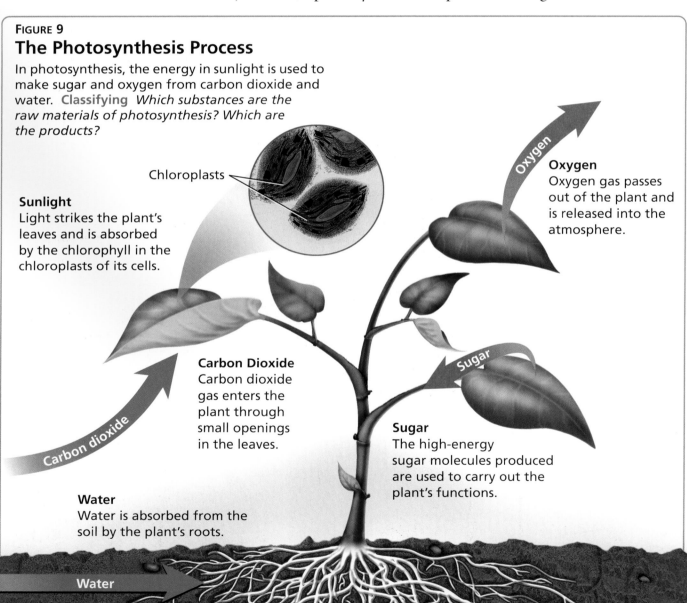

Chloroplasts

Sunlight
Light strikes the plant's leaves and is absorbed by the chlorophyll in the chloroplasts of its cells.

Oxygen
Oxygen gas passes out of the plant and is released into the atmosphere.

Carbon Dioxide
Carbon dioxide gas enters the plant through small openings in the leaves.

Sugar
The high-energy sugar molecules produced are used to carry out the plant's functions.

Water
Water is absorbed from the soil by the plant's roots.

Water

The Photosynthesis Equation Scientists write equations to describe chemical reactions. A chemical equation shows raw materials and products. **The many chemical reactions of photosynthesis can be summarized by this equation:**

$$\text{carbon dioxide} + \text{water} \xrightarrow{\text{light energy}} \text{sugar} + \text{oxygen}$$
$$(CO_2) \quad + (H_2O) \quad\quad\quad\quad (C_6H_{12}O_6) + (O_2)$$

You can read this equation as, "carbon dioxide and water combine in the presence of light to produce sugar and oxygen." Photosynthesis takes place in the parts of a plant that contain chlorophyll.

Like all organisms, plants need a steady supply of energy to grow and develop, respond, and reproduce. The food made by plants during photosynthesis supplies energy for these processes. Any excess food made by plants is stored in their roots, stems, leaves, or fruits. Carrot plants, for example, store excess food in their roots. When you eat a carrot, you are eating the plant's stored food.

The other product of photosynthesis is oxygen. Most of the oxygen produced during photosynthesis passes out of the plant and into the air. It can then be used by other organisms for their body processes.

FIGURE 10
Food Made by Plants
You can enjoy the results of photosynthesis in a salad. When you eat cucumbers, tomatoes, and other plant products, you are eating food made and stored by plants.

✔ **Reading Checkpoint** What are the products of photosynthesis?

Section 2 Assessment

⟳ **Target Reading Skill** Previewing Visuals Refer to your questions and answers about photosynthesis to help you answer Question 2.

Reviewing Key Concepts

1. a. **Listing** What are three things that might happen to light when it strikes an object?
   b. **Relating Cause and Effect** What happens when light strikes a green leaf? How does this explain why leaves appear green?
   c. **Predicting** Predict whether a plant would grow better when exposed to green light or to blue light. Explain.
2. a. **Reviewing** What is the overall equation for photosynthesis?
   b. **Summarizing** In a sentence, summarize what happens during each of the two stages of photosynthesis.

c. **Applying Concepts** Explain how each of these conditions could affect photosynthesis in a plant: (a) cloudy weather, (b) drought, (c) bright sunlight.

Lab zone **At-Home Activity**

Reflecting on Light With a family member, look around your kitchen for objects that transmit, reflect, and absorb white light. Explain to your family member what happens to white light when it strikes each object. Then, choose one of the objects and explain why you see it as the color you do.

Eye on Photosynthesis

Problem

What raw materials and conditions are involved in photosynthesis?

Skills Focus

observing, controlling variables, designing experiments

Materials

- *Elodea* plants
- water (boiled, then cooled)
- wide-mouthed container
- sodium bicarbonate solution
- 2 test tubes
- wax pencil
- lamp (optional)

Procedure

PART 1 Observing Photosynthesis

1. Use a wax pencil to label two test tubes *1* and *2*. Fill test tube 1 with sodium bicarbonate solution. Sodium bicarbonate provides a source of carbon dioxide for photosynthesis.

2. Fill the wide-mouthed container about three-fourths full of sodium bicarbonate solution.

3. Hold your thumb over the mouth of test tube 1. Turn the test tube over, and lower it to the bottom of the container. Do not let in any air. If necessary, repeat this step so that test tube 1 contains no air pockets. **CAUTION:** *Glass test tubes are fragile. Handle the test tubes carefully. Do not touch broken glass.*

4. Fill test tube 2 with sodium bicarbonate solution. Place an *Elodea* plant in the tube with the cut stem at the bottom. Put your thumb over the mouth of the test tube, and lower it into the container without letting in any air. Wash your hands.

5. Place the container with the two test tubes in bright light. After a few minutes, examine both test tubes for bubbles.

6. If bubbles form in test tube 2, observe the *Elodea* stem to see if it is producing the bubbles. The bubbles are oxygen bubbles. The production of oxygen signals that photosynthesis is taking place.

7. Leave the setup in bright light for 30 minutes. Observe what happens to any bubbles that form. Record your observations.

PART 2 Is Carbon Dioxide Needed for Photosynthesis?

8. Your teacher will provide a supply of water that has been boiled and then cooled. Boiling removes gases that are dissolved in the water, including carbon dioxide.

9. Based on what you learned in Part 1, design an experiment to show whether or not carbon dioxide is needed for photosynthesis. Obtain your teacher's approval before carrying out your experiment. Record all your observations.

PART 3 What Other Conditions Are Needed for Photosynthesis?

10. Make a list of other conditions that may affect photosynthesis. For example, think about factors such as light, the size of the plant, and the number of leaves.

11. Choose one factor from your list. Then design an experiment to show how the factor affects photosynthesis. Obtain your teacher's approval before carrying out your experiment. Record all your observations.

Analyze and Conclude

1. **Observing** What process produced the bubbles you observed in Part 1?

2. **Controlling Variables** In Part 1, what was the purpose of test tube 1?

3. **Designing Experiments** For the experiments you carried out in Parts 2 and 3, identify the manipulated variable and the responding variable. Explain whether or not your experiments were controlled experiments.

4. **Drawing Conclusions** Based on your results in Part 2, is carbon dioxide necessary for photosynthesis?

5. **Posing Questions** What question about photosynthesis did you explore in Part 3? What did you learn?

6. **Communicating** In a paragraph, summarize what you learned about photosynthesis from this investigation. Be sure to support each of your conclusions with evidence from your experiments.

More to Explore

A small animal in a closed container will die, even if it has enough water and food. A small animal in a closed container with a plant, water, and food will not die. Use what you have learned from this experiment to explain these facts.

Mosses, Liverworts, and Hornworts

Reading Preview

Key Concept
- What characteristics do the three groups of nonvascular plants share?

Key Terms
- rhizoid • bog • peat

Target Reading Skill
Identifying Main Ideas As you read this section, write the main idea—the biggest or most important idea—in a graphic organizer like the one below. Then write three supporting details that give examples of the main idea.

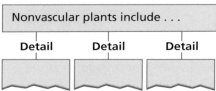

Main Idea

Nonvascular plants include . . .

Detail	Detail	Detail

Lab zone Discover **Activity**

Will Mosses Absorb Water?

1. Place 20 mL of sand into a plastic graduated cylinder. Place 20 mL of peat moss into a second plastic graduated cylinder.
2. Predict what would happen if you were to pour 10 mL of water slowly into each of the two graduated cylinders and then wait five minutes.
3. To test your prediction, use a third graduated cylinder to add 10 mL of water slowly to the sand. Then add 10 mL of water to the moss. After five minutes, record your observations.

Think It Over
Predicting How did your prediction compare with your results? What did you learn about moss from this investigation?

You pause from your hike to look at the forest around you. As far as you can see, you are surrounded by a living carpet of mosses. They are growing everywhere—up tree trunks, on rocks along the banks of the stream, and on the forest floor. Mosses make up one group of nonvascular plants. **The three major groups of nonvascular plants are mosses, liverworts, and hornworts. These low-growing plants live in moist environments where they can absorb water and other nutrients directly from their environment.** The watery surroundings also enable sperm cells to swim to egg cells during reproduction.

Mosses

Have you ever seen mosses growing in the cracks of a sidewalk or in a shady spot? With more than 10,000 species, mosses are by far the most diverse group of nonvascular plants.

The Structure of a Moss If you were to look closely at a moss, you would see a plant that looks something like the one in Figure 11. The familiar green, fuzzy moss is the gameto- phyte generation of the plant. Structures that look like tiny leaves grow off a small, stemlike structure. Thin, rootlike struc- tures called **rhizoids** anchor the moss and absorb water and nutrients. The sporophyte generation grows out of the game- tophyte. The sporophyte grows a long, slender stalk with a cap- sule at the end. The capsule contains spores.

The Importance of Mosses Many people use peat moss in agriculture and gardening. The peat moss that gardeners use contains sphagnum (SFAG num) moss. Sphagnum moss grows in a type of wetland called a **bog.** The still water in a bog is so acidic that decomposers cannot live in the water. Thus when the plants die, they do not decay. Instead, the dead plants accu- mulate at the bottom of the bog. Over time, the mosses become compressed into layers and form a blackish-brown material called **peat.** Large deposits of peat exist in North America, Europe, and Asia. In Europe and Asia, people use peat as a fuel to heat homes and to cook food.

✔ **Reading Checkpoint** How does peat form?

FIGURE 11
A Moss Plant
A moss gametophyte is low- growing and has structures that look like roots, stems, and leaves. The stalklike sporophyte generation remains attached to the gametophyte.
Interpreting Diagrams
What structures anchor the gametophyte?

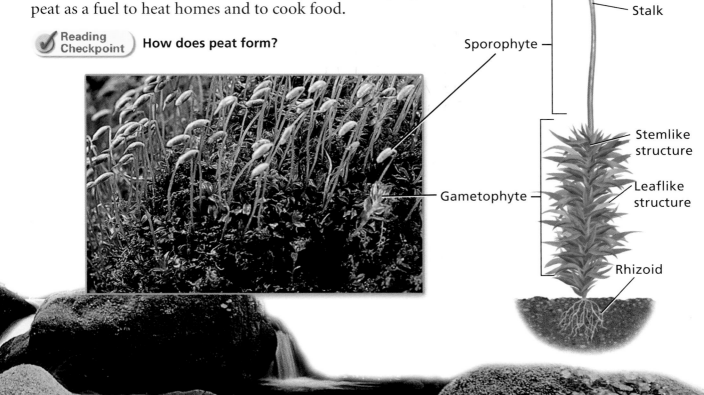

Capsule

Stalk

Sporophyte

Gametophyte

Stemlike structure

Leaflike structure

Rhizoid

FIGURE 12
Liverworts and Hornworts
Liverworts (left) have sporophytes that are too small to see. The leaf-like and treelike structures are part of the plants' gametophytes. Hornworts (right) have gametophytes that lie flat on the ground. The hornlike sporophytes are about one centimeter long.

For: Links on nonvascular plants
Visit: www.SciLinks.org
Web Code: scn-0143

Liverworts and Hornworts

Figure 12 shows examples of two other groups of nonvascular plants—liverworts and hornworts. There are more than 8,000 species of liverworts. This group of plants is named for the shape of the plant's body, which looks somewhat like a human liver. *Wort* is an old English word for "plant." Liverworts are often found growing as a thick crust on moist rocks or soil along the sides of a stream.

There are fewer than 100 species of hornworts. If you look closely at a hornwort, you can see slender, curved structures that look like horns growing out of the gametophytes. These hornlike structures, which give these plants their names, are the sporophytes. Unlike mosses or liverworts, hornworts are seldom found on rocks or tree trunks. Instead, hornworts usually live in moist soil, often mixed in with grass plants.

 **Reading Checkpoint** **What does a hornwort sporophyte look like?**

Section 3 Assessment

Target Reading Skill Identifying Main Ideas Use your graphic organizer about nonvascular plants to help you answer the questions below.

Reviewing Key Concepts

1. **a. Describing** Describe two characteristics that nonvascular plants share.
   b. Relating Cause and Effect Explain how the two characteristics of nonvascular plants are related.
   c. Comparing and Contrasting In what ways are mosses, liverworts, and hornworts similar? In what ways do they differ?

Lab zone **At-Home Activity**

Moss Hunt With a family member, go on a moss hunt in your neighborhood. Look for mosses in sidewalk cracks, on trees, or on other objects. For each location in which you find mosses, observe and record the sunlight and moisture conditions. Explain why mosses grow in the environments they do.

Masses of Mosses

Problem

How is a moss plant adapted to carry out its life activities?

Skills Focus

observing, measuring

Materials

- clump of moss
- hand lens
- metric ruler
- toothpicks
- plastic dropper
- water

Procedure

1. Your teacher will give you a clump of moss. Examine the clump from all sides. Draw a diagram of what you see. Measure the size of the overall clump and the main parts of the clump. Record your observations.

2. Using toothpicks, gently separate five individual moss plants from the clump. Be sure to pull them totally apart so that you can observe each plant separately. If the moss plants start to dry out as you are working, moisten them with a few drops of water.

3. Measure the length of the leaflike, stemlike, and rootlike structures on each plant. If brown stalks and capsules are present, measure them. Find the average length of each structure.

4. Make a drawing of a single moss plant. Label the parts, give their sizes, and record the color of each part. When you are finished observing the moss, return it to your teacher. Wash your hands thoroughly.

5. Obtain class averages for the sizes of the structures you measured in Step 3. Also, if the moss that you observed had brown stalks and capsules, share your observations about those structures.

Analyze and Conclude

1. **Observing** Describe the overall appearance of the moss clump, including its color, size, and texture.

2. **Measuring** What was the typical size of the leaflike portion of the moss plants, the typical height of the stemlike portion, and the typical length of the rootlike portion?

3. **Inferring** In which part(s) of the moss does photosynthesis occur? How do you know?

4. **Communicating** Write a paragraph explaining what you learned about mosses from this investigation. Include explanations of why mosses cannot grow tall and why they live in moist environments.

More to Explore

Select a moss plant with stalks and capsules. Use toothpicks to release some of the spores, which can be as small as dust particles. Examine the spores under a microscope. Create a labeled drawing of what you see.

Ferns, Club Mosses, and Horsetails

Reading Preview

Key Concept
• What are the main characteristics of seedless vascular plants?

Key Term
• frond

Target Reading Skill
Asking Questions Before you read, preview the red headings. In a graphic organizer like the one below, ask a *what, how,* or *where* question for each heading. As you read, answer your questions.

Ferns, Club Mosses, and Horsetails

Question	Answer
What are the characteristics of seedless vascular plants?	Seedless vascular plants have . . .

Lab zone **Discover Activity**

How Quickly Can Water Move Upward?

1. Put on your goggles. Your teacher will give you a plastic petri dish as well as a narrow glass tube that is open at both ends.
2. Fill the petri dish half full of water. Add a drop of food coloring to the water.
3. Stand the tube on end in the water and hold it upright. Observe what happens. Record your observations.

Think It Over
Inferring Why might it be an advantage for the transporting cells of plants to be arranged in a tubelike way?

The time is 340 million years ago—long before the dinosaurs lived. The place is somewhere in the forests that covered most of Earth's land. If you could have walked through one of these ancient forests, it would have looked very strange to you. You might have recognized the mosses and liverworts that carpeted the moist soil. But overhead you would have seen very tall, odd-looking trees.

Among the trees were huge, tree-sized ferns. Other trees resembled giant sticks with leaves up to one meter long. The huge leaves stuck out from the branches. When the leaves dropped off, they left diamond-shaped scars that looked like the scales that cover a fish.

Characteristics of Seedless Vascular Plants

The odd-looking plants in the ancient forests were the ancestors of three groups of smaller plants alive today. **Ferns, club mosses, and horsetails share two characteristics. They have true vascular tissue and they do not produce seeds. Instead of seeds, these plants reproduce by releasing spores.**

Vascular Tissue What adaptations allowed the ancient trees to grow so tall? Unlike mosses, the trees were vascular plants. Vascular plants can grow tall because their vascular tissue provides an effective way of transporting materials throughout the plant.

The vascular tissue also strengthens the plants' bodies. The cells making up the vascular tissue have strong cell walls. Imagine a handful of drinking straws bundled together with rubber bands. The bundle of straws is stronger and more stable than a single straw would be. Arranged in a similar way, the strong tubelike structures in vascular plants give the plants strength and stability.

Spores for Reproduction Ferns, club mosses, and horsetails need to grow in moist surroundings just as mosses do. This is because the plants release spores into their surroundings, where they grow into gametophytes. When the gametophytes produce egg cells and sperm cells, there must be enough water available for the sperm to swim toward the eggs.

✓ **Reading Checkpoint** What adaptations allowed plants to grow tall?

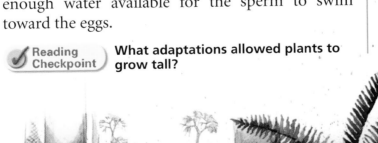

FIGURE 13
An Ancient Forest
Giant ferns, club mosses, and horsetails dominated ancient forests on Earth.

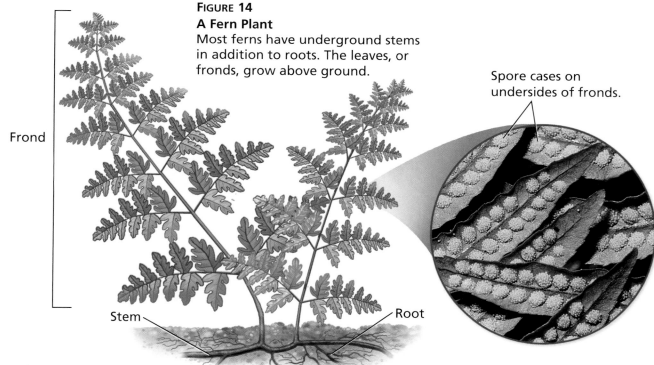

Lab zone Try This **Activity**

Examining a Fern

1. Your teacher will give you a fern plant to observe.

2. Draw a diagram of the plant and label the structures that you see.

3. Use a hand lens to observe the top and lower surfaces of the leaf. Run a finger over both surfaces.

4. With a plastic dropper, add a few drops of water to the top surface of the leaf. Note what happens.

Inferring Use your observations to explain how ferns are adapted to life on land.

Ferns

There are more than 12,000 species of ferns alive today. They range in size from tiny plants about the size of this letter "M" to tree ferns that grow up to 5 meters tall.

The Structure of Ferns Like other vascular plants, ferns have true stems, roots, and leaves. The stems of most ferns are underground. Leaves grow upward from the top side of the stems, while roots grow downward from the bottom of the stems. Roots are structures that anchor the fern to the ground and absorb water and nutrients from the soil. These substances enter the root's vascular tissue and travel through the tissue into the stems and leaves.

Figure 14 shows a fern's structure. Notice that the fern's leaves, or **fronds,** are divided into many smaller parts that look like small leaves. The upper surface of each frond is coated with a cuticle that helps the plant retain water. In many ferns, the developing leaves are coiled at first. Because they resemble the top of a violin, these young leaves are often called fiddleheads. As they mature, the fiddleheads uncurl.

Reproduction in Ferns The familiar fern, with its visible fronds, is the sporophyte stage of the plant. On the underside of mature fronds, spores develop in tiny spore cases. Wind and water can carry the spores great distances. If a spore lands in moist, shaded soil, it develops into a gametophyte. Fern gametophytes are tiny plants that grow low to the ground.

FIGURE 14
A Fern Plant
Most ferns have underground stems in addition to roots. The leaves, or fronds, grow above ground.

Spore cases on undersides of fronds.

Frond

Stem

Root

Club Mosses and Horsetails

Like ferns, club mosses and horsetails have true stems, roots, and leaves. They also have a similar life cycle. However, there are relatively few species of club mosses and horsetails alive today.

Do not be confused by the name *club mosses*. Unlike true mosses, club mosses have vascular tissue. You may be familiar with the club moss in Figure 15. The plant, which looks a little like the small branch of a pine tree, is sometimes called ground pine or princess pine. Club mosses usually grow in moist woodlands and near streams.

There are about 30 species of horsetails on Earth today. As you can see in Figure 15, the stems of horsetails are jointed. Long, coarse, needlelike branches grow in a circle around each joint. Small leaves grow flat against the stem just above each joint. The whorled pattern of growth somewhat resembles the appearance of a horse's tail. The stems contain silica, a gritty substance also found in sand. During colonial times, Americans used the plants to scrub their pots and pans. Another common name for horsetails is scouring rushes.

FIGURE 15
Club Mosses and Horsetails
Club mosses (left) look like tiny pine trees. Horsetails (right) have branches and leaves that grow in a circle around each joint. **Inferring** *Which grows taller—true mosses or club mosses?*

 **Reading Checkpoint** **Where do club mosses usually grow?**

Section 4 Assessment

🔁 **Target Reading Skill** Asking Questions Use the answers to the questions you wrote about the headings to help you answer the questions below.

Reviewing Key Concepts

1. a. **Listing** What two characteristics do ferns, club mosses, and horsetails share?
   b. **Comparing and Contrasting** In what ways do ferns, club mosses, and horsetails differ from true mosses? In what way are they similar to true mosses?
   c. **Inferring** Although ferns have vascular tissue, they still must live in moist, shady environments. Explain why.

Writing in Science

Product Label Create a product label to be attached to pots of fern plants for sale at a garden shop. Describe the structure of ferns and growing instructions. Include other helpful information or diagrams.

Study Guide

1 The Plant Kingdom

Key Concepts

- Nearly all plants are autotrophs, organisms that produce their own food. All plants are eukaryotes that contain many cells. In addition, all plant cells are surrounded by cell walls.

- For plants to survive on land, they must have ways to obtain water and other nutrients from their surroundings, retain water, transport materials in their bodies, support their bodies, and reproduce.

- Scientists informally group plants into two major groups—nonvascular plants and vascular plants.

- Plants have complex life cycles that include two different stages, the sporophyte stage and the gametophyte stage.

Key Terms

photosynthesis	zygote
tissue	nonvascular plant
chloroplast	vascular plant
vacuole	chlorophyll
cuticle	sporophyte
vascular tissue	gametophyte
fertilization	

2 Photosynthesis and Light

Key Concepts

- When light strikes the green leaves of a plant, most of the green part of the spectrum is reflected. Most of the other colors of light are absorbed.

- The many chemical reactions of photosynthesis can be summarized by this equation:

$$(CO_2) + (H_2O) \xrightarrow{\text{light energy}} (C_6H_{12}O_6) + (O_2)$$

Carbon dioxide and water combine in the presence of light to produce sugar and oxygen.

Key Terms

transmission	absorption
reflection	accessory pigment

3 Mosses, Liverworts, and Hornworts

Key Concept

- The three major groups of nonvascular plants are mosses, liverworts, and hornworts. These low-growing plants live in moist environments where they can absorb water and other nutrients directly from their environment.

Key Terms
rhizoid
bog
peat

4 Ferns, Club Mosses, and Horsetails

Key Concept

- Ferns, club mosses, and horsetails share two characteristics. They have true vascular tissue and they do not produce seeds. Instead of seeds, these plants reproduce by releasing spores.

Key Term
frond

Review and Assessment

Go Online
PHSchool.com

For: Self-Assessment
Visit: PHSchool.com
Web Code: cea-1040

Organizing Information

Comparing and Contrasting Copy the graphic organizer about mosses and ferns onto a separate sheet of paper. Then complete it and add a title. (For more on Comparing and Contrasting, see the Skills Handbook.)

Characteristic	Moss	Fern
Size	a. _____ ? _____	Can be tall
Environment	Moist	b. _____ ? _____
Body parts	Rootlike, stemlike, and leaflike structures	c. _____ ? _____
Familiar generation	d. _____ ? _____	Sporophyte
Is true vascular tissue present?	No	e. _____ ? _____

Reviewing Key Terms

Choose the letter of the best answer.

1. Mosses and trees are both
   a. vascular plants.
   b. nonvascular plants.
   c. seed plants.
   d. plants.

2. The structures in plant cells in which food is made are called
   a. cuticles.
   b. chloroplasts.
   c. vacuoles.
   d. vascular tissues.

3. When visible light strikes a green leaf, most of the green light is
   a. reflected.
   b. absorbed.
   c. transmitted.
   d. stored.

4. The familiar green, fuzzy moss is the
   a. frond.
   b. rhizoid.
   c. gametophyte.
   d. sporophyte.

5. The leaves of ferns are called
   a. rhizoids.   b. sporophytes.
   c. fronds.   d. cuticles.

If the statement is true, write *true*. If it is false, change the underlined word or words to make the statement true.

6. <u>Vascular tissue</u> is a system of tubelike structures through which water and food move.

7. The waxy, waterproof layer that covers the leaves of most plants is called the <u>cell wall</u>.

8. Leaves are green due to <u>accessory pigments</u>.

9. Sugars and oxygen are the products of <u>fertilization</u>.

10. Mosses are <u>vascular</u> plants.

Writing in Science

Firsthand Account You are a biologist who has studied plant life in various environments. Select one environment and describe in detail the plant life you found there. What features allowed the plants to survive?

Introduction to Plants
Video Preview
Video Field Trip
▶ Video Assessment

Review and Assessment

Checking Concepts

11. Name one adaptation that distinguishes plants from algae.

12. Briefly describe the life cycle of a typical plant.

13. Explain why a yellow school bus appears yellow in color.

14. What role does chlorophyll play in the photosynthesis process?

15. What are two functions of rhizoids? In what plants are they found?

16. In what two ways is vascular tissue important to a fern plant?

17. In what ways do mosses and club mosses differ from each other? In what ways are they similar?

Thinking Critically

18. **Relating Cause and Effect** After a patch of land becomes bare, small plants often appear. Soon, slightly taller plants start to grow, while the small ones die. The new plants may be replaced by even taller plants. How might light play a role in these changes?

19. **Comparing and Contrasting** How does the sporophyte generation of a plant differ from the gametophyte generation?

20. **Predicting** Explain what would happen to light if it were to strike each object shown.

A   B

21. **Applying Concepts** A friend tells you that he has seen moss plants that are about 2 meters tall. Is your friend correct? Explain.

22. **Inferring** People have observed that mosses tend to grow on the north side of a tree rather than the south side. Why might this be so?

Applying Skills

Use the data table to answer Questions 23–27.

A scientist exposed a green plant to different colors of light. She then measured how much of each light the plant absorbed.

Absorption of Light by a Plant

Color of Light	Percentage of Light Absorbed
Red	55
Orange	10
Yellow	2
Green	1
Blue	85
Violet	40

23. **Graphing** Create a bar graph using the information in the data table. (For information on creating bar graphs, see the Skills Handbook.)

24. **Interpreting Data** What color of light did the plant absorb the most?

25. **Drawing Conclusions** List the three colors of light that are most important for photosynthesis in this plant.

26. **Predicting** If the plant were exposed only to yellow light, how might the plant be affected? Explain.

27. **Inferring** If a plant with reddish leaves were used in a similar experiment, how might the results differ? Explain.

Lab zone Chapter **Project**

Performance Assessment Present your exhibit to your classmates. Describe your original exhibit and how you changed it based on the feedback you received. Explain what you learned by doing this project. What factors are most important in creating a successful educational exhibit for children?

Standardized Test Prep

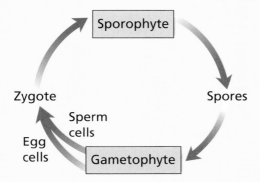
Choose the letter of the best answer.

1. Based on the diagram above, which of these statements about a plant's life cycle is true?
   A Plants spend part of their lives producing spores.
   B Plants spend part of their lives producing sperm and egg cells.
   C A zygote develops into the spore-producing stage of the plant.
   D all of the above

2. You examine plant cells under a microscope and notice many green round bodies within the cells.

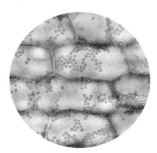

   The green structures are most likely involved in
   F directing the cell's functions.
   G photosynthesis.
   H storing food and water.
   J making proteins.

3. Both mosses and ferns
   A have true vascular tissue.
   B reproduce with spores.
   C have roots, stems, and leaves.
   D can only grow low to the ground.

4. Which of the following statements best explains why mosses and liverworts cannot grow tall?
   F They have no rootlike structures.
   G Taller plants in their surroundings release chemicals that slow down their growth.
   H They cannot take in enough oxygen from their surroundings.
   J They do not have true vascular tissue.

5. A houseplant that has not been watered for several days is droopy and wilted. What can you infer has happened to the plant's cells?
   A Water has filled the plant's nucleus.
   B Water has filled the plant's contractile vacuoles.
   C Water has filled the plant's chloroplasts.
   D Water has left the plant's vacuoles.

Constructed Response

6. Describe three adaptations that plants have for living on land. Explain why each adaptation is important for a plant to be able to survive on land.

Chapter
5

Seed Plants

interactive Textbook

The *Passiflora* plant produces delicate, highly scented flowers. ▶

Lab zone™ Chapter **Project**

Cycle of a Lifetime

How long is a seed plant's life? Redwood trees can live for thousands of years. Tomato plants die after only one season. Can organisms that seem so different have anything in common? In this chapter, you'll find out. Some answers will come from this chapter's project. In this project, you'll grow plants from seeds and then care for the plants until they produce seeds.

Your Goal To care for and observe a plant throughout its life cycle

To complete this project, you must

- grow a plant from a seed
- observe and describe key parts of your plant's life cycle, such as seed germination and pollination
- harvest and plant the seeds that your growing plant produces
- follow the safety guidelines in Appendix A

Plan It! Observe the seeds that your teacher gives you. In a small group, discuss what conditions the seeds might need to grow. What should you look for after you plant the seeds? What changes do you expect your plant to undergo during its life cycle? When you are ready, plant your seeds.

The Characteristics of Seed Plants

Reading Preview

Key Concepts
- What characteristics do seed plants share?
- How do seeds become new plants?
- What are the main functions of roots, stems, and leaves?

Key Terms
- phloem • xylem • pollen
- seed • embryo • cotyledon
- germination • root cap
- cambium • stomata
- transpiration

Target Reading Skill

Outlining As you read, make an outline about seed plants that you can use for review. Use the red headings for the main ideas and the blue headings for the supporting ideas.

The Characteristics of Seed Plants
I. What is a seed plant?
A. Vascular tissue
B.
II. How seeds become new plants
A.
B.

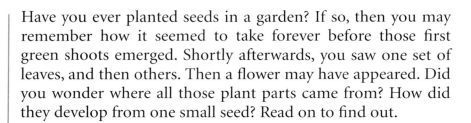

Lab zone **Discover Activity**

Which Plant Part Is It?
1. With a partner, carefully observe the items of food your teacher gives you.
2. Make a list of the food items.
3. For each food item, write the name of the plant part—root, stem, or leaf— from which you think it is obtained.

Think It Over
Classifying Classify the items into groups depending on the plant part from which the food is obtained. Compare your groupings with those of your classmates.

Have you ever planted seeds in a garden? If so, then you may remember how it seemed to take forever before those first green shoots emerged. Shortly afterwards, you saw one set of leaves, and then others. Then a flower may have appeared. Did you wonder where all those plant parts came from? How did they develop from one small seed? Read on to find out.

What Is a Seed Plant?

The plant growing in your garden was a seed plant. So are most of the other plants around you. In fact, seed plants outnumber seedless plants by more than ten to one. You eat many seed plants—rice, peas, and squash, for example. You wear clothes made from seed plants, such as cotton and flax. You may live in a home built from seed plants—oak, pine, or maple trees. In addition, seed plants produce much of the oxygen you breathe.

Seed plants share two important characteristics. They have vascular tissue, and they use pollen and seeds to reproduce. In addition, all seed plants have body plans that include roots, stems, and leaves. Like seedless plants, seed plants have complex life cycles that include the sporophyte and the gametophyte stages. In seed plants, the plants that you see are the sporophytes. The gametophytes are microscopic.

Vascular Tissue Most seed plants live on land. Recall from Chapter 4 that land plants face many challenges, including standing upright and supplying all their cells with food and water. Like ferns, seed plants meet these two challenges with vascular tissue. The thick walls of the cells in the vascular tissue help support the plants. In addition, food, water, and nutrients are transported throughout the plants in vascular tissue.

There are two types of vascular tissue. **Phloem** (FLOH um) is the vascular tissue through which food moves. When food is made in the leaves, it enters the phloem and travels to other parts of the plant. Water and minerals, on the other hand, travel in the vascular tissue called **xylem** (ZY lum). The roots absorb water and minerals from the soil. These materials enter the root's xylem and move upward into the stems and leaves.

Pollen and Seeds Unlike seedless plants, seed plants can live in a wide variety of environments. Recall that seedless plants need water in their surroundings for fertilization to occur. Seed plants do not need water for sperm to swim to the eggs. Instead, seed plants produce **pollen,** tiny structures that contain the cells that will later become sperm cells. Pollen delivers sperm cells directly near the eggs. After sperm cells fertilize the eggs, seeds develop. A **seed** is a structure that contains a young plant inside a protective covering. Seeds protect the young plant from drying out.

FIGURE 1
Harvesting Wild Rice
Like all seed plants, wild rice plants have vascular tissue and use seeds to reproduce. The seeds develop in shallow bodies of water, and the plants grow up above the water's surface. These men are harvesting the mature rice grains.

 **Reading Checkpoint** What material travels in phloem? What materials travel in xylem?

FIGURE 2

Seed Structure

The structures of three different seeds are shown here.
Inferring *How is the stored food used?*

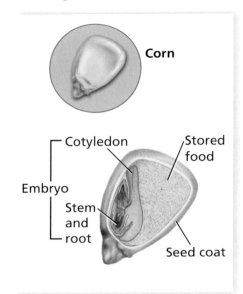

Corn

Cotyledon
Stored food
Embryo
Stem and root
Seed coat

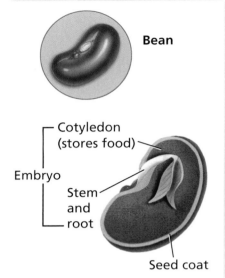

Bean

Cotyledon (stores food)
Embryo
Stem and root
Seed coat

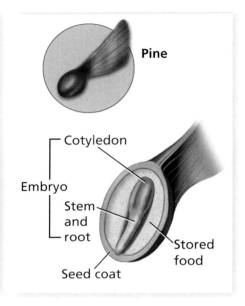

Pine

Cotyledon
Embryo
Stem and root
Seed coat
Stored food

Lab zone **Try This Activity**

The In-Seed Story

1. Your teacher will give you a hand lens and two different seeds that have been soaked in water.

2. Carefully observe the outside of each seed. Draw what you see.

3. Gently remove the coverings of the seeds. Then carefully separate the parts of each seed. Use a hand lens to examine the inside of each seed. Draw what you see.

Observing Based on your observations, label the parts of each seed. Then describe the function of each part next to its label.

How Seeds Become New Plants

All seeds share important similarities. **Inside a seed is a partially developed plant. If a seed lands in an area where conditions are favorable, the plant sprouts out of the seed and begins to grow.**

Seed Structure A seed has three main parts—an embryo, stored food, and a seed coat. The young plant that develops from the zygote, or fertilized egg, is called the **embryo.** The embryo already has the beginnings of roots, stems, and leaves. In the seeds of most plants, the embryo stops growing when it is quite small. When the embryo begins to grow again, it uses the food stored in the seed until it can make its own food by photosynthesis. In all seeds, the embryo has one or more seed leaves, or **cotyledons** (kaht uh LEED unz). In some seeds, food is stored in the cotyledons. In others, food is stored outside the embryo. Figure 2 compares the structure of corn, bean, and pine seeds.

The outer covering of a seed is called the seed coat. Some familiar seed coats are the "skins" on lima beans and peanuts. The seed coat acts like plastic wrap, protecting the embryo and its food from drying out. This allows a seed to remain inactive for a long time. In many plants, the seeds are surrounded by a structure called a fruit, which you will learn more about in Section 3.

Seed Dispersal After seeds have formed, they are usually scattered, sometimes far from where they were produced. The scattering of seeds is called seed dispersal. Seeds are dispersed in many ways. One method involves other organisms. For example, some animals eat fruits, such as cherries or grapes. The seeds inside the fruits pass through the animal's digestive system and are deposited in new areas. Other seeds are enclosed in barblike structures that hook onto an animal's fur or a person's clothes. The structures then fall off the fur or clothes in a new area.

A second means of dispersal is water. Water can disperse seeds that fall into oceans and rivers. A third dispersal method involves wind. Wind disperses lightweight seeds that often have structures to catch the wind, such as those of dandelions and maple trees. Finally, some plants eject their seeds in a way that might remind you of popping popcorn. The force scatters the seeds in many directions.

FIGURE 3
Seed Dispersal
The seeds of these plants are enclosed in fruits with adaptations that help them disperse.

Dispersal by wind: Dandelion fruits with "parachutes" ▶

◀ **Dispersal by animals:** Barblike fruits

Dispersal by water: Floating coconut palm fruit ▶

Seed Plants

Video Preview
▶ **Video Field Trip**
Video Assessment

Germination After a seed is dispersed, it may remain inactive for a while before it germinates. **Germination** (jur muh NAY shun) occurs when the embryo begins to grow again and pushes out of the seed. Germination begins when the seed absorbs water from the environment. Then the embryo uses its stored food to begin to grow. As shown in Figure 4, the embryo's roots first grow downward; then its stem and leaves grow upward. Once you can see a plant's leaves, the plant is called a seedling.

A seed that is dispersed far from its parent plant has a better chance of survival. When a seed does not have to compete with its parent for light, water, and nutrients, it has a better chance of becoming a seedling.

Reading Checkpoint **What must happen in order for germination to begin?**

Roots

Have you ever tried to pull a dandelion out of the soil? It's not easy, is it? That is because most roots are good anchors. Roots have three main functions. **Roots anchor a plant in the ground, absorb water and minerals from the soil, and sometimes store food.** The more root area a plant has, the more water and minerals it can absorb.

Types of Roots The two main types of root systems are shown in Figure 5. A fibrous root system consists of many similarly sized roots that form a dense, tangled mass. Plants with fibrous roots take much soil with them when you pull them out of the ground. Lawn grass, corn, and onions have fibrous root systems. In contrast, a taproot system has one long, thick main root. Many smaller roots branch off the main root. A plant with a taproot system is hard to pull out of the ground. Carrots, dandelions, and cacti have taproots.

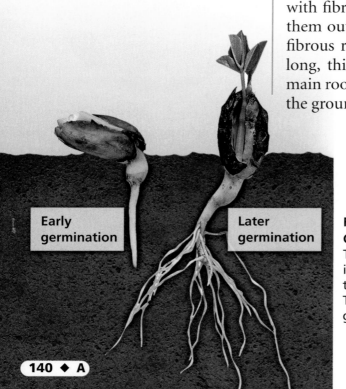

Early germination

Later germination

FIGURE 4
Germination
The embryo in this peanut seed uses its stored food to germinate. First, the embryo's roots grow downward. Then, its stem and leaves begin to grow upward.

The Structure of a Root In Figure 5, you can see the structure of a typical root. Notice that the tip of the root is rounded and is covered by a structure called the root cap. The **root cap** protects the root from injury from rocks as the root grows through the soil. Behind the root cap are the cells that divide to form new root cells.

Root hairs grow out of the root's surface. These tiny hairs can enter the spaces between soil particles, where they absorb water and minerals. By increasing the surface area of the root that touches the soil, root hairs help the plant absorb large amounts of substances. The root hairs also help to anchor the plant in the soil.

Locate the vascular tissue in the center of the root. The water and nutrients that are absorbed from the soil quickly move into the xylem. From there, these substances are transported upward to the plant's stems and leaves.

Phloem transports food manufactured in the leaves to the root. The root tissues may then use the food for growth or store it for future use by the plant.

 **Reading Checkpoint** What is a root cap?

FIGURE 5
Root Structure

Some plants have fibrous roots while others have taproots. A root's structure is adapted for absorbing water and minerals from the soil. **Relating Cause and Effect** *How do root hairs help absorb water and minerals?*

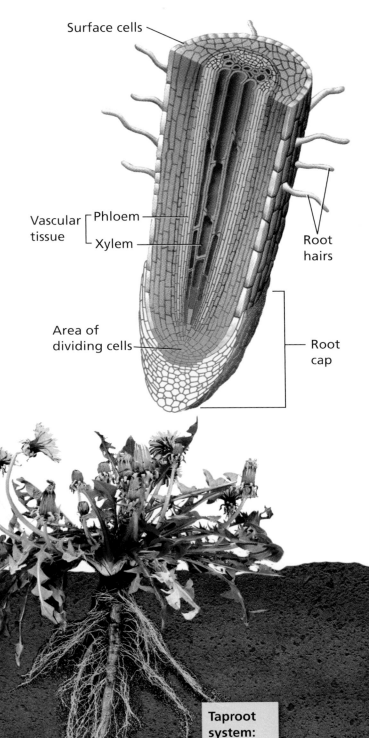

Surface cells

Vascular tissue ⎡Phloem
⎣Xylem

Root hairs

Area of dividing cells

Root cap

Fibrous root system: Onion

Taproot system: Dandelion

In this activity, you will calculate the speed at which water moves up a celery stalk.

1.  Pour about 1 cm of water into a tall plastic container. Stir in several drops of red food coloring.

2. Place the freshly cut end of a celery stalk in the water. Lean the stalk against the container's side.

3. After 20 minutes, remove the celery. Use a metric ruler to measure the height of the water in the stalk.

4. Use the measurement and the following formula to calculate how fast the water moved up the stalk.

$$\text{Speed} = \frac{\text{Height}}{\text{Time}}$$

Based on your calculation, predict how far the water would move in 2 hours. Then test your prediction.

Stems

The stem of a plant has two main functions. **The stem carries substances between the plant's roots and leaves. The stem also provides support for the plant and holds up the leaves so they are exposed to the sun.** In addition, some stems, such as those of asparagus, store food.

The Structure of a Stem Stems can be either herbaceous (hur BAY shus) or woody. Herbaceous stems contain no wood and are often soft. Coneflowers and pepper plants have herbaceous stems. In contrast, woody stems are hard and rigid. Maple trees and roses have woody stems.

Both herbaceous and woody stems consist of phloem and xylem tissue as well as many other supporting cells. Figure 6 shows the inner structure of one type of herbaceous stem.

As you can see in Figure 7, a woody stem contains several layers of tissue. The outermost layer is bark. Bark includes an outer protective layer and an inner layer of living phloem, which transports food through the stem. Next is a layer of cells called the **cambium** (KAM bee um), which divide to produce new phloem and xylem. It is xylem that makes up most of what you call "wood." Sapwood is active xylem that transports water and minerals through the stem. The older, darker, heartwood is inactive but provides support.

✓ Reading Checkpoint **What function does the bark of a woody stem perform?**

FIGURE 6
A Herbaceous Stem
Herbaceous stems, like those on these coneflowers, are often soft. The inset shows the inner structure of one type of herbaceous stem.

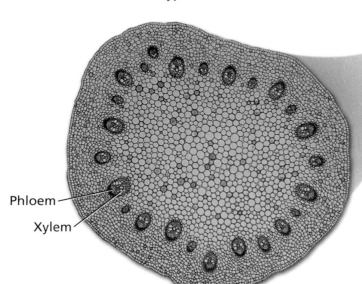

Phloem

Xylem

Annual Rings Have you ever looked at a tree stump and seen a pattern of circles that looks something like a target? These circles are called annual rings because they represent a tree's yearly growth. Annual rings are made of xylem. Xylem cells that form in the spring are large and have thin walls because they grow rapidly. They produce a wide, light brown ring. Xylem cells that form in the summer grow slowly and, therefore, are small and have thick walls. They produce a thin, dark ring. One pair of light and dark rings represents one year's growth. You can estimate a tree's age by counting its annual rings.

The width of a tree's annual rings can provide important clues about past weather conditions, such as rainfall. In rainy years, more xylem is produced, so the tree's annual rings are wide. In dry years, rings are narrow. By examining annual rings from some trees in the southwestern United States, scientists were able to infer that severe droughts occurred in the years 840, 1067, 1379, and 1632.

FIGURE 7
A Woody Stem

Trees like these maples have woody stems. A typical woody stem is made up of many layers. The layers of xylem form annual rings that can reveal the age of the tree and the growing conditions it has experienced.
Interpreting Diagrams *Where is the cambium located?*

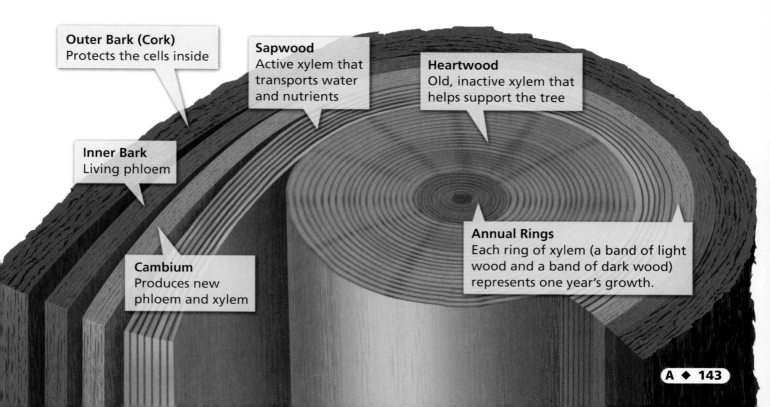

Outer Bark (Cork)
Protects the cells inside

Sapwood
Active xylem that transports water and nutrients

Heartwood
Old, inactive xylem that helps support the tree

Inner Bark
Living phloem

Cambium
Produces new phloem and xylem

Annual Rings
Each ring of xylem (a band of light wood and a band of dark wood) represents one year's growth.

FIGURE 8
The Structure of a Leaf

A leaf is a well-adapted food factory. Each structure helps the leaf produce food.

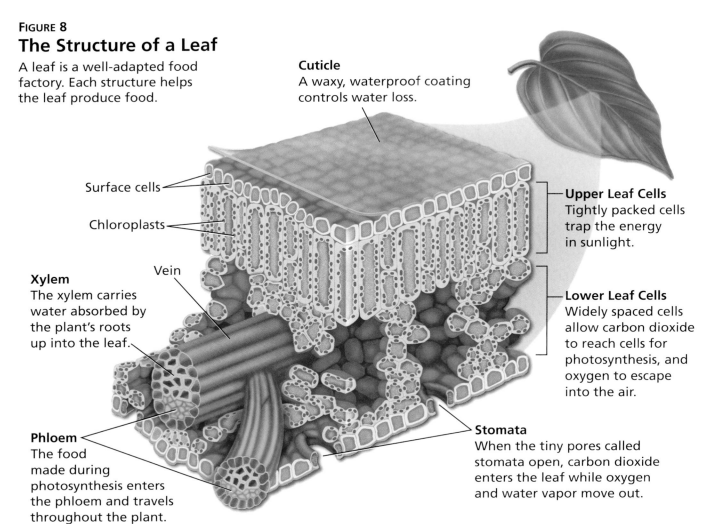

Cuticle
A waxy, waterproof coating controls water loss.

Surface cells

Chloroplasts

Upper Leaf Cells
Tightly packed cells trap the energy in sunlight.

Lower Leaf Cells
Widely spaced cells allow carbon dioxide to reach cells for photosynthesis, and oxygen to escape into the air.

Xylem
The xylem carries water absorbed by the plant's roots up into the leaf.

Vein

Phloem
The food made during photosynthesis enters the phloem and travels throughout the plant.

Stomata
When the tiny pores called stomata open, carbon dioxide enters the leaf while oxygen and water vapor move out.

Leaves

Leaves vary greatly in size and shape. Pine trees, for example, have needle-shaped leaves. Birch trees have small rounded leaves with jagged edges. Regardless of their shape, leaves play an important role in a plant. **Leaves capture the sun's energy and carry out the food-making process of photosynthesis.**

The Structure of a Leaf If you were to cut through a leaf and look at the edge under a microscope, you would see the structures in Figure 8. The leaf's top and bottom surface layers protect the cells inside. Between the layers of cells are veins that contain xylem and phloem.

The surface layers of the leaf have small openings, or pores, called **stomata** (STOH muh tuh) (singular *stoma*). The Greek word *stoma* means "mouth"—and stomata do look like tiny mouths. The stomata open and close to control when gases enter and leave the leaf. When the stomata are open, carbon dioxide enters the leaf, and oxygen and water vapor exit.

Go Online
PHSchool.com

For: More on leaves
Visit: PHSchool.com
Web Code: ced-1051

The Leaf and Photosynthesis The structure of a leaf is ideal for carrying out photosynthesis. The cells that contain the most chloroplasts are located near the leaf's upper surface, where they get the most light. The chlorophyll in the chloroplasts traps the sun's energy.

Carbon dioxide enters the leaf through open stomata. Water, which is absorbed by the plant's roots, travels up the stem to the leaf through the xylem. During photosynthesis, sugar and oxygen are produced from the carbon dioxide and water. Oxygen passes out of the leaf through the open stomata. The sugar enters the phloem and then travels throughout the plant.

Controlling Water Loss Because such a large area of a leaf is exposed to the air, water can quickly evaporate, or be lost, from a leaf into the air. The process by which water evaporates from a plant's leaves is called **transpiration.** A plant can lose a lot of water through transpiration. A corn plant, for example, can lose almost 4 liters of water on a hot summer day. Without a way to slow down the process of transpiration, a plant would shrivel up and die.

Fortunately, plants have ways to slow down transpiration. One way that plants retain water is by closing the stomata. The stomata often close when leaves start to dry out.

 **Reading Checkpoint** How does water get into a leaf?

FIGURE 9
Stomata
Stomata open (top) and close (bottom) to control when gases enter and exit the leaf.
Relating Cause and Effect *What gases enter and exit when the stomata open?*

Section 1 Assessment

Target Reading Skill Outlining Use the information in your outline about seed plants to help you answer the questions below.

Reviewing Key Concepts

1. **a. Reviewing** What two characteristics do all seed plants share?
   b. Relating Cause and Effect What characteristics enable seed plants to live in a wide variety of environments? Explain.

2. **a. Listing** Name the three main parts of a seed.
   b. Sequencing List the steps in the sequence in which they must occur for a seed to grow into a new plant.
   c. Applying Concepts If a cherry seed were to take root right below its parent tree, what three challenges might the cherry seedling face?

3. **a. Identifying** What are the main functions of a plant's roots, stems, and leaves?
   b. Comparing and Contrasting Compare the path on which water moves through a plant to the path on which sugar moves through a plant.
   c. Applying Concepts How are the structures of a tree's roots and leaves well-suited for their roles in supplying the tree with water and sugar?

Writing in Science

Product Label Write a "packaging label" for a seed. Include a name and description for each part of the seed. Be sure to describe the role of each part in producing a new plant.

Gymnosperms

Reading Preview

Key Concepts
- What are the characteristics of gymnosperms?
- How do gymnosperms reproduce?
- What important products come from gymnosperms?

Key Terms
- gymnosperm • cone • ovule
- pollination

Target Reading Skill
Previewing Visuals Before you read, preview Figure 11. Then write two questions that you have about the diagram in a graphic organizer like the one below. As you read, answer your questions.

The Life Cycle of a Gymnosperm

Q.	How does gymnosperm pollination occur?
A.	
Q.	

Go Online

SCi LINKS NSTA

For: Links on gymnosperms
Visit: www.SciLinks.org
Web Code: scn-0152

Lab zone Discover **Activity**

Are All Leaves Alike?
1. Your teacher will give you a hand lens, a ruler, and the leaves from some seed plants.
2. Using the hand lens, examine each leaf. Sketch each leaf in your notebook.
3. Measure the length and width of each leaf. Record your measurements in your notebook.

Think It Over
Classifying Divide the leaves into two groups on the basis of your observations. Explain why you grouped the leaves as you did.

Have you ever seen a tree that is wider than a car? Do trees this huge really exist? The answer is yes. Some giant sequoia trees, which grow almost exclusively in central California, are more than 10 meters wide. You can understand why giant sequoias are commonly referred to as "giants of the forest." It takes a long time for a tree to grow so big. Scientists think that the largest giant sequoias may be about 2,000 years old. One reason they live so long is because their bark is fire resistant.

What Are Gymnosperms?

The giant sequoia trees belong to the group of seed plants known as gymnosperms. A **gymnosperm** (JIM nuh spurm) is a seed plant that produces naked seeds. The seeds of gymnosperms are referred to as "naked" because they are not enclosed by a protective fruit.

Every gymnosperm produces naked seeds. In addition, many gymnosperms have needle-like or scalelike leaves, and deep-growing root systems. Gymnosperms are the oldest type of seed plant. According to fossil evidence, gymnosperms first appeared on Earth about 360 million years ago. Fossils also indicate that there were many more species of gymnosperms on Earth in the past than there are today. Four groups of gymnosperms exist today.

FIGURE 10
Types of Gymnosperms
Gymnosperms are the oldest seed plants. Cycads, conifers, ginkgoes, and gnetophytes are the only groups that exist today.

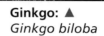

Gnetophyte: ▲
Welwitschia

Ginkgo: ▲
Ginkgo biloba

Cycad: ▲
Sago palm

Conifer: ▶
Giant sequoia

Cycads About 175 million years ago, the majority of plants were cycads. Today, cycads (SY kadz) grow mainly in tropical and subtropical areas. Cycads look like palm trees with cones. A cycad cone can grow as large as a football.

Conifers Conifers (KAHN uh furz), or cone-bearing plants, are the largest and most diverse group of gymnosperms today. Most conifers, such as pines, sequoias, and junipers, are evergreens—plants that keep their leaves, or needles, year-round. When needles drop off, they are replaced by new ones.

Ginkgoes Ginkgoes (GING kohz) also grew hundreds of millions of years ago, but today, only one species of ginkgo, *Ginkgo biloba*, exists. It probably survived only because the Chinese and Japanese cared for it in their gardens. Today, ginkgo trees are planted along city streets because they can tolerate air pollution.

Gnetophytes Gnetophytes (NEE tuh fyts) live in hot deserts and in tropical rain forests. Some gnetophytes are trees, some are shrubs, and others are vines. The *Welwitschia* shown in Figure 10 grows in the deserts of West Africa and can live for more than 1,000 years.

 **Reading Checkpoint** **What are the four types of gymnosperms?**

Reproduction in Gymnosperms

Most gymnosperms have reproductive structures called **cones.** Cones are covered with scales. Most gymnosperms produce two types of cones: male cones and female cones. Usually, a single plant produces both male and female cones. In some types of gymnosperms, however, individual trees produce either male cones or female cones. A few types of gymnosperms produce no cones at all.

In Figure 11, you can see the male and female cones of a Ponderosa pine. Male cones produce tiny grains of pollen—the male gametophyte. Pollen contains the cells that will later become sperm cells. Each scale on a male cone produces thousands of pollen grains.

The female gametophyte develops in structures called ovules. An **ovule** (OH vyool) is a structure that contains an egg cell. Female cones contain at least one ovule at the base of each scale. After fertilization occurs, the ovule develops into a seed.

You can follow the process of gymnosperm reproduction in Figure 11. **First, pollen falls from a male cone onto a female cone. In time, a sperm cell and an egg cell join together in an ovule on the female cone.** After fertilization occurs, the seed develops on the scale of the female cone.

Pollination The transfer of pollen from a male reproductive structure to a female reproductive structure is called **pollination.** In gymnosperms, wind often carries the pollen from the male cones to the female cones. The pollen collects in a sticky substance produced by each ovule.

Fertilization Once pollination has occurred, the ovule closes and seals in the pollen. The scales also close, and a sperm cell fertilizes an egg cell inside each ovule. The fertilized egg then develops into the embryo part of the seed.

Seed Development Female cones remain on the tree while the seeds mature. As the seeds develop, the female cone increases in size. It can take up to two years for the seeds of some gymnosperms to mature. Male cones, however, usually fall off the tree after they have shed their pollen.

Seed Dispersal When the seeds are mature, the scales open. The wind shakes the seeds out of the cone and carries them away. Only a few seeds will land in suitable places and grow into new plants.

 Reading Checkpoint **What is pollen and where is it produced?**

FIGURE 11
The Life Cycle of a Gymnosperm

Ponderosa pines have a typical life cycle for a gymnosperm. Follow the steps of pollination, fertilization, seed development, and dispersal in the pine tree.
Interpreting Diagrams *Where do the pine seeds develop?*

1 A pine tree produces male and female cones.

2 **A** A male cone produces pollen grains, which contain cells that will mature into sperm cells.

Scale on male cone

Scale on female cone

Egg cells

Ovule

2 **B** Each scale on a female cone has two ovules at its base.

3 In time, two egg cells form inside each ovule.

4 The wind scatters pollen grains. Some become trapped in a sticky substance produced by the ovule.

7 Wind disperses the pine seeds. A seed grows into a seedling and then into a tree.

6 The ovule develops into a seed. The fertilized egg becomes the seed's embryo. Other parts of the ovule develop into the seed coat and the seed's stored food.

5 The ovule closes, and a pollen grain produces a tube that grows into the ovule. A sperm cell moves through the tube and fertilizes the egg cell.

Gymnosperms in Everyday Life

Gymnosperms, especially conifers, provide many useful products. **Paper and other products, such as the lumber used to build homes, come from conifers.** The rayon fibers in clothes as well as the cellophane wrappers on some food products also come from conifers. Other products, such as turpentine and the rosin used by baseball pitchers, gymnasts, and musicians, are made from the sap produced by some conifers.

Because conifers are so useful to humans, they are grown in large, managed forests in many regions of the United States. When adult trees in managed forests are cut down, young trees are planted to replace them. Since different parts of the forest are usually cut at different times, there are always adult trees that can be harvested. These management efforts help ensure a steady supply of these important trees.

FIGURE 12
Uses of Gymnosperms
Conifers provided the lumber for this new house.

 **Reading Checkpoint** What are two products made from the sap of conifers?

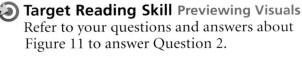

Section 2 Assessment

Target Reading Skill Previewing Visuals Refer to your questions and answers about Figure 11 to answer Question 2.

Reviewing Key Concepts

1. **a.** Listing What characteristics do all gymnosperms share? What other characteristics do many gymnosperms have?
   b. Comparing and Contrasting In what way do gymnosperm seeds differ from corn or bean seeds, which are not gymnosperms?
   c. Predicting Do you think that the seeds of gymnosperms would likely be dispersed by animals? Why or why not?
2. **a.** Reviewing What is a cone?
   b. Comparing and Contrasting What are the two different types of cones? What role does each cone play in gymnosperm reproduction?
   c. Sequencing Briefly describe the steps in the reproduction of a gymnosperm.

3. **a.** Identifying Name two important products that come from conifers.
   b. Making Judgments Do you think that managed forests guarantee that there will be a steady supply of conifers? Why or why not?

Lab zone At-Home Activity

Everyday Gymnosperms Describe the characteristics of gymnosperms to a family member. Then, with that family member, make a list of things in your home that are made from gymnosperms. Also list the gymnosperms that grow where you live.

Section 3 Angiosperms

Reading Preview

Key Concepts
- What characteristics do angiosperms share?
- What is the function of an angiosperm's flowers?
- How do angiosperms reproduce?
- How do monocots differ from dicots?

Key Terms
- angiosperm • flower • sepal
- petal • stamen • pistil
- ovary • fruit • monocot
- dicot

Target Reading Skill
Building Vocabulary Using a word in a sentence helps you think about how best to explain the word. After you read the section, reread the paragraphs that contain definitions of Key Terms. Use all the information you have learned to write a meaningful sentence using each Key Term.

◀ Rafflesia

Lab zone Discover Activity

What Is a Fruit?

1. Your teacher will give you three different fruits that have been cut in half.
2. Use a hand lens to carefully observe the outside of each fruit. For each fruit, record its color, shape, size, and other external features. Record your observations in your notebook.
3. Carefully observe the structures inside the fruit. Record your observations.

Think It Over
Forming Operational Definitions Based on your observations, how would you define the term *fruit*?

You probably associate the word *flower* with a sweet-smelling plant growing in a garden. You certainly wouldn't think of something that smells like rotting meat. But that's exactly what the corpse flower, or rafflesia, smells like. These flowers, which grow on vines in Asia, are huge—nearly 1 meter across! You won't be seeing rafflesia in your local florist shop any time soon.

Rafflesia belongs to the group of seed plants known as **angiosperms** (AN jee uh spurmz). **All angiosperms, or flowering plants, share two important characteristics. First, they produce flowers. Second, in contrast to gymnosperms, which produce uncovered seeds, angiosperms produce seeds that are enclosed in fruits.**

Angiosperms live almost everywhere on Earth. They grow in frozen areas in the Arctic, tropical jungles, and barren deserts. A few angiosperms, such as mangrove trees, can live at the ocean's edge.

FIGURE 13
The Structure of a Flower

Like most flowers, this lily contains both male and female reproductive structures.

Pistils
Pistils are the female reproductive parts of a flower. A pistil consists of a sticky stigma, a slender tube called the style, and a hollow structure, called the ovary, at the base.

Stamens
Stamens are the male reproductive parts of a flower. Pollen is produced in the anther, at the top of the stalklike filament.

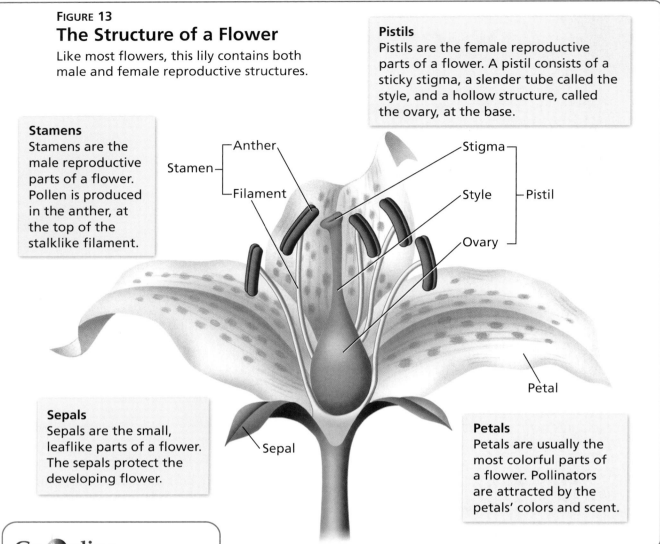

Stamen — Anther, Filament
Stigma, Style, Ovary — Pistil
Petal
Sepal

Sepals
Sepals are the small, leaflike parts of a flower. The sepals protect the developing flower.

Petals
Petals are usually the most colorful parts of a flower. Pollinators are attracted by the petals' colors and scent.

Go Online
active art

For: The Structure of a Flower activity
Visit: PHSchool.com
Web Code: cep-1053

The Structure of Flowers

Flowers come in all sorts of shapes, sizes, and colors. But, despite their differences, all flowers have the same function—reproduction. A **flower** is the reproductive structure of an angiosperm. Figure 13 shows the parts of a typical flower. As you read about the parts, keep in mind that some flowers lack one or more of the parts. For example, some flowers have only male reproductive parts, and some flowers lack petals.

Sepals and Petals When a flower is still a bud, it is enclosed by leaflike structures called **sepals** (SEE pulz). Sepals protect the developing flower and are often green in color. When the sepals fold back, they reveal the flower's colorful, leaflike **petals.** The petals are generally the most colorful parts of a flower. The shapes, sizes, and number of petals vary greatly from flower to flower.

Stamens Within the petals are the flower's male and female reproductive parts. The **stamens** (STAY munz) are the male reproductive parts. Locate the stamens inside the flower in Figure 13. The thin stalk of the stamen is called the filament. Pollen is produced in the anther, at the top of the filament.

Pistils The female parts, or **pistils** (PIS tulz), are found in the center of most flowers. Some flowers have two or more pistils; others have only one. The sticky tip of the pistil is called the stigma. A slender tube, called a style, connects the stigma to a hollow structure at the base of the flower. This hollow structure is the **ovary,** which protects the seeds as they develop. An ovary contains one or more ovules.

Pollinators The colors and shapes of most petals and the scents produced by most flowers attract insects and other animals. These organisms ensure that pollination occurs. Pollinators include birds, bats, and insects such as bees and flies. The rafflesia flower you read about at the beginning of the section is pollinated by flies. The flies are attracted by the strong smell of rotting meat.

 **Reading Checkpoint** What are the male and female reproductive parts of a flower?

FIGURE 14
Pollinators
Pollinators, such as insects, birds, and bats, are attracted to a flower's color, shape, or scent. *Inferring How might the white color of the cactus flower aid in attracting bats?*

◄ A honeybee is covered in the pollen of an orange flower.

▲ A hummingbird pollinates a bright red flower.

A bat pollinates an organ ► pipe cactus flower at night.

Reproduction in Angiosperms

You can follow the process of angiosperm reproduction in Figure 16. **First, pollen falls on a flower's stigma. In time, the sperm cell and egg cell join together in the flower's ovule. The zygote develops into the embryo part of the seed.**

Pollination A flower is pollinated when a grain of pollen falls on the stigma. Like gymnosperms, some angiosperms are pollinated by the wind. But most angiosperms rely on birds, bats, or insects for pollination. Nectar, a sugar-rich food, is located deep inside a flower. When an animal enters a flower to obtain the nectar, it brushes against the anthers and becomes coated with pollen. Some of the pollen can drop onto the flower's stigma as the animal leaves the flower. The pollen can also be brushed onto the sticky stigma of the next flower the animal visits.

Fertilization If the pollen falls on the stigma of a similar plant, fertilization can occur. A sperm cell joins with an egg cell inside an ovule within the ovary at the base of the flower. The zygote then begins to develop into the seed's embryo. Other parts of the ovule develop into the rest of the seed.

Fruit Development and Seed Dispersal As the seed develops after fertilization, the ovary changes into a **fruit**—a ripened ovary and other structures that enclose one or more seeds. Apples and cherries are fruits. So are many foods you usually call vegetables, such as tomatoes and squash. Fruits are the means by which angiosperm seeds are dispersed. Animals that eat fruits help to disperse their seeds.

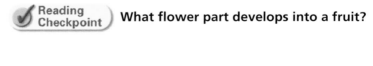 **Reading Checkpoint** What flower part develops into a fruit?

FIGURE 15
Fruits
The seeds of angiosperms are enclosed in fruits, which protect and help disperse the seeds.

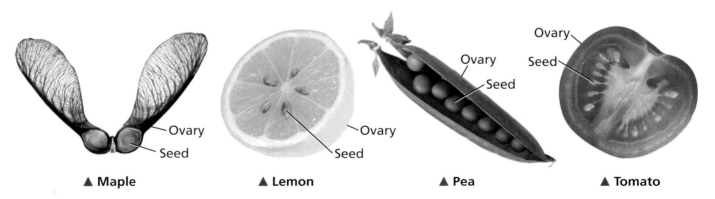

▲ Maple ▲ Lemon ▲ Pea ▲ Tomato

Ovary
Seed
Ovary
Seed
Ovary
Seed
Ovary
Seed

FIGURE 16

The Life Cycle of an Angiosperm

All angiosperms have a similar life cycle. Follow the steps of pollination, fertilization, seed development, and dispersal in this apple tree.

Interpreting Diagrams *What plant part does the ovule develop into?*

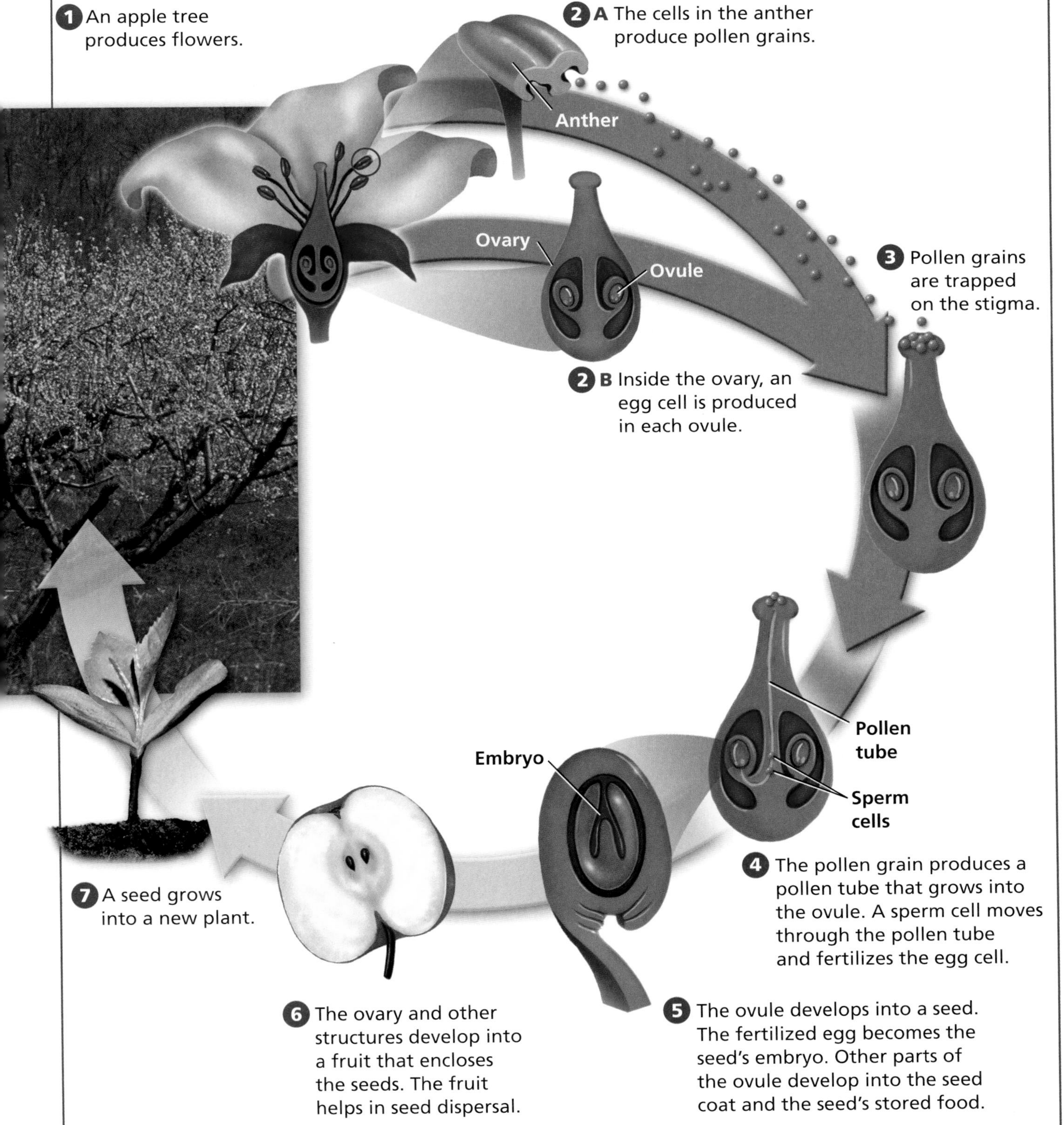

❶ An apple tree produces flowers.

❷ A The cells in the anther produce pollen grains.

Anther

Ovary

Ovule

❸ Pollen grains are trapped on the stigma.

❷ B Inside the ovary, an egg cell is produced in each ovule.

Embryo

Pollen tube

Sperm cells

❹ The pollen grain produces a pollen tube that grows into the ovule. A sperm cell moves through the pollen tube and fertilizes the egg cell.

❼ A seed grows into a new plant.

❻ The ovary and other structures develop into a fruit that encloses the seeds. The fruit helps in seed dispersal.

❺ The ovule develops into a seed. The fertilized egg becomes the seed's embryo. Other parts of the ovule develop into the seed coat and the seed's stored food.

FIGURE 17

Monocots and Dicots
Monocots and dicots differ in the number of cotyledons, the pattern of veins and vascular tissue, and the number of petals.

Interpreting Tables
How do monocot and dicot leaves differ?

Comparing Monocots and Dicots		
Plant Part	**Monocots**	**Dicots**
Seed	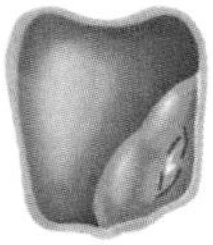 One cotyledon	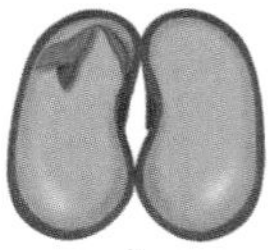 Two cotyledons
Leaf	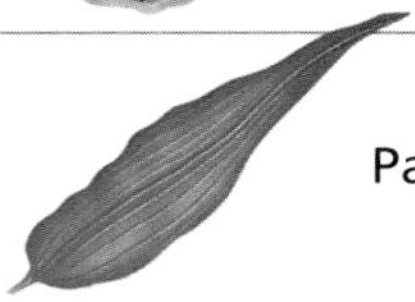 Parallel veins	 Branching veins
Stem	 Bundles of vascular tissue scattered throughout stem	 Bundles of vascular tissue arranged in a ring
Flower	 Flower parts in threes	 Flower parts in fours or fives

Types of Angiosperms

Angiosperms are divided into two major groups: monocots and dicots. "Cot" is short for *cotyledon*. Recall from Section 1 that the cotyledon, or seed leaf, provides food for the embryo. *Mono* means "one" and *di* means "two." **Monocots** are angiosperms that have only one seed leaf. **Dicots,** on the other hand, produce seeds with two seed leaves. In Figure 17, you can compare the characteristics of monocots and dicots.

Monocots Grasses, including corn, wheat, and rice, and plants such as lilies and tulips are monocots. The flowers of a monocot usually have either three petals or a multiple of three petals. Monocots usually have long, slender leaves with veins that run parallel to one another like train rails. The bundles of vascular tissue in monocot stems are usually scattered randomly throughout the stem.

Dicots Dicots include plants such as roses and violets, as well as dandelions. Both oak and maple trees are dicots, as are food plants such as beans and apples. The flowers of dicots often have either four or five petals or multiples of these numbers. The leaves are usually wide, with veins that branch many times. Dicot stems usually have bundles of vascular tissue arranged in a ring.

 **Reading Checkpoint** How do the petals of monocots and dicots differ in number?

Math Skills

Multiples

Is a flower with 6 petals a monocot? To answer this question, you need to determine if 6 is a multiple of 3. A number is a multiple of 3 if there is a nonzero whole number that, when multiplied by 3, gives you that number.

In this case, 6 is a multiple of 3 because you can multiply 2 (a nonzero whole number) by 3 to get 6.

$$2 \times 3 = 6$$

Therefore, a flower with 6 petals is a monocot. Other multiples of 3 include 9 and 12.

Practice Problem Which of these numbers are multiples of 4?

6, 10, 12, 16

Angiosperms in Everyday Life

Angiosperms are an important source of food, clothing, and medicine for other organisms. Plant-eating animals, such as cows, elephants, and beetles, eat flowering plants such as grasses as well as the leaves of trees. People eat vegetables, fruits, and cereals, all of which are angiosperms.

People also produce clothing and other products from angiosperms. For example, the seeds of cotton plants, like the ones you see in Figure 18, are covered with cotton fibers. The stems of flax plants provide linen fibers. The sap of rubber trees is used to make rubber for tires and other products. Furniture is often made from the wood of maple, cherry, and oak trees. Some important medications come from angiosperms, too. For example, the heart medication digitalis comes from the leaves of the foxglove plant.

FIGURE 18
Cotton Bolls
Angiosperms, such as cotton plants, provide many important products. Cotton seeds, which develop in fruits called bolls, are covered with fibers that are manufactured into cotton fabric.

 **Reading Checkpoint** **What are two angiosperms from which people produce clothing?**

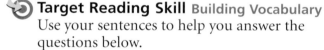

Section 3 Assessment

Target Reading Skill Building Vocabulary Use your sentences to help you answer the questions below.

Reviewing Key Concepts

1. a. **Reviewing** What two characteristics do all angiosperms share?
   b. **Comparing and Contrasting** Do gymnosperms share either of the two characteristics with angiosperms? Explain.
2. a. **Identifying** What is the function of an angiosperm's flowers?
   b. **Describing** Describe the role of a flower's sepals, petals, stamens, and pistil.
3. a. **Reviewing** On what part of a flower must pollen land for pollination to occur?
   b. **Sequencing** Briefly describe the steps in the reproduction of an angiosperm, from pollination to seed dispersal.
   c. **Making Judgments** Do you agree or disagree with the following statement? Animals are essential in order for reproduction in angiosperms to occur. Explain your answer.

4. a. **Listing** Name the two major groups of angiosperms.
   b. **Comparing and Contrasting** How do the seeds, leaves, stems, and flowers of these two groups differ?
   c. **Classifying** A plant's leaves have parallel veins, and each of its flowers has six petals. To which group does it belong? Explain.

Math Practice

5. **Multiples** Which of the following numbers are multiples of 3? Which of the numbers are multiples of 4?

   5, 6, 8, 10, 12, 15

6. **Multiples** Suppose you found a flower with 12 petals. Would you know from the number of petals whether the flower is a monocot or a dicot? Explain.

A Close Look at Flowers

Problem

What is the function of a flower, and what roles do its different parts play?

Skills Focus

observing, inferring, measuring

Materials

- paper towels
- plastic dropper
- hand lens
- microscope
- slide
- large flower
- coverslip
- scalpel
- tape
- water
- metric ruler
- lens paper

Procedure

PART 1   The Outer Parts of the Flower

1. Tape four paper towel sheets on your work area. Obtain a flower from your teacher. While handling the flower gently, observe its shape and color. Use the ruler to measure it. Notice whether the petals have any spots or other markings. Does the flower have a scent? Record your observations with sketches and descriptions.

2. Observe the sepals. How many are there? How do they relate to the rest of the flower? (*Hint:* The sepals are often green, but not always.) Record your observations.

3. Use a scalpel to carefully cut off the sepals without damaging the structures beneath them. **CAUTION:** *Scalpels are sharp. Cut in a direction away from yourself and others.*

4. Observe the petals. How many are there? Are all the petals the same, or are they different? Record your observations.

PART 2   The Male Part of the Flower

5. Carefully pull off the petals to examine the male part of the flower. Try not to damage the structures beneath the petals.

6. Observe the stamens. How many are there? How are they shaped? How tall are they? Record your observations.

7. Use a scalpel to carefully cut the stamens away from the rest of the flower without damaging the structures beneath them. Lay the stamens on the paper towel.

8. Obtain a clean slide and coverslip. Hold a stamen over the slide, and gently tap some pollen grains from the anther onto the slide. Add a drop of water to the pollen. Then place the coverslip over the water and pollen.

9. Observe the pollen under both the low-power objective and the high-power objective of a microscope. Draw and label a pollen grain.

PART 3 The Female Part of the Flower

10. Use a scalpel to cut the pistil away from the rest of the flower. Measure the height of the pistil. Examine its shape. Observe the top of the pistil. Determine if that surface will stick to and lift a tiny piece of lens paper. Record your observations.

11. Lay the pistil on the paper towel. Holding it firmly at its base, use a scalpel to cut the pistil in half at its widest point, as shown in the diagram below. **CAUTION:** *Cut away from your fingers.* How many compartments do you see? How many ovules do you see? Record your observations.

Analyze and Conclude

1. **Observing** Based on your observations, describe how the sepals, petals, stamens, and pistils of a flower are arranged.

2. **Inferring** How are the sepals, petals, stamens, and pistil involved in the function of this flower?

3. **Measuring** Based on your measurements of the heights of the pistil and stamens, how do you think the flower you examined is pollinated? Use additional observations to support your answer.

4. **Classifying** Did you find any patterns in the number of sepals, petals, stamens, or other structures in your flower? If so, describe that pattern. Is your flower a monocot or a dicot?

5. **Communicating** Write a paragraph explaining all you can learn about a plant by examining one of its flowers. Use your observations in this lab to support your conclusions.

More to Explore

Some kinds of flowers do not have all the parts found in the flower in this lab. Obtain a different flower. Find out which parts that flower has, and which parts are missing. *Obtain your teacher's permission before carrying out your investigation.*

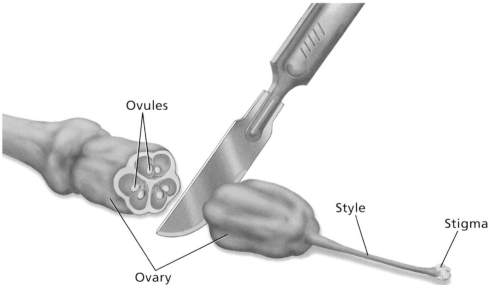

Ovules

Ovary

Style

Stigma

Plant Responses and Growth

Reading Preview

Key Concepts
- What are three stimuli that produce plant responses?
- How do plants respond to seasonal changes?
- How long do different angiosperms live?

Key Terms
- tropism • hormone
- auxin • photoperiodism
- short-day plant
- long-day plant
- critical night length
- day-neutral plant • dormancy
- annual • biennial • perennial

Target Reading Skill
Relating Cause and Effect
A cause makes something happen. An effect is what happens. As you read through the paragraphs under the heading Hormones and Tropisms, identify four effects of plant hormones. Write the information in a graphic organizer like the one below.

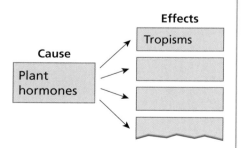

Effects

Cause

| Plant hormones |

Tropisms

Discover **Activity**

Can a Plant Respond to Touch?
1. Your teacher will give you two plants. Observe the first plant. Gently touch a leaf with the tip of a pencil. Observe what happens over the next three minutes. Record your observations.
2. Repeat Step 1 with the second plant. Record your observations.
3. Wash your hands with soap and water.

Think It Over
Inferring What advantage might a plant have if its leaves responded to touch?

The bladderwort is a freshwater plant with small yellow flowers. Attached to its floating stems are open structures called bladders. When a water flea touches a sensitive hair on a bladder, the bladder flicks open. Faster than you can blink, the water flea is sucked inside, and the bladder snaps shut. The plant then digests the trapped flea.

A bladderwort responds quickly—faster than many animals respond to a similar stimulus. You may be surprised to learn that some plants have lightning-quick responses. In fact, you might have thought that plants do not respond to stimuli at all. But plants do respond to some stimuli, although they usually do so more slowly than the bladderwort.

Tropisms

Animals usually respond to stimuli by moving. Unlike animals, plants commonly respond by growing either toward or away from a stimulus. A plant's growth response toward or away from a stimulus is called a **tropism** (TROH piz um). If a plant grows toward the stimulus, it is said to show a positive tropism. If a plant grows away from a stimulus, it shows a negative tropism. **Touch, light, and gravity are three important stimuli to which plants show growth responses, or tropisms.**

Touch Some plants, such as bladderworts, show a response to touch called thigmotropism. The prefix *thigmo-* comes from a Greek word that means "touch." The stems of many vines, such as grapes and morning glories, show a positive thigmotropism. As the vines grow, they coil around any object that they touch.

Light Have you ever noticed plants on a windowsill with their leaves and stems facing the sun? All plants exhibit a response to light called phototropism. The leaves, stems, and flowers of plants grow toward light, showing a positive phototropism. By growing towards the light, a plant receives more energy for photosynthesis.

Gravity Plants also respond to gravity. This response is called gravitropism. Roots show positive gravitropism—they grow downward. Stems, on the other hand, show negative gravitropism—they grow upward.

Hormones and Tropisms Plants are able to respond to touch, light, and gravity because they produce hormones. A **hormone** produced by a plant is a chemical that affects how the plant grows and develops.

One important plant hormone is named **auxin** (AWK sin). Auxin speeds up the rate at which a plant's cells grow. Auxin controls a plant's response to light. When light shines on one side of a plant's stem, auxin builds up in the shaded side of the stem. The cells on the shaded side begin to grow faster. Eventually, the cells on the stem's shaded side are longer than those on its sunny side. So the stem bends toward the light.

In addition to tropisms, plant hormones also control many other plant activities. Some of these activities are germination, the formation of flowers, stems, and leaves, the shedding of leaves, and the development and ripening of fruit.

Reading Checkpoint What is one role that the plant hormone auxin plays?

FIGURE 19

Tropisms

Touch, light, and gravity are three stimuli to which plants show growth responses, or tropisms.

▲ **Touch** A vine coiling around a wire shows positive thigmotropism.

▲ **Light** A plant's stems and flowers growing toward light show positive phototropism.

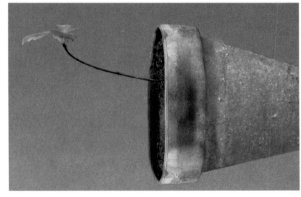

▲ **Gravity** A plant's stem growing upward, against the pull of gravity, shows negative gravitropism.

FIGURE 20
Short-day and Long-day Plants
A short-day plant flowers when nights are longer than the critical night length. A long-day plant flowers when nights are shorter than the critical night length.
Applying Concepts *Which plant—chrysanthemum or iris—would most likely flower in the early summer?*

Short-Day Plant	
Longer than critical night length	Shorter than critical night length
Chrysanthemum	Chrysanthemum

Long-Day Plant	
Longer than critical night length	Shorter than critical night length
Iris	Iris

Seasonal Changes

You may have heard the saying "April showers bring May flowers," but have you ever wondered whether it's true? Do all flowers bloom in May? Is it really rain that makes flowers bloom?

People have long observed that plants respond to the changing seasons. Some plants bloom in early spring, while others don't bloom until summer. The leaves on some trees change color in autumn and then fall off by winter.

Photoperiodism What environmental factor triggers a plant to flower? **The amount of darkness a plant receives determines the time of flowering in many plants.** A plant's response to seasonal changes in length of night and day is called **photoperiodism.**

Plants differ in how they respond to the length of nights. **Short-day plants** flower when nights are *longer* than a critical length. **Long-day plants** flower when nights are *shorter* than a critical length. This critical length, called the **critical night length,** is the number of hours of darkness that determines whether or not a plant will flower. For example, if a short-day plant has a critical night length of 11 hours, it will flower only when nights are longer than 11 hours.

Short-day plants bloom in the fall or winter, when nights are growing longer. Chrysanthemums and poinsettias are short-day plants. In contrast, long-day plants flower in the spring or summer, when nights are getting shorter. Long-day plants include irises and lettuce.

Other plants, such as dandelions, rice, and tomatoes, are **day-neutral plants.** Their flowering cycle is not sensitive to periods of light and dark.

Go Online
SciLINKS NSTA

For: Links on plant responses
Visit: www.SciLinks.org
Web Code: scn-0154

FIGURE 21
Winter Dormancy
As winter approaches, the leaves on this sugar maple turn color and then fall to the ground.

Winter Dormancy As winter draws near, many plants prepare to go into a state of dormancy. **Dormancy is a period when an organism's growth or activity stops. Dormancy helps plants survive freezing temperatures and the lack of liquid water.**

With many trees, the first change is that the leaves begin to turn color. Cooler weather and shorter days cause the leaves to stop making chlorophyll. As chlorophyll breaks down, yellow and orange pigments become visible. In addition, the plant begins to produce new red pigments. The brilliant colors of autumn leaves result.

Over the next few weeks, all of the remaining sugar and water are transported out of the tree's leaves. The leaves then fall to the ground, and the tree is ready for winter.

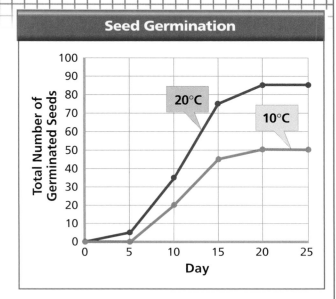

 **Reading Checkpoint** What is dormancy?

Math Analyzing Data

Germination and Temperature

One hundred radish seeds were planted in each of two identical trays of soil. One tray was kept at 10°C, and one tray was kept at 20°C. The trays received equal amounts of water and sunlight. The graph shows how many seeds germinated over time at each temperature.

1. **Reading Graphs** What variable is plotted on the horizontal axis? What variable is plotted on the vertical axis?

2. **Interpreting Data** How did the number of seeds that germinated change between day 20 and day 25 at 10°C? At 20°C?

3. **Drawing Conclusions** According to the graph, at which temperature did more seeds eventually germinate? What can you conclude about the relationship between temperature and germination?

Seed Germination

Total Number of Germinated Seeds (vertical axis: 0–100)
Day (horizontal axis: 0–25)
20°C
10°C

4. **Predicting** Predict what the graph would look like for a tray of 100 radish seeds kept at 5°C. Give a reason for your prediction.

▲ **Annual:**
Morning glory

Biennial: ▶
Foxglove

FIGURE 22
Life Spans of Angiosperms
Annuals live for one year. Biennials live for two years, and perennials live for many years.

▲ **Perennial:**
Peony

Life Spans of Angiosperms

Angiosperms are classified as annuals, biennials, or perennials based on the length of their life cycles. Flowering plants that complete a life cycle within one growing season are called **annuals.** Most annuals have herbaceous stems. Annuals include marigolds, petunias, wheat, and cucumbers.

Angiosperms that complete their life cycle in two years are called **biennials** (by EN ee ulz). In the first year, biennials germinate and grow roots, very short stems, and leaves. During their second year, biennials lengthen their stems, grow new leaves, and then produce flowers and seeds. Once the flowers produce seeds, the plant dies. Parsley, celery, and foxglove are biennials.

Flowering plants that live for more than two years are called **perennials.** Most perennials flower every year. Some perennials, such as peonies, have herbaceous stems. The leaves and stems of these plants die each winter, and new ones are produced each spring. Most perennials, however, have woody stems that live through the winter. Maple trees are examples of woody perennials.

 **Reading Checkpoint** **How long does a biennial live?**

Section 4 Assessment

⊙ Target Reading Skill Relating Cause and Effect Refer to your graphic organizer about plant hormones to help you answer Question 1 below.

Reviewing Key Concepts

1. **a. Describing** Describe three tropisms that take place in plants.
   b. Explaining How does auxin control a plant's response to light?
   c. Developing Hypotheses The stems of your morning glory plants have wrapped around your garden fence. Explain why this has occurred.
2. **a. Defining** What is photoperiodism? What is winter dormancy?
   b. Comparing and Contrasting How do short-day plants and long-day plants differ?
   c. Sequencing List in order the changes that a tree undergoes as winter approaches.

3. **a. Defining** How do annuals, biennials, and perennials differ?
   b. Applying Concepts Is the grass that grows on most lawns an annual, a biennial, or a perennial? Explain.

Lab zone **At-Home Activity**

Sun Seekers With a family member, soak some corn seeds or lima bean seeds in water overnight. Then push them gently into some soil in a paper cup until they are just covered. Keep the soil moist. When you see the stems break through the soil, place the cup in a sunny window. After a few days, explain to your family member why the plants grew in the direction they did.

Feeding the World

Reading Preview

Key Concept
• What technologies may help farmers produce more crops?

Key Terms
• precision farming • hydroponics
• genetic engineering

Target Reading Skill
Identifying Main Ideas As you read the section, write the main idea in a graphic organizer like the one below. Then write three supporting details that give examples of the main idea.

Main Idea

Technologies that may help produce more food include . . .

Detail	Detail	Detail

Discover Activity

Will There Be Enough to Eat?

1. Choose a numbered tag from the bag that your teacher provides. If you pick a tag with the number *1* on it, you're from a wealthy country. If you pick a tag with the number *2*, you're from a middle-income country. If you pick a tag with the number *3*, you're from a poor country.
2. Find classmates that have the same number on their tag. Sit down as a group.
3. Your teacher will serve your group a meal. The amount of food you receive will depend on the number on your tag.
4. As you eat, observe the people in your group and in the other groups. After you eat, record your observations. Also, record how you felt and what you were thinking during the meal.

Think It Over
Predicting Based on this activity, predict what effect an increase in the world's population would have on the world's food supply.

More than 6 billion people live on Earth today. By the year 2050, the population could grow as large as 10 billion. Think about how much food will be needed to feed the growing population. How will farmers be able to grow enough food?

Farmers and scientists are hard at work trying to find answers to this question. Farmers are using new technologies that make farming more efficient. People are developing methods for growing crops in areas with poor soil. In addition, scientists are developing plants that are more resistant to insects, diseases, and drought.

◀ A food market in Turkey

Precision Farming

On the farms of the future, satellite images and computers will be just as important as tractors and harvesters. Such technologies will allow farmers to practice **precision farming,** a farming method in which farmers fine-tune the amount of water and fertilizer they use to the requirements of a specific field.

First, satellite images of a farmer's fields are taken. Then, a computer analyzes the images to determine the makeup of the soil in the different fields. The computer uses the data to prepare a watering and fertilizing plan for each field.

Precision farming can benefit farmers by saving time and money. It also increases crop yields by helping farmers maintain ideal conditions in all fields. Precision farming would also benefit the environment because farmers use only as much fertilizer as the soil needs. When less fertilizer is used, fewer nutrients wash off the land into lakes and rivers. As you read in Chapter 3, reducing the use of fertilizers is one way to prevent algal blooms from damaging bodies of water.

Hydroponics

In some areas, people cannot grow crops because the soil is so poor. For example, on some islands in the Pacific Ocean, the soil contains large amounts of salt from the surrounding ocean. Food crops will not grow in salty soil.

On these islands, people may soon use hydroponics to grow food crops. **Hydroponics** (hy druh PAHN iks) is a farming method in which plants are grown in solutions of nutrients instead of in soil. Usually, the plants are grown in containers in which their roots are anchored in gravel or sand. The nutrient solution is pumped through the gravel or sand. **Hydroponics allows people to grow crops in areas with poor soil to help feed a growing population.** Unfortunately, hydroponics is a costly method of growing food crops.

FIGURE 23
Precision Farming
The map on this tractor's computer screen shows the makeup of the soil in a farm's fields. The map was obtained by satellite imaging.
Relating Cause and Effect *How can precision farming benefit the environment?*

 **What is hydroponics?**

Engineering Better Plants

Wheat, corn, rice, and potatoes are the major sources of food today. To feed more people, the yields of these crops must be increased. This is not an easy task. One challenge facing farmers is that these crops grow only in certain climates. Another challenge is that the size and structure of these plants limit how much food they can produce.

One technique scientists are using to address these challenges is called genetic engineering. In **genetic engineering,** scientists alter an organism's genetic material to produce an organism with qualities that people find useful.

Scientists are using genetic engineering to produce plants that can grow in a wider range of climates. They are also engineering plants to be more resistant to damage from insects. For example, scientists have inserted genetic material from a bacterium into corn and tomato plants. This bacterium is harmless to humans. But its genetic material enables the plants to produce substances that kill insects. Caterpillars or other insects that bite into the leaves of these plants are killed. Today, farmers grow many kinds of genetically engineered plants.

 **Reading Checkpoint** What is one way that genetic engineering can help farmers produce more food?

Go Online

For: Links on plants as food
Visit: www.SciLinks.org
Web Code: scn-0155

Section 5 Assessment

Target Reading Skill Identifying Main Ideas Use your graphic organizer to help you answer the questions below.

Reviewing Key Concepts

1. **a. Listing** Name three technologies that farmers can use to increase crop yields.
   b. Explaining Describe one farming challenge that each technology addresses.
   c. Making Judgments Which technology do you think holds the most promise for the future? Support your answer with reasons.

Writing in Science

Interview Suppose you could interview a farmer who uses precision farming. Write a one-page interview in which you ask the farmer to explain the technology and its benefits.

Technology Lab
· Tech & Design ·

Design and Build a Hydroponic Garden

Problem

Can you design and build a system for growing plants without soil?

Skills Focus

designing a solution, redesigning

Materials

- potted plant
- 2 different types of seedlings
- nutrient solution
- empty 2-liter soda bottles
- paper towels
- optional materials provided by your teacher

Procedure

PART 1 Research and Investigate

1. Copy the data table onto a sheet of paper.

2. Carefully examine the potted plant your teacher gives you. Think about all the factors that are required in order for the plant to grow. List these factors in the first column of the data table.

3. Use your knowledge of plants and additional research to fill in the second column of the data table.

4. For each factor listed in the table, decide whether or not it is "essential" for plant growth. Write this information in the third column of the data table.

PART 2 Design and Build

5. To test whether soil is essential for plant growth, design a "garden" system for growing plants without soil. Your garden must
   - include at least two different types of seedlings
   - use only the amount of nutrient solution provided by your teacher
   - be built using materials that are small and lightweight, yet durable

6. Sketch your garden design on a sheet of paper and make a list of the materials you will use. Then obtain your teacher's approval and build your garden.

PART 3 Evaluate and Redesign

7. Test your garden design by growing your plants for 2 weeks. Each day, measure and record the height of your plants and the number of leaves. Also note the overall appearance of your plants.

8. Evaluate your design by comparing your garden and plants with those of your classmates. Based on your comparison, decide how you might improve your garden's design. Then make any needed changes and monitor plant growth for one more week.

Data Table		
Factor Required for Plant Growth	What This Factor Provides for the Plant	Essential or Nonessential?

Analyze and Conclude

1. **Identifying a Need** In Part 1, did you list soil as a factor required for plant growth? If so, did you think it was an essential or nonessential factor? Explain your thinking.

2. **Designing a Solution** How did the information you gathered in Part 1 help you in designing your garden in Part 2? How did your garden design provide for each of the essential growth factors you listed?

3. **Redesigning** What changes did you make to your garden design and why? Did the changes lead to improved plant growth?

4. **Working With Design Constraints** How did the design constraints in Step 5 limit your design? How did you overcome those limitations?

5. **Evaluating the Impact on Society** Hydroponic gardens are planned for future space flights and as a way to grow plants in cold climates. Explain why hydroponic gardens are a good choice for each of these situations. Then, identify two more situations in which hydroponic gardens would be a good choice and explain why.

Communicate

Create a brochure highlighting the benefits of hydroponic gardening. Be sure to provide details about how a plant's needs are met and about the problems that hydroponic gardens could solve.

Chapter 5

Study Guide

1 The Characteristics of Seed Plants

Key Concepts

- Seed plants have vascular tissue and use pollen and seeds to reproduce.
- Inside a seed is a partially developed plant. If a seed lands in an area where conditions are favorable, it can begin to develop into a plant.
- Roots anchor a plant in the ground and absorb water and minerals. Stems carry substances between roots and leaves, provide support, and hold up the leaves. Leaves capture the sun's energy for photosynthesis.

Key Terms

phloem	germination
xylem	root cap
pollen	cambium
seed	stomata
embryo	transpiration
cotyledon	

2 Gymnosperms

Key Concepts

- Every gymnosperm produces naked seeds. In addition, many gymnosperms have needle-like or scalelike leaves, and deep-growing roots.
- During reproduction, pollen falls from a male cone onto a female cone. In time, sperm and egg cells join in an ovule on the female cone.
- Paper and other products, such as the lumber used to build homes, come from conifers.

Key Terms

gymnosperm	ovule
cone	pollination

3 Angiosperms

Key Concepts

- All angiosperms produce flowers and fruits.
- All flowers function in reproduction.
- During reproduction, pollen falls on a flower's stigma. In time, sperm and egg cells join in the flower's ovule. The zygote develops into the embryo part of the seed.
- Angiosperms are divided into two major groups: monocots and dicots.

Key Terms

angiosperm	pistil
flower	ovary
sepal	fruit
petal	monocot
stamen	dicot

4 Plant Responses and Growth

Key Concepts

- Touch, light, and gravity are stimuli to which plants have growth responses, or tropisms.
- The amount of darkness that a plant receives determines the time of flowering in many plants.
- Dormancy helps plants survive winter.
- Angiosperms are classified as annuals, biennials, or perennials.

Key Terms

tropism	critical night length
hormone	day-neutral plant
auxin	dormancy
photoperiodism	annual
short-day plant	biennial
long-day plant	perennial

5 Feeding the World

Key Concept

- Precision farming, hydroponics, and genetic engineering can help farmers produce more crops to feed the world's population.

Key Terms

precision farming	genetic engineering
hydroponics	

Review and Assessment

Go Online
PHSchool.com

For: Self-Assessment
Visit: PHSchool.com
Web Code: cea-1050

Organizing Information

Concept Mapping Copy the concept map about seed plants onto a sheet of paper. Then complete it and add a title. (For more on Concept Mapping, see the Skills Handbook.)

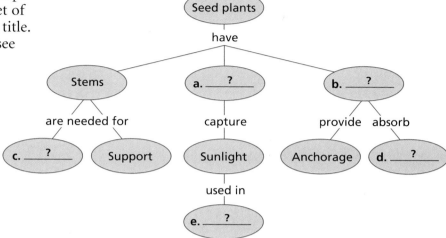

Reviewing Key Terms

Choose the letter of the best answer.

1. The process by which a seed sprouts is called
   a. pollination.
   b. fertilization.
   c. dispersal.
   d. germination.

2. In woody stems, new xylem cells are produced by the
   a. bark.
   b. cambium.
   c. phloem.
   d. pith.

3. Which of the following is the male part of a flower?
   a. pistil
   b. ovule
   c. stamen
   d. petal

4. What kind of tropism do roots display when they grow downward into the soil?
   a. positive gravitropism
   b. negative gravitropism
   c. phototropism
   d. thigmotropism

5. The process of growing crops in a nutrient solution is called
   a. genetic engineering.
   b. hydroponics.
   c. precision farming.
   d. satellite imaging.

If the statement is true, write *true*. If it is false, change the underlined word or words to make the statement true.

6. <u>Stems</u> anchor plants in the soil.

7. The needles of a pine tree are actually its <u>leaves</u>.

8. <u>Gymnosperm</u> seeds are dispersed in fruits.

9. Flowering plants that live for more than two years are called <u>annuals</u>.

10. <u>Precision farming</u> uses technology to fine-tune water and fertilizer requirements.

Writing in Science

Firsthand Account Write a story from the viewpoint of a seedling. Describe how you were dispersed as a seed and how you grew into a seedling.

Discovery CHANNEL SCHOOL™

Seed Plants
Video Preview
Video Field Trip
▶ Video Assessment

Review and Assessment

Checking Concepts

11. Describe four different ways that seeds can be dispersed.

12. Explain the role that stomata play in leaves.

13. Describe the structure of a female cone.

14. What is the difference between pollination and fertilization?

15. What role does a fruit play in an angiosperm's life cycle?

16. What role do plant hormones play in phototropism?

17. How can the use of hydroponics help increase the amount of food that can be grown on Earth?

Thinking Critically

18. **Inferring** Sometimes undersea volcanoes erupt, and new islands form far away from other land masses. Years later, seed plants may be found growing on those islands. How can the presence of those plants be explained?

19. **Relating Cause and Effect** When a strip of bark is removed all the way around the trunk of a tree, the tree dies. Explain why.

20. **Predicting** Pesticides are designed to kill harmful insects. Sometimes, however, pesticides kill helpful insects as well. What effect could this have on angiosperms?

21. **Comparing and Contrasting** Which of the plants below is a monocot? Which is a dicot? Explain your conclusions.

A　　　　**B**

22. **Applying Concepts** Explain why people who grow houseplants on windowsills should turn the plants every week or so.

Math Practice

23. **Multiples** Use what you know about multiples to determine which flower is a monocot and which is a dicot: a flower with nine petals; a flower with ten petals. Explain.

Applying Skills

Use the data in the graph below to answer Questions 24–26.

A scientist measured transpiration in an ash tree over an 18-hour period. She also measured how much water the tree's roots took up in the same period.

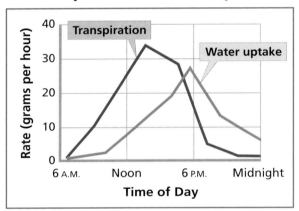

Transpiration and Water Uptake

24. **Interpreting Data** At what time is the rate of transpiration highest? At what time is the rate of water uptake highest?

25. **Inferring** Why do you think the transpiration rate increases and decreases as it does during the 18-hour period?

26. **Drawing Conclusions** Based on the graph, what is one conclusion you can reach about the pattern of water loss and gain in the ash tree?

Lab zone Chapter **Project**

Performance Assessment Design a poster that shows the results of your investigation. You may wish to use a cycle diagram to show the main events in the plant's life. What new information did you learn about seed plants by doing this project?

Standardized Test Prep

Choose the letter of the best answer.

1. The diagram below shows the parts of a flower. In which flower part does pollen formation take place?

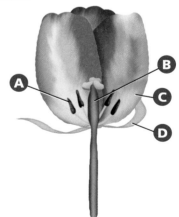

    A part A   **B** part B
    C part C   **D** part D

2. Which of the following is the correct path that water takes once it enters a plant?
    F leaves, stems, roots
    G roots, leaves, stems
    H stems, roots, leaves
    J roots, stems, leaves

3. A scientist examining the annual rings of a tree observes a section with wide rings. What inference can be made from this observation?
    A There was a drought during the years the wide rings were produced.
    B Rainfall was plentiful during the years the wide rings were produced.
    C Forest fires produced the wide rings.
    D There were severe springtime frosts during the years the wide rings were produced.

4. Which would a student expect to find when examining a dicot?
    F one cotyledon
    G flower parts in multiples of threes
    H stems with bundles of vascular tissue arranged in a ring
    J leaves with parallel veins

5. Which of the following statements is a valid comparison of gymnosperms and angiosperms?
    A Both gymnosperms and angiosperms produce flowers.
    B Gymnosperms produce flowers, while angiosperms produce cones.
    C Most gymnosperms have broad leaves, while angiosperms do not.
    D Angiosperm seeds are enclosed within fruits, while gymnosperm seeds are not.

Constructed Response

6. Explain how positive phototropism can help a plant survive. Use the following terms in your answer: food, leaves, photosynthesis, energy, and sunlight.

Corn—The Amazing Grain

What common grain is—

- dried, then popped and eaten at the movies?
- ground into meal?
- eaten in flakes for breakfast?

People have been eating corn in hundreds of different ways for thousands of years—since corn was first grown for food by ancient cultures in Mexico.

Because corn is useful, people have valued it throughout history. It tastes good, is nourishing, and stores well. Over time, knowledge of corn has spread among people and cultures. Christopher Columbus introduced corn to Europe. Columbus called it *mahiz,* meaning "a kind of grain."

Today in many countries of the world, corn is a basic part of people's diet, whether in the form of kernels, meal, oil, syrup, or flour. The United States grows billions of bushels a year. But people eat only a tiny portion of this yield as corn. About 80 percent of the United States corn crop is fed to livestock to supply eggs, milk, and meat. Hundreds of other products—from chewing gum to fireworks—are also made from parts of the plant.

Machu Picchu
The ruins of Machu Picchu, an Incan city, are in the Andes Mountains of Peru.

Village Market
A Peruvian farmer sells different types of corn.

Maize Through the Ages

Some people say, "Wherever corn went, civilization followed." Corn—or maize—was probably cultivated from a wild grass in Mexico around 8000 B.C. Early farmers planted seeds and harvested crops in planned spaces. They passed on their knowledge of corn to their children and to other farmers. Having plenty of corn is believed to be one reason the ancient agricultural empires of the Mayas and Incas developed and flourished.

In Central America, the Mayan civilization was at its height between A.D. 300 and A.D. 800. In Mayan cities, the people built pyramid-shaped temples where they worshipped gods of the sun, rain, and corn. Maize was grown in fields around the cities. The timing of the stages for growing corn affected all Mayan activities. The life cycle of maize and its plant parts— leaves, silk, tassels, and kernels—became the basis for words in the Mayan language.

In South America, the Incan empire thrived between the 1400s and 1535. A powerful ruler of the Incas came to power in Peru in 1438. In less than a century, the Incas expanded their territory from a small area around Cuzco, Peru, to a vast empire. The Inca empire stretched through the Andes Mountains, from Chile to Ecuador. It was the last of Peru's thriving ancient civilizations. The Incan empire was destroyed by Spaniards who arrived in the 1530s in search of gold. In Cuzco, they found an eye-dazzling garden where corn stalks, leaves, husks, and cobs were crafted in silver and gold. To the Incas, corn was more precious than the metal the Spaniards sought.

Though the empires of the Mayas and Incas collapsed, corn-growing spread to other regions. Eventually, the plant was brought north to the Mississippi and Ohio river valleys and east to the Caribbean islands.

Civilizations of the Americas
The Mayan civilization in Central America and the Incan civilization in South America flourished before Europeans arrived.

Social Studies Activity

Use a map of Central and South America today.

- Trace the approximate boundaries of the Mayan and Incan empires.

- Name the countries that are now located in these areas.

- Identify the geographical features within the empires.

- Find out about the climate. Why were these lands well suited to growing corn?

A Kernel Goes a Long Way

Did you know that corn and corn products are used as fuel? Or, did you know that corn is found in some brands of baby food, crayons, soap, and tires? It's even found in ketchup, hot dogs, and toothpaste.

Today, only a small portion of the corn that is planted is sweet corn. Sweet corn is sold fresh or used to produce canned or frozen corn. But millions of bushels of field corn, which is less sweet, are trucked to refineries. There, the kernels are turned into oil, starch, sugar, or fuel.

When ears of field corn arrive at a refinery, the corn is cleaned and soaked. Next, corn kernels are milled—crushed and ground. The milled substance is spun in giant tanks to separate out the embryos. Oil is extracted from the embryo of the kernel. The seed coat may be removed by sifting and can be dried to produce corn bran.

The remaining substance—the stored food—is ground into corn meal. One part of the ground meal is rich in proteins and is used for animal feed. The other part of the corn meal is the starch.

From cornstarch, corn sugars and syrups are processed. You eat these in breads, breakfast cereals, colas, ice cream, and salad dressings, to name only a few products. Cornstarch is also processed into glues and powders for the paper and textile industries, and into ethanol, a fuel.

Corn Ear
Corn plants grow from kernels on corn ears like this one.

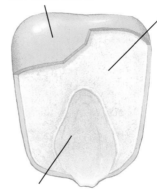

Seed Coat
The seed coat protects the kernel. Bran is made from the seed coat.

Stored Food
The stored food is the inner starchy part that feeds the embryo. Many things are made from the starchy part of the corn kernel, including
• cornstarch
• corn sugar
• corn syrups
• ice cream
• animal feed
• glue
• fuel

Embryo
The embryo is the part of the seed that will develop into a new corn plant. Corn oil is made from the embryo.

Science Activity

When you're at the supermarket, how do you decide which brand of a particular product to buy? What criteria do you use? Working with a partner, choose a corn product, such as tortillas, corn flakes, or popcorn, to investigate.

• Collect several brands of the product to test.

• Decide what you will test for. For example, you might want to test which brand of popcorn produces more popped kernels.

• Before you begin, predict what your results will be.

• Design your own experiment. Write out the step-by-step procedure you will follow. Make sure that you keep all variables the same as you test each product.

• Make observations and collect data.

• Interpret the data and draw your conclusion. How did your results compare with your prediction?

Mind-Boggling Corn Data

Every continent in the world except Antarctica produces some corn each year. The largest corn-producing country is the United States, growing 42 percent of the world's corn. The graph shows the leading corn-producing countries. China is next largest, growing 19 percent. The other countries in the world grow smaller amounts.

In the United States, corn is grown in nearly every state, producing about 9 billion bushels of corn a year. A bushel of corn contains about 72,800 kernels. Most of that corn is grown in a group of midwestern states known as the "Corn Belt." Iowa, Illinois, Nebraska, and Minnesota are the four major corn-growing states. Indiana, Missouri, Kansas, Ohio, South Dakota, Wisconsin, Michigan, and Kentucky are the other Corn Belt states.

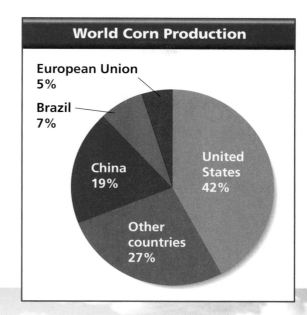

World Corn Production

European Union 5%
Brazil 7%
China 19%
United States 42%
Other countries 27%

Math Activity

Make a circle graph to show corn production in the United States. To create your graph, follow the steps in the Skills Handbook.

- Use the data in the table below to set up proportions to find the number of degrees in each slice. Then figure percents for Major Corn Belt States, Other Corn Belt States, and States Outside the Corn Belt. Round to the nearest tenth.

- Use a compass to draw a circle.

- Determine the size of each of the three slices.

- Measure out and mark off each slice in the circle.

What percent should you get when you add up these numbers?

United States Corn Production	
	Billions of Bushels
Major Corn Belt States (Iowa, Illinois, Nebraska, Minnesota)	5.45
Other Corn Belt States (Indiana, Missouri, Kansas, Ohio, South Dakota, Wisconsin, Michigan, and Kentucky)	2.49
States Outside the Corn Belt	1.06
Total for the United States	9.00

From the Garden in the Sky

The word for corn in some Native American languages means "that which gives us life." No one knows how humans discovered corn. But many cultures have myths and stories to explain how the plant came to be. To the Pawnee on the Nebraska plains, corn was Evening Star, the mother of all things. The Navajo in the southwestern United States tell a story of a turkey hen that flew in a straight line. As it traveled, it shook an ear of corn from its feathers. The following folk tale comes from the Iroquois in Canada.

The Corn Goddess

The Great Spirit gave seeds of corn to a mysterious maiden who became the wife of a great hunter. The wife taught the hunter's people how to plant and harvest the corn, and how to grind it and bake it into bread. The people were pleased.

But the great hunter's brother disliked the bread and threw it to the ground. The wife was alarmed that he had dishonored the gift of the Great Spirit. That night she told her husband that she must leave his people.

Shortly before dawn, the people heard the sound of falling rain. But it was not rain. It was the sound of thousands of kernels dropping from the ears of corn. Soon all the stalks were empty.

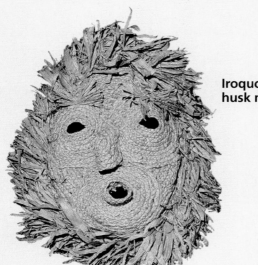

Iroquois corn husk mask

The men hunted but found little game. Before long the children cried because they were so hungry. The great hunter was sad. He decided to leave and find his wife. She had told him, "If ever you want to find me, walk east. When you reach a lake, rest and listen for the cry of a child. Then you should plant an arrow in the ground, point it in the direction of the sound, and sleep. When you wake, the arrow will show you the way."

The great hunter went east to the big lake and lit a fire. Late that night he heard crying. He planted his arrow and lay down to sleep. At dawn, he walked as the arrow pointed. He walked all day, then stopped to rest at night. He lit another fire. Again he heard crying, placed his arrow, and slept. On the third night, his wife appeared.

He said his people were starving and he asked for her help. When winter passed, the great hunter returned to his people with corn from his wife. That year, the harvest was abundant. He rejoiced, but he missed his wife and left to find her again. He traveled to the lake and listened for crying, but he did not hear it. He traveled another day, and another, thinking he knew the direction to go. He searched day after day, listening for the cry. Perhaps he is still looking for her.

—————Adapted from *The Corn Goddess and Other Tales from Indian Canada*, National Museum, Canada

Language Arts Activity

A folk tale is a story that is passed down from person to person. It may explain something in nature, as this story does, or teach a lesson. Find words and phrases that show that this tale was created a long time ago.

Write your own story about how corn came to be found in nature. Use a modern-day setting and characters in your story.

Tie It Together

Plan a Corn Ball

Organize a corn carnival for your school. To advertise the carnival, create a huge popcorn ball with popped corn and glue made from a cornstarch and water mixture. (The largest popcorn ball on record weighed over a ton.)

Here are some suggestions for activities.

- Display a variety of products made from corn.
- Bring in food made from corn.
- Set up a booth to explain how popcorn pops.
- Have a contest for visitors to guess the number of popcorn kernels.
- Set up a booth for telling corny jokes.
- Collect corn facts, pictures, and photographs that show corn in art or in history.
- Collect information on agriculture in the Mayan or Incan cultures.

Corn on the Cob
It's a favorite American food.

Think Like a Scientist

Scientists have a particular way of looking at the world, or scientific habits of mind. Whenever you ask a question and explore possible answers, you use many of the same skills that scientists do. Some of these skills are described on this page.

Observing

When you use one or more of your five senses to gather information about the world, you are **observing.** Hearing a dog bark, counting twelve green seeds, and smelling smoke are all observations. To increase the power of their senses, scientists sometimes use microscopes, telescopes, or other instruments that help them make more detailed observations.

An observation must be an accurate report of what your senses detect. It is important to keep careful records of your observations in science class by writing or drawing in a notebook. The information collected through observations is called evidence, or data.

Inferring

When you interpret an observation, you are **inferring,** or making an inference. For example, if you hear your dog barking, you may infer that someone is at your front door. To make this inference, you combine the evidence— the barking dog—and your experience or knowledge—you know that your dog barks when strangers approach—to reach a logical conclusion.

Notice that an inference is not a fact; it is only one of many possible interpretations for an observation. For example, your dog may be barking because it wants to go for a walk. An inference may turn out to be incorrect even if it is based on accurate observations and logical reasoning. The only way to find out if an inference is correct is to investigate further.

Predicting

When you listen to the weather forecast, you hear many predictions about the next day's weather—what the temperature will be, whether it will rain, and how windy it will be. Weather forecasters use observations and knowledge of weather patterns to predict the weather. The skill of **predicting** involves making an inference about a future event based on current evidence or past experience.

Because a prediction is an inference, it may prove to be false. In science class, you can test some of your predictions by doing experiments. For example, suppose you predict that larger paper airplanes can fly farther than smaller airplanes. How could you test your prediction?

Activity

Use the photograph to answer the questions below.

Observing Look closely at the photograph. List at least three observations.

Inferring Use your observations to make an inference about what has happened. What experience or knowledge did you use to make the inference?

Predicting Predict what will happen next. On what evidence or experience do you base your prediction?

Classifying

Could you imagine searching for a book in the library if the books were shelved in no particular order? Your trip to the library would be an all-day event! Luckily, librarians group together books on similar topics or by the same author. Grouping together items that are alike in some way is called **classifying.** You can classify items in many ways: by size, by shape, by use, and by other important characteristics.

Like librarians, scientists use the skill of classifying to organize information and objects. When things are sorted into groups, the relationships among them become easier to understand.

Activity

Classify the objects in the photograph into two groups based on any characteristic you choose. Then use another characteristic to classify the objects into three groups.

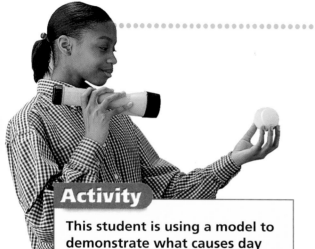

Making Models

Have you ever drawn a picture to help someone understand what you were saying? Such a drawing is one type of model. A model is a picture, diagram, computer image, or other representation of a complex object or process. **Making models** helps people understand things that they cannot observe directly.

Scientists often use models to represent things that are either very large or very small, such as the planets in the solar system, or the parts of a cell. Such models are physical models—drawings or three-dimensional structures that look like the real thing. Other models are mental models—mathematical equations or words that describe how something works.

Activity

This student is using a model to demonstrate what causes day and night on Earth. What do the flashlight and the tennis ball in the model represent?

Communicating

Whenever you talk on the phone, write a report, or listen to your teacher at school, you are communicating. **Communicating** is the process of sharing ideas and information with other people. Communicating effectively requires many skills, including writing, reading, speaking, listening, and making models.

Scientists communicate to share results, information, and opinions. Scientists often communicate about their work in journals, over the telephone, in letters, and on the Internet.

They also attend scientific meetings where they share their ideas with one another in person.

Activity

On a sheet of paper, write out clear, detailed directions for tying your shoe. Then exchange directions with a partner. Follow your partner's directions exactly. How successful were you at tying your shoe? How could your partner have communicated more clearly?

Making Measurements

By measuring, scientists can express their observations more precisely and communicate more information about what they observe.

Measuring in SI

The standard system of measurement used by scientists around the world is known as the International System of Units, which is abbreviated as SI (**Système International d'Unités,** in French). SI units are easy to use because they are based on multiples of 10. Each unit is ten times larger than the next smallest unit and one tenth the size of the next largest unit. The table lists the prefixes used to name the most common SI units.

Common SI Prefixes		
Prefix	Symbol	Meaning
kilo-	k	1,000
hecto-	h	100
deka-	da	10
deci-	d	0.1 (one tenth)
centi-	c	0.01 (one hundredth)
milli-	m	0.001 (one thousandth)

Length To measure length, or the distance between two points, the unit of measure is the **meter (m).** The distance from the floor to a doorknob is approximately one meter. Long distances, such as the distance between two cities, are measured in kilometers (km). Small lengths are measured in centimeters (cm) or millimeters (mm). Scientists use metric rulers and meter sticks to measure length.

Common Conversions	
1 km	=	1,000 m
1 m	=	100 cm
1 m	=	1,000 mm
1 cm	=	10 mm

Activity

The larger lines on the metric ruler in the picture show centimeter divisions, while the smaller, unnumbered lines show millimeter divisions. How many centimeters long is the shell? How many millimeters long is it?

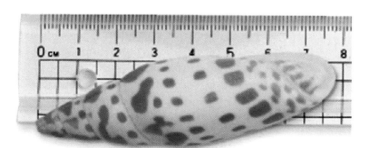

Liquid Volume To measure the volume of a liquid, or the amount of space it takes up, you will use a unit of measure known as the **liter (L).** One liter is the approximate volume of a medium-size carton of milk. Smaller volumes are measured in milliliters (mL). Scientists use graduated cylinders to measure liquid volume.

Activity

The graduated cylinder in the picture is marked in milliliter divisions. Notice that the water in the cylinder has a curved surface. This curved surface is called the *meniscus.* To measure the volume, you must read the level at the lowest point of the meniscus. What is the volume of water in this graduated cylinder?

Common Conversion
1 L = 1,000 mL

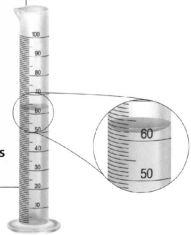

Mass To measure mass, or the amount of matter in an object, you will use a unit of measure known as the **gram (g).** One gram is approximately the mass of a paper clip. Larger masses are measured in kilograms (kg). Scientists use a balance to find the mass of an object.

Common Conversion

1 kg = 1,000 g

Activity

The mass of the potato in the picture is measured in kilograms. What is the mass of the potato? Suppose a recipe for potato salad called for one kilogram of potatoes. About how many potatoes would you need?

Temperature To measure the temperature of a substance, you will use the **Celsius scale.** Temperature is measured in degrees Celsius (°C) using a Celsius thermometer. Water freezes at 0°C and boils at 100°C.

Time The unit scientists use to measure time is the **second (s).**

Activity

What is the temperature of the liquid in degrees Celsius?

Converting SI Units

To use the SI system, you must know how to convert between units. Converting from one unit to another involves the skill of **calculating,** or using mathematical operations. Converting between SI units is similar to converting between dollars and dimes because both systems are based on multiples of ten.

Suppose you want to convert a length of 80 centimeters to meters. Follow these steps to convert between units.

1. Begin by writing down the measurement you want to convert—in this example, 80 centimeters.

2. Write a conversion factor that represents the relationship between the two units you are converting. In this example, the relationship is 1 meter = 100 centimeters. Write this conversion factor as a fraction, making sure to place the units you are converting from (centimeters, in this example) in the denominator.

3. Multiply the measurement you want to convert by the fraction. When you do this, the units in the first measurement will cancel out with the units in the denominator. Your answer will be in the units you are converting to (meters, in this example).

Example

80 centimeters = ▪ meters

$$80 \text{ centimeters} \times \frac{1 \text{ meter}}{100 \text{ centimeters}} = \frac{80 \text{ meters}}{100}$$
$$= 0.8 \text{ meters}$$

Activity

Convert between the following units.

1. 600 millimeters = ▪ meters
2. 0.35 liters = ▪ milliliters
3. 1,050 grams = ▪ kilograms

Conducting a Scientific Investigation

In some ways, scientists are like detectives, piecing together clues to learn about a process or event. One way that scientists gather clues is by carrying out experiments. An experiment tests an idea in a careful, orderly manner. Although experiments do not all follow the same steps in the same order, many follow a pattern similar to the one described here.

Posing Questions

Experiments begin by asking a scientific question. A scientific question is one that can be answered by gathering evidence. For example, the question "Which freezes faster—fresh water or salt water?" is a scientific question because you can carry out an investigation and gather information to answer the question.

Developing a Hypothesis

The next step is to form a hypothesis. A **hypothesis** is a possible explanation for a set of observations or answer to a scientific question. In science, a hypothesis must be something that can be tested. A hypothesis can be worded as an *If . . . then . . .* statement. For example, a hypothesis might be *"If I add salt to fresh water, then the water will take longer to freeze."* A hypothesis worded this way serves as a rough outline of the experiment you should perform.

Designing an Experiment

Next you need to plan a way to test your hypothesis. Your plan should be written out as a step-by-step procedure and should describe the observations or measurements you will make.

Two important steps involved in designing an experiment are controlling variables and forming operational definitions.

Controlling Variables In a well-designed experiment, you need to keep all variables the same except for one. A **variable** is any factor that can change in an experiment. The factor that you change is called the **manipulated variable**. In this experiment, the manipulated variable is the amount of salt added to the water. Other factors, such as the amount of water or the starting temperature, are kept constant.

The factor that changes as a result of the manipulated variable is called the **responding variable.** The responding variable is what you measure or observe to obtain your results. In this experiment, the responding variable is how long the water takes to freeze.

An experiment in which all factors except one are kept constant is called a **controlled experiment.** Most controlled experiments include a test called the control. In this experiment, Container 3 is the control. Because no salt is added to Container 3, you can compare the results from the other containers to it. Any difference in results must be due to the addition of salt alone.

Forming Operational Definitions Another important aspect of a well-designed experiment is having clear operational definitions. An **operational definition** is a statement that describes how a particular variable is to be measured or how a term is to be defined. For example, in this experiment, how will you determine if the water has frozen? You might decide to insert a stick in each container at the start of the experiment. Your operational definition of "frozen" would be the time at which the stick can no longer move.

Experimental Procedure
1. Fill 3 containers with 300 milliliters of cold tap water.
2. Add 10 grams of salt to Container 1; stir. Add 20 grams of salt to Container 2; stir. Add no salt to Container 3.
3. Place the 3 containers in a freezer.
4. Check the containers every 15 minutes. Record your observations.

Interpreting Data

The observations and measurements you make in an experiment are called **data.** At the end of an experiment, you need to analyze the data to look for any patterns or trends. Patterns often become clear if you organize your data in a data table or graph. Then think through what the data reveal. Do they support your hypothesis? Do they point out a flaw in your experiment? Do you need to collect more data?

Drawing Conclusions

A **conclusion** is a statement that sums up what you have learned from an experiment. When you draw a conclusion, you need to decide whether the data you collected support your hypothesis or not. You may need to repeat an experiment several times before you can draw any conclusions from it. Conclusions often lead you to pose new questions and plan new experiments to answer them.

Activity

Is a ball's bounce affected by the height from which it is dropped? Using the steps just described, plan a controlled experiment to investigate this problem.

Technology Design Skills

Engineers are people who use scientific and technological knowledge to solve practical problems. To design new products, engineers usually follow the process described here, even though they may not follow these steps in the exact order. As you read the steps, think about how you might apply them in technology labs.

Identify a Need

Before engineers begin designing a new product, they must first identify the need they are trying to meet. For example, suppose you are a member of a design team in a company that makes toys. Your team has identified a need: a toy boat that is inexpensive and easy to assemble.

Research the Problem

Engineers often begin by gathering information that will help them with their new design. This research may include finding articles in books, magazines, or on the Internet. It may also include talking to other engineers who have solved similar problems. Engineers often perform experiments related to the product they want to design.

For your toy boat, you could look at toys that are similar to the one you want to design. You might do research on the Internet. You could also test some materials to see whether they will work well in a toy boat.

Drawing for a boat design ▼

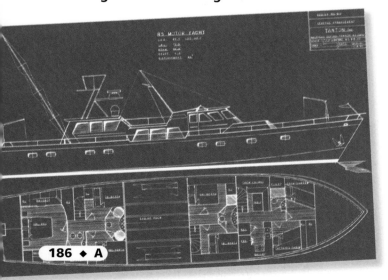

Design a Solution

Research gives engineers information that helps them design a product. When engineers design new products, they usually work in teams.

Generating Ideas Often design teams hold brainstorming meetings in which any team member can contribute ideas. **Brainstorming** is a creative process in which one team member's suggestions often spark ideas in other group members. Brainstorming can lead to new approaches to solving a design problem.

Evaluating Constraints During brainstorming, a design team will often come up with several possible designs. The team must then evaluate each one.

As part of their evaluation, engineers consider constraints. **Constraints** are factors that limit or restrict a product design. Physical characteristics, such as the properties of materials used to make your toy boat, are constraints. Money and time are also constraints. If the materials in a product cost a lot, or if the product takes a long time to make, the design may be impractical.

Making Trade-offs Design teams usually need to make trade-offs. In a **trade-off,** engineers give up one benefit of a proposed design in order to obtain another. In designing your toy boat, you will have to make trade-offs. For example, suppose one material is sturdy but not fully waterproof. Another material is more waterproof, but breakable. You may decide to give up the benefit of sturdiness in order to obtain the benefit of waterproofing.

Build and Evaluate a Prototype

Once the team has chosen a design plan, the engineers build a prototype of the product. A **prototype** is a working model used to test a design. Engineers evaluate the prototype to see whether it works well, is easy to operate, is safe to use, and holds up to repeated use.

Think of your toy boat. What would the prototype be like? Of what materials would it be made? How would you test it?

Troubleshoot and Redesign

Few prototypes work perfectly, which is why they need to be tested. Once a design team has tested a prototype, the members analyze the results and identify any problems. The team then tries to **troubleshoot,** or fix the design problems. For example, if your toy boat leaks or wobbles, the boat should be redesigned to eliminate those problems.

Communicate the Solution

A team needs to communicate the final design to the people who will manufacture and use the product. To do this, teams may use sketches, detailed drawings, computer simulations, and word descriptions.

Activity

You can use the technology design process to design and build a toy boat.

Research and Investigate

1. Visit the library or go online to research toy boats.

2. Investigate how a toy boat can be powered, including wind, rubber bands, or baking soda and vinegar.

3. Brainstorm materials, shapes, and steering for your boat.

Design and Build

4. Based on your research, design a toy boat that
   • is made of readily available materials
   • is no larger than 15 cm long and 10 cm wide

   • includes a power system, a rudder, and an area for cargo
   • travels 2 meters in a straight line carrying a load of 20 pennies

5. Sketch your design and write a step-by-step plan for building your boat. After your teacher approves your plan, build your boat.

Evaluate and Redesign

6. Test your boat, evaluate the results, and troubleshoot any problems.

7. Based on your evaluation, redesign your toy boat so it performs better.

Creating Data Tables and Graphs

How can you make sense of the data in a science experiment?
The first step is to organize the data to help you understand them.
Data tables and graphs are helpful tools for organizing data.

Data Tables

You have gathered your materials and set up your experiment. But before you start, you need to plan a way to record what happens during the experiment. By creating a data table, you can record your observations and measurements in an orderly way.

Suppose, for example, that a scientist conducted an experiment to find out how many Calories people of different body masses burn while doing various activities. The data table shows the results.

Notice in this data table that the manipulated variable (body mass) is the heading of one column. The responding variable (for

Calories Burned in 30 Minutes			
Body Mass	Experiment 1: Bicycling	Experiment 2: Playing Basketball	Experiment 3: Watching Television
30 kg	60 Calories	120 Calories	21 Calories
40 kg	77 Calories	164 Calories	27 Calories
50 kg	95 Calories	206 Calories	33 Calories
60 kg	114 Calories	248 Calories	38 Calories

Experiment 1, the number of Calories burned while bicycling) is the heading of the next column. Additional columns were added for related experiments.

Bar Graphs

To compare how many Calories a person burns doing various activities, you could create a bar graph. A bar graph is used to display data in a number of separate, or distinct, categories. In this example, bicycling, playing basketball, and watching television are the three categories.

To create a bar graph, follow these steps.

1. On graph paper, draw a horizontal, or *x*-, axis and a vertical, or *y*-, axis.

2. Write the names of the categories to be graphed along the horizontal axis. Include an overall label for the axis as well.

3. Label the vertical axis with the name of the responding variable. Include units of measurement. Then create a scale along the axis by marking off equally spaced numbers that cover the range of the data collected.

4. For each category, draw a solid bar using the scale on the vertical axis to determine the height. Make all the bars the same width.

5. Add a title that describes the graph.

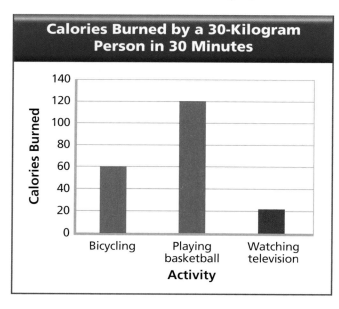

Line Graphs

To see whether a relationship exists between body mass and the number of Calories burned while bicycling, you could create a line graph. A line graph is used to display data that show how one variable (the responding variable) changes in response to another variable (the manipulated variable). You can use a line graph when your manipulated variable is **continuous,** that is, when there are other points between the ones that you tested. In this example, body mass is a continuous variable because there are other body masses between 30 and 40 kilograms (for example, 31 kilograms). Time is another example of a continuous variable.

Line graphs are powerful tools because they allow you to estimate values for conditions that you did not test in the experiment. For example, you can use the line graph to estimate that a 35-kilogram person would burn 68 Calories while bicycling.

To create a line graph, follow these steps.

1. On graph paper, draw a horizontal, or x-, axis and a vertical, or y-, axis.

2. Label the horizontal axis with the name of the manipulated variable. Label the vertical axis with the name of the responding variable. Include units of measurement.

3. Create a scale on each axis by marking off equally spaced numbers that cover the range of the data collected.

4. Plot a point on the graph for each piece of data. In the line graph above, the dotted lines show how to plot the first data point (30 kilograms and 60 Calories). Follow an imaginary vertical line extending up from the horizontal axis at the 30-kilogram mark. Then follow an imaginary horizontal line extending across from the vertical axis at the 60-Calorie mark. Plot the point where the two lines intersect.

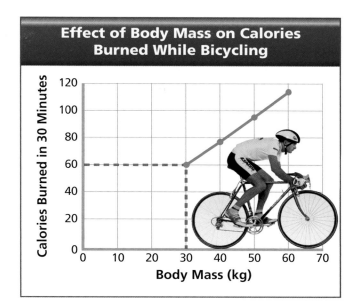

Effect of Body Mass on Calories Burned While Bicycling

5. Connect the plotted points with a solid line. (In some cases, it may be more appropriate to draw a line that shows the general trend of the plotted points. In those cases, some of the points may fall above or below the line. Also, not all graphs are linear. It may be more appropriate to draw a curve to connect the points.)

6. Add a title that identifies the variables or relationship in the graph.

Activity

Create line graphs to display the data from Experiment 2 and Experiment 3 in the data table.

Activity

You read in the newspaper that a total of 4 centimeters of rain fell in your area in June, 2.5 centimeters fell in July, and 1.5 centimeters fell in August. What type of graph would you use to display these data? Use graph paper to create the graph.

Circle Graphs

Like bar graphs, circle graphs can be used to display data in a number of separate categories. Unlike bar graphs, however, circle graphs can only be used when you have data for *all* the categories that make up a given topic. A circle graph is sometimes called a pie chart. The pie represents the entire topic, while the slices represent the individual categories. The size of a slice indicates what percentage of the whole a particular category makes up.

The data table below shows the results of a survey in which 24 teenagers were asked to identify their favorite sport. The data were then used to create the circle graph at the right.

Favorite Sports

Sport	Students
Soccer	8
Basketball	6
Bicycling	6
Swimming	4

To create a circle graph, follow these steps.

1. Use a compass to draw a circle. Mark the center with a point. Then draw a line from the center point to the top of the circle.

2. Determine the size of each "slice" by setting up a proportion where x equals the number of degrees in a slice. (*Note:* A circle contains 360 degrees.) For example, to find the number of degrees in the "soccer" slice, set up the following proportion:

$$\frac{\text{Students who prefer soccer}}{\text{Total number of students}} = \frac{x}{\text{Total number of degrees in a circle}}$$

$$\frac{8}{24} = \frac{x}{360}$$

Cross-multiply and solve for x.

$$24x = 8 \times 360$$
$$x = 120$$

The "soccer" slice should contain 120 degrees.

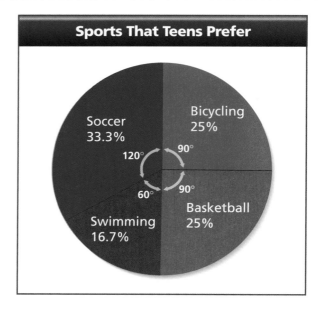

Sports That Teens Prefer

3. Use a protractor to measure the angle of the first slice, using the line you drew to the top of the circle as the 0° line. Draw a line from the center of the circle to the edge for the angle you measured.

4. Continue around the circle by measuring the size of each slice with the protractor. Start measuring from the edge of the previous slice so the wedges do not overlap. When you are done, the entire circle should be filled in.

5. Determine the percentage of the whole circle that each slice represents. To do this, divide the number of degrees in a slice by the total number of degrees in a circle (360), and multiply by 100%. For the "soccer" slice, you can find the percentage as follows:

$$\frac{120}{360} \times 100\% = 33.3\%$$

6. Use a different color for each slice. Label each slice with the category and with the percentage of the whole it represents.

7. Add a title to the circle graph.

Activity

In a class of 28 students, 12 students take the bus to school, 10 students walk, and 6 students ride their bicycles. Create a circle graph to display these data.

Math Review

Scientists use math to organize, analyze, and present data. This appendix will help you review some basic math skills.

Mean, Median, and Mode

The **mean** is the average, or the sum of the data divided by the number of data items. The middle number in a set of ordered data is called the **median**. The **mode** is the number that appears most often in a set of data.

> **Example**
>
> A scientist counted the number of distinct songs sung by seven different male birds and collected the data shown below.
>
> | Male Bird Songs | | | | | | | |
> |---|---|---|---|---|---|---|---|
> | **Bird** | A | B | C | D | E | F | G |
> | **Number of Songs** | 36 | 29 | 40 | 35 | 28 | 36 | 27 |
>
> To determine the mean number of songs, add the total number of songs and divide by the number of data items—in this case, the number of male birds.
>
> $$\text{Mean} = \frac{231}{7} = 33 \text{ songs}$$
>
> To find the median number of songs, arrange the data in numerical order and find the number in the middle of the series.
>
> **27 28 29 35 36 36 40**
>
> The number in the middle is 35, so the median number of songs is 35.
>
> The mode is the value that appears most frequently. In the data, 36 appears twice, while each other item appears only once. Therefore, 36 songs is the mode.

> **Practice**
>
> Find out how many minutes it takes each student in your class to get to school. Then find the mean, median, and mode for the data.

Probability

Probability is the chance that an event will occur. Probability can be expressed as a ratio, a fraction, or a percentage. For example, when you flip a coin, the probability that the coin will land heads up is 1 in 2, or $\frac{1}{2}$, or 50 percent.

The probability that an event will happen can be expressed in the following formula.

$$P(\text{event}) = \frac{\text{Number of times the event can occur}}{\text{Total number of possible events}}$$

> **Example**
>
> A paper bag contains 25 blue marbles, 5 green marbles, 5 orange marbles, and 15 yellow marbles. If you close your eyes and pick a marble from the bag, what is the probability that it will be yellow?
>
> $$P(\text{yellow marbles}) = \frac{15 \text{ yellow marbles}}{50 \text{ marbles total}}$$
>
> $$P = \frac{15}{50}, \text{ or } \frac{3}{10}, \text{ or } 30\%$$

> **Practice**
>
> Each side of a cube has a letter on it. Two sides have *A*, three sides have *B*, and one side has *C*. If you roll the cube, what is the probability that *A* will land on top?

Area

The **area** of a surface is the number of square units that cover it. The front cover of your textbook has an area of about 600 cm².

Area of a Rectangle and a Square To find the area of a rectangle, multiply its length times its width. The formula for the area of a rectangle is

$$A = \ell \times w, \text{ or } A = \ell w$$

Since all four sides of a square have the same length, the area of a square is the length of one side multiplied by itself, or squared.

$$A = s \times s, \text{ or } A = s^2$$

Example

A scientist is studying the plants in a field that measures 75 m × 45 m. What is the area of the field?

$$A = \ell \times w$$
$$A = 75 \text{ m} \times 45 \text{ m}$$
$$A = 3{,}375 \text{ m}^2$$

Area of a Circle The formula for the area of a circle is

$$A = \pi \times r \times r, \text{ or } A = \pi r^2$$

The length of the radius is represented by r, and the value of π is approximately $\frac{22}{7}$.

Example

Find the area of a circle with a radius of 14 cm.

$$A = \pi r^2$$
$$A = 14 \times 14 \times \frac{22}{7}$$
$$A = 616 \text{ cm}^2$$

Practice

Find the area of a circle that has a radius of 21 m.

Circumference

The distance around a circle is called the circumference. The formula for finding the circumference of a circle is

$$C = 2 \times \pi \times r, \text{ or } C = 2\pi r$$

Example

The radius of a circle is 35 cm. What is its circumference?

$$C = 2\pi r$$
$$C = 2 \times 35 \times \frac{22}{7}$$
$$C = 220 \text{ cm}$$

Practice

What is the circumference of a circle with a radius of 28 m?

Volume

The volume of an object is the number of cubic units it contains. The volume of a wastebasket, for example, might be about 26,000 cm³.

Volume of a Rectangular Object To find the volume of a rectangular object, multiply the object's length times its width times its height.

$$V = \ell \times w \times h, \text{ or } V = \ell w h$$

Example

Find the volume of a box with length 24 cm, width 12 cm, and height 9 cm.

$$V = \ell w h$$
$$V = 24 \text{ cm} \times 12 \text{ cm} \times 9 \text{ cm}$$
$$V = 2{,}592 \text{ cm}^3$$

Practice

What is the volume of a rectangular object with length 17 cm, width 11 cm, and height 6 cm?

Fractions

A **fraction** is a way to express a part of a whole. In the fraction $\frac{4}{7}$, 4 is the numerator and 7 is the denominator.

Adding and Subtracting Fractions To add or subtract two or more fractions that have a common denominator, first add or subtract the numerators. Then write the sum or difference over the common denominator.

To find the sum or difference of fractions with different denominators, first find the least common multiple of the denominators. This is known as the least common denominator. Then convert each fraction to equivalent fractions with the least common denominator. Add or subtract the numerators. Then write the sum or difference over the common denominator.

> **Example**
> $$\frac{5}{6} - \frac{3}{4} = \frac{10}{12} - \frac{9}{12} = \frac{10-9}{12} = \frac{1}{12}$$

Multiplying Fractions To multiply two fractions, first multiply the two numerators, then multiply the two denominators.

> **Example**
> $$\frac{5}{6} \times \frac{2}{3} = \frac{5 \times 2}{6 \times 3} = \frac{10}{18} = \frac{5}{9}$$

Dividing Fractions Dividing by a fraction is the same as multiplying by its reciprocal. Reciprocals are numbers whose numerators and denominators have been switched. To divide one fraction by another, first invert the fraction you are dividing by—in other words, turn it upside down. Then multiply the two fractions.

> **Example**
> $$\frac{2}{5} \div \frac{7}{8} = \frac{2}{5} \times \frac{8}{7} = \frac{2 \times 8}{5 \times 7} = \frac{16}{35}$$

> **Practice**
> Solve the following: $\frac{3}{7} \div \frac{4}{5}$.

Decimals

Fractions whose denominators are 10, 100, or some other power of 10 are often expressed as decimals. For example, the fraction $\frac{9}{10}$ can be expressed as the decimal 0.9, and the fraction $\frac{7}{100}$ can be written as 0.07.

Adding and Subtracting With Decimals To add or subtract decimals, line up the decimal points before you carry out the operation.

> **Example**
>
> | 27.4 | 278.635 |
> |---|---|
> | + 6.19 | − 191.4 |
> | 33.59 | 87.235 |

Multiplying With Decimals When you multiply two numbers with decimals, the number of decimal places in the product is equal to the total number of decimal places in each number being multiplied.

> **Example**
>
> 46.2 (one decimal place)
> × 2.37 (two decimal places)
> 109.494 (three decimal places)

Dividing With Decimals To divide a decimal by a whole number, put the decimal point in the quotient above the decimal point in the dividend.

> **Example**
>
> $15.5 \div 5$
>
> $$5\overline{)15.5} \quad = 3.1$$

To divide a decimal by a decimal, you need to rewrite the divisor as a whole number. Do this by multiplying both the divisor and dividend by the same multiple of 10.

> **Example**
>
> $1.68 \div 4.2 = 16.8 \div 42$
>
> $$42\overline{)16.8} \quad = 0.4$$

> **Practice**
> Multiply 6.21 by 8.5.

Ratio and Proportion

A **ratio** compares two numbers by division. For example, suppose a scientist counts 800 wolves and 1,200 moose on an island. The ratio of wolves to moose can be written as a fraction, $\frac{800}{1,200}$, which can be reduced to $\frac{2}{3}$. The same ratio can also be expressed as 2 to 3 or 2 : 3.

A **proportion** is a mathematical sentence saying that two ratios are equivalent. For example, a proportion could state that $\frac{800 \text{ wolves}}{1,200 \text{ moose}} = \frac{2 \text{ wolves}}{3 \text{ moose}}$. You can sometimes set up a proportion to determine or estimate an unknown quantity. For example, suppose a scientist counts 25 beetles in an area of 10 square meters. The scientist wants to estimate the number of beetles in 100 square meters.

Example

1. Express the relationship between beetles and area as a ratio: $\frac{25}{10}$, simplified to $\frac{5}{2}$.

2. Set up a proportion, with x representing the number of beetles. The proportion can be stated as $\frac{5}{2} = \frac{x}{100}$.

3. Begin by cross-multiplying. In other words, multiply each fraction's numerator by the other fraction's denominator.

$$5 \times 100 = 2 \times x, \text{ or } 500 = 2x$$

4. To find the value of x, divide both sides by 2. The result is 250, or 250 beetles in 100 square meters.

Practice

Find the value of x in the following proportion: $\frac{6}{7} = \frac{x}{49}$.

Percentage

A **percentage** is a ratio that compares a number to 100. For example, there are 37 granite rocks in a collection that consists of 100 rocks. The ratio $\frac{37}{100}$ can be written as 37%. Granite rocks make up 37% of the rock collection.

You can calculate percentages of numbers other than 100 by setting up a proportion.

Example

Rain falls on 9 days out of 30 in June. What percentage of the days in June were rainy?

$$\frac{9 \text{ days}}{30 \text{ days}} = \frac{d\%}{100\%}$$

To find the value of d, begin by cross-multiplying, as for any proportion:

$$9 \times 100 = 30 \times d \qquad d = \frac{900}{30} \qquad d = 30$$

Practice

There are 300 marbles in a jar, and 42 of those marbles are blue. What percentage of the marbles are blue?

Significant Figures

The **precision** of a measurement depends on the instrument you use to take the measurement. For example, if the smallest unit on the ruler is millimeters, then the most precise measurement you can make will be in millimeters.

The sum or difference of measurements can only be as precise as the least precise measurement being added or subtracted. Round your answer so that it has the same number of digits after the decimal as the least precise measurement. Round up if the last digit is 5 or more, and round down if the last digit is 4 or less.

Example

Subtract a temperature of 5.2°C from the temperature 75.46°C.

75.46 − 5.2 = 70.26

5.2 has the fewest digits after the decimal, so it is the least precise measurement. Since the last digit of the answer is 6, round up to 3. The most precise difference between the measurements is 70.3°C.

Practice

Add 26.4 m to 8.37 m. Round your answer according to the precision of the measurements.

Significant figures are the number of nonzero digits in a measurement. Zeroes between nonzero digits are also significant. For example, the measurements 12,500 L, 0.125 cm, and 2.05 kg all have three significant figures. When you multiply and divide measurements, the one with the fewest significant figures determines the number of significant figures in your answer.

Example

Multiply 110 g by 5.75 g.

110 × 5.75 = 632.5

Because 110 has only two significant figures, round the answer to 630 g.

Scientific Notation

A **factor** is a number that divides into another number with no remainder. In the example, the number 3 is used as a factor four times.

An **exponent** tells how many times a number is used as a factor. For example, $3 \times 3 \times 3 \times 3$ can be written as 3^4. The exponent 4 indicates that the number 3 is used as a factor four times. Another way of expressing this is to say that 81 is equal to 3 to the fourth power.

Example

$$3^4 = 3 \times 3 \times 3 \times 3 = 81$$

Scientific notation uses exponents and powers of ten to write very large or very small numbers in shorter form. When you write a number in scientific notation, you write the number as two factors. The first factor is any number between 1 and 10. The second factor is a power of 10, such as 10^3 or 10^6.

Example

The average distance between the planet Mercury and the sun is 58,000,000 km. To write the first factor in scientific notation, insert a decimal point in the original number so that you have a number between 1 and 10. In the case of 58,000,000, the number is 5.8.

To determine the power of 10, count the number of places that the decimal point moved. In this case, it moved 7 places.

58,000,000 km = 5.8 × 10^7 km

Practice

Express 6,590,000 in scientific notation.

Reading Comprehension Skills

Each section in your textbook introduces a Target Reading Skill. You will improve your reading comprehension by using the Target Reading Skills described below.

Using Prior Knowledge

Your prior knowledge is what you already know before you begin to read about a topic. Building on what you already know gives you a head start on learning new information. Before you begin a new assignment, think about what you know. You might look at the headings and the visuals to spark your memory. You can list what you know. Then, as you read, consider questions like these.

• How does what you learn relate to what you know?

• How did something you already know help you learn something new?

• Did your original ideas agree with what you have just learned?

Asking Questions

Asking yourself questions is an excellent way to focus on and remember new information in your textbook. For example, you can turn the text headings into questions. Then your questions can guide you to identify the important information as you read. Look at these examples:

Heading: Using Seismographic Data

Question: How are seismographic data used?

Heading: Kinds of Faults

Question: What are the kinds of faults?

You do not have to limit your questions to text headings. Ask questions about anything that you need to clarify or that will help you understand the content. *What* and *how* are probably the most common question words, but you may also ask *why*, *who*, *when*, or *where* questions.

Previewing Visuals

Visuals are photographs, graphs, tables, diagrams, and illustrations. Visuals contain important information. Before you read, look at visuals and their labels and captions. This preview will help you prepare for what you will be reading.

Often you will be asked what you want to learn about a visual. For example, after you look at the normal fault diagram below, you might ask: What is the movement along a normal fault? Questions about visuals give you a purpose for reading—to answer your questions.

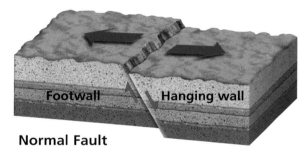

Footwall   **Hanging wall**

Normal Fault

Outlining

An outline shows the relationship between main ideas and supporting ideas. An outline has a formal structure. You write the main ideas, called topics, next to Roman numerals. The supporting ideas, called subtopics, are written under the main ideas and labeled A, B, C, and so on. An outline looks like this:

Technology and Society
I. Technology through history
II. The impact of technology on society
A.
B.

Identifying Main Ideas

When you are reading science material, it is important to try to understand the ideas and concepts that are in a passage. Each paragraph has a lot of information and detail. Good readers try to identify the most important—or biggest—idea in every paragraph or section. That's the main idea. The other information in the paragraph supports or further explains the main idea.

Sometimes main ideas are stated directly. In this book, some main ideas are identified for you as key concepts. These are printed in bold-face type. However, you must identify other main ideas yourself. In order to do this, you must identify all the ideas within a paragraph or section. Then ask yourself which idea is big enough to include all the other ideas.

Comparing and Contrasting

When you compare and contrast, you examine the similarities and differences between things. You can compare and contrast in a Venn diagram or in a table.

Venn Diagram A Venn diagram consists of two overlapping circles. In the space where the circles overlap, you write the characteristics that the two items have in common. In one of the circles outside the area of overlap, you write the differing features or characteristics of one of the items. In the other circle outside the area of overlap, you write the differing characteristics of the other item.

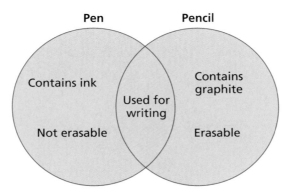

Table In a compare/contrast table, you list the characteristics or features to be compared across the top of the table. Then list the items to be compared in the left column. Complete the table by filling in information about each characteristic or feature.

Blood Vessel	Function	Structure of Wall
Artery	Carries blood away from heart	
Capillary		
Vein		

Identifying Supporting Evidence

A hypothesis is a possible explanation for observations made by scientists or an answer to a scientific question. Scientists must carry out investigations and gather evidence that either supports or disproves the hypothesis.

Identifying the supporting evidence for a hypothesis or theory can help you understand the hypothesis or theory. Evidence consists of facts—information whose accuracy can be confirmed by testing or observation.

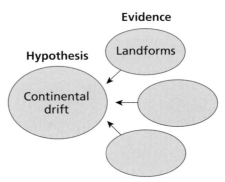

Sequencing

A sequence is the order in which a series of events occurs. A flowchart or a cycle diagram can help you visualize a sequence.

Flowchart To make a flowchart, write a brief description of each step or event in a box. Place the boxes in order, with the first event at the top of the page. Then draw an arrow to connect each step or event to the next.

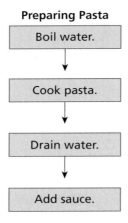

Preparing Pasta

Boil water.

Cook pasta.

Drain water.

Add sauce.

Cycle Diagram A cycle diagram shows a sequence that is continuous, or cyclical. A continuous sequence does not have an end because when the final event is over, the first event begins again. To create a cycle diagram, write the starting event in a box placed at the top of a page in the center. Then, moving in a clockwise direction, write each event in a box in its proper sequence. Draw arrows that connect each event to the one that occurs next.

Seasons of the Year

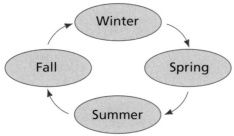

Winter

Spring

Fall

Summer

Relating Cause and Effect

Science involves many cause-and-effect relationships. A cause makes something happen. An effect is what happens. When you recognize that one event causes another, you are relating cause and effect.

Words like *cause, because, effect, affect,* and *result* often signal a cause or an effect. Sometimes an effect can have more than one cause, or a cause can produce several effects.

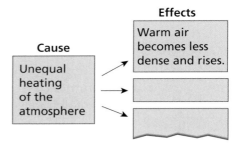

Cause

Unequal heating of the atmosphere

Effects

Warm air becomes less dense and rises.

Concept Mapping

Concept maps are useful tools for organizing information on any topic. A concept map begins with a main idea or core concept and shows how the idea can be subdivided into related subconcepts or smaller ideas.

You construct a concept map by placing concepts (usually nouns) in ovals and connecting them with linking words (usually verbs). The biggest concept or idea is placed in an oval at the top of the map. Related concepts are arranged in ovals below the big idea. The linking words connect the ovals.

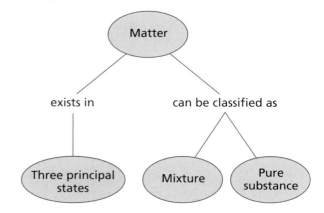

Matter

exists in

can be classified as

Three principal states

Mixture

Pure substance

Building Vocabulary

Knowing the meaning of these prefixes, suffixes, and roots will help you understand the meaning of words you do not recognize.

Word Origins Many science words come to English from other languages, such as Greek and Latin. By learning the meaning of a few common Greek and Latin roots, you can determine the meaning of unfamiliar science words.

Prefixes A prefix is a word part that is added at the beginning of a root or base word to change its meaning.

Suffixes A suffix is a word part that is added at the end of a root word to change the meaning.

Greek and Latin Roots		
Greek Roots	**Meaning**	**Example**
ast-	star	astronaut
geo-	Earth	geology
metron-	measure	kilometer
opt-	eye	optician
photo-	light	photograph
scop-	see	microscope
therm-	heat	thermostat
Latin Roots	**Meaning**	**Example**
aqua-	water	aquarium
aud-	hear	auditorium
duc-, duct-	lead	conduct
flect-	bend	reflect
fract-, frag-	break	fracture
ject-	throw	reject
luc-	light	lucid
spec-	see	inspect

Prefixes and Suffixes		
Prefix	**Meaning**	**Example**
com-, con-	with	communicate, concert
de-	from; down	decay
di-	two	divide
ex-, exo-	out	exhaust
in-, im-	in, into; not	inject, impossible
re-	again; back	reflect, recall
trans-	across	transfer
Suffix	**Meaning**	**Example**
-al	relating to	natural
-er, -or	one who	teacher, doctor
-ist	one who practices	scientist
-ity	state of	equality
-ology	study of	biology
-tion, -sion	state or quality of	reaction, tension

Safety Symbols

These symbols warn of possible dangers in the laboratory and remind you to work carefully.

 Safety Goggles Wear safety goggles to protect your eyes in any activity involving chemicals, flames or heating, or glassware.

 Lab Apron Wear a laboratory apron to protect your skin and clothing from damage.

 Breakage Handle breakable materials, such as glassware, with care. Do not touch broken glassware.

 Heat-Resistant Gloves Use an oven mitt or other hand protection when handling hot materials such as hot plates or hot glassware.

 Plastic Gloves Wear disposable plastic gloves when working with harmful chemicals and organisms. Keep your hands away from your face, and dispose of the gloves according to your teacher's instructions.

 Heating Use a clamp or tongs to pick up hot glassware. Do not touch hot objects with your bare hands.

 Flames Before you work with flames, tie back loose hair and clothing. Follow instructions from your teacher about lighting and extinguishing flames.

 No Flames When using flammable materials, make sure there are no flames, sparks, or other exposed heat sources present.

 Corrosive Chemical Avoid getting acid or other corrosive chemicals on your skin or clothing or in your eyes. Do not inhale the vapors. Wash your hands after the activity.

 Poison Do not let any poisonous chemical come into contact with your skin, and do not inhale its vapors. Wash your hands when you are finished with the activity.

 Fumes Work in a ventilated area when harmful vapors may be involved. Avoid inhaling vapors directly. Only test an odor when directed to do so by your teacher, and use a wafting motion to direct the vapor toward your nose.

 Sharp Object Scissors, scalpels, knives, needles, pins, and tacks can cut your skin. Always direct a sharp edge or point away from yourself and others.

 Animal Safety Treat live or preserved animals or animal parts with care to avoid harming the animals or yourself. Wash your hands when you are finished with the activity.

 Plant Safety Handle plants only as directed by your teacher. If you are allergic to certain plants, tell your teacher; do not do an activity involving those plants. Avoid touching harmful plants such as poison ivy. Wash your hands when you are finished with the activity.

 Electric Shock To avoid electric shock, never use electrical equipment around water, or when the equipment is wet or your hands are wet. Be sure cords are untangled and cannot trip anyone. Unplug equipment not in use.

 Physical Safety When an experiment involves physical activity, avoid injuring yourself or others. Alert your teacher if there is any reason you should not participate.

 Disposal Dispose of chemicals and other laboratory materials safely. Follow the instructions from your teacher.

 Hand Washing Wash your hands thoroughly when finished with the activity. Use antibacterial soap and warm water. Rinse well.

 General Safety Awareness When this symbol appears, follow the instructions provided. When you are asked to develop your own procedure in a lab, have your teacher approve your plan before you go further.

Science Safety Rules

General Precautions

Follow all instructions. Never perform activities without the approval and supervision of your teacher. Do not engage in horseplay. Never eat or drink in the laboratory. Keep work areas clean and uncluttered.

Dress Code

Wear safety goggles whenever you work with chemicals, glassware, heat sources such as burners, or any substance that might get into your eyes. If you wear contact lenses, notify your teacher.

Wear a lab apron or coat whenever you work with corrosive chemicals or substances that can stain. Wear disposable plastic gloves when working with organisms and harmful chemicals. Tie back long hair. Remove or tie back any article of clothing or jewelry that can hang down and touch chemicals, flames, or equipment. Roll up long sleeves. Never wear open shoes or sandals.

First Aid

Report all accidents, injuries, or fires to your teacher, no matter how minor. Be aware of the location of the first-aid kit, emergency equipment such as the fire extinguisher and fire blanket, and the nearest telephone. Know whom to contact in an emergency.

Heating and Fire Safety

Keep all combustible materials away from flames. When heating a substance in a test tube, make sure that the mouth of the tube is not pointed at you or anyone else. Never heat a liquid in a closed container. Use an oven mitt to pick up a container that has been heated.

Using Chemicals Safely

Never put your face near the mouth of a container that holds chemicals. Never touch, taste, or smell a chemical unless your teacher tells you to.

Use only those chemicals needed in the activity. Keep all containers closed when chemicals are not being used. Pour all chemicals over the sink or a container, not over your work surface. Dispose of excess chemicals as instructed by your teacher.

Be extra careful when working with acids or bases. When mixing an acid and water, always pour the water into the container first and then add the acid to the water. Never pour water into an acid. Wash chemical spills and splashes immediately with plenty of water.

Using Glassware Safely

If glassware is broken or chipped, notify your teacher immediately. Never handle broken or chipped glass with your bare hands.

Never force glass tubing or thermometers into a rubber stopper or rubber tubing. Have your teacher insert the glass tubing or thermometer if required for an activity.

Using Sharp Instruments

Handle sharp instruments with extreme care. Never cut material toward you; cut away from you.

Animal and Plant Safety

Never perform experiments that cause pain, discomfort, or harm to animals. Only handle animals if absolutely necessary. If you know that you are allergic to certain plants, molds, or animals, tell your teacher before doing an activity in which these are used. Wash your hands thoroughly after any activity involving animals, animal parts, plants, plant parts, or soil.

During field work, wear long pants, long sleeves, socks, and closed shoes. Avoid poisonous plants and fungi as well as plants with thorns.

End-of-Experiment Rules

Unplug all electrical equipment. Clean up your work area. Dispose of waste materials as instructed by your teacher. Wash your hands after every experiment.

The microscope is an essential tool in the study of life science. It allows you to see things that are too small to be seen with the unaided eye.

You will probably use a compound microscope like the one you see here. The compound microscope has more than one lens that magnifies the object you view.

Typically, a compound microscope has one lens in the eyepiece, the part you look through. The eyepiece lens usually magnifies 10 ×. Any object you view through this lens would appear 10 times larger than it is.

The compound microscope may contain one or two other lenses called objective lenses. If there are two objective lenses, they are called the low-power and high-power objective lenses. The low-power objective lens usually magnifies 10 ×. The high-power objective lens usually magnifies 40 ×.

To calculate the total magnification with which you are viewing an object, multiply the magnification of the eyepiece lens by the magnification of the objective lens you are using. For example, the eyepiece's magnification of 10 × multiplied by the low-power objective's magnification of 10 × equals a total magnification of 100 ×.

Use the photo of the compound microscope to become familiar with the parts of the microscope and their functions.

The Parts of a Compound Microscope

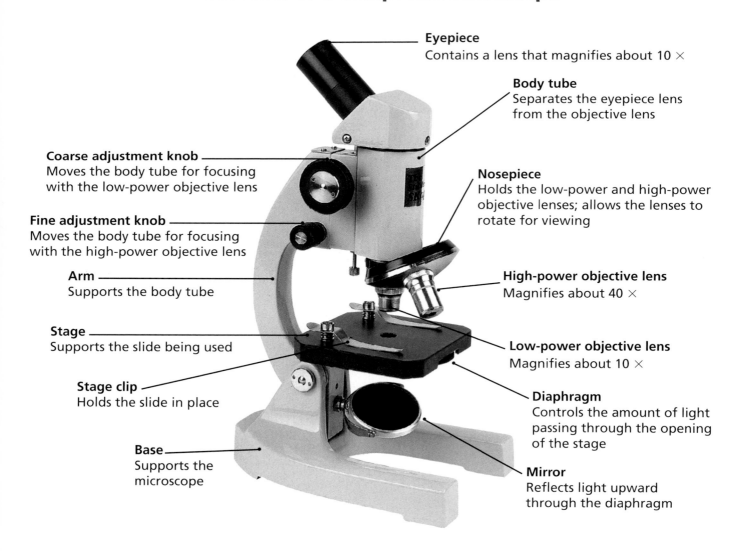

Eyepiece
Contains a lens that magnifies about 10 ×

Body tube
Separates the eyepiece lens from the objective lens

Coarse adjustment knob
Moves the body tube for focusing with the low-power objective lens

Nosepiece
Holds the low-power and high-power objective lenses; allows the lenses to rotate for viewing

Fine adjustment knob
Moves the body tube for focusing with the high-power objective lens

High-power objective lens
Magnifies about 40 ×

Arm
Supports the body tube

Stage
Supports the slide being used

Low-power objective lens
Magnifies about 10 ×

Stage clip
Holds the slide in place

Diaphragm
Controls the amount of light passing through the opening of the stage

Base
Supports the microscope

Mirror
Reflects light upward through the diaphragm

Using the Microscope

Use the following procedures when you are working with a microscope.

1. To carry the microscope, grasp the microscope's arm with one hand. Place your other hand under the base.
2. Place the microscope on a table with the arm toward you.
3. Turn the coarse adjustment knob to raise the body tube.
4. Revolve the nosepiece until the low-power objective lens clicks into place.
5. Adjust the diaphragm. While looking through the eyepiece, also adjust the mirror until you see a bright white circle of light. **CAUTION:** *Never use direct sunlight as a light source.*
6. Place a slide on the stage. Center the specimen over the opening on the stage. Use the stage clips to hold the slide in place. **CAUTION:** *Glass slides are fragile.*
7. Look at the stage from the side. Carefully turn the coarse adjustment knob to lower the body tube until the low-power objective almost touches the slide.
8. Looking through the eyepiece, very slowly turn the coarse adjustment knob until the specimen comes into focus.
9. To switch to the high-power objective lens, look at the microscope from the side. Carefully revolve the nosepiece until the high-power objective lens clicks into place. Make sure the lens does not hit the slide.
10. Looking through the eyepiece, turn the fine adjustment knob until the specimen comes into focus.

Making a Wet-Mount Slide

Use the following procedures to make a wet-mount slide of a specimen.

1. Obtain a clean microscope slide and a coverslip. **CAUTION:** *Glass slides and coverslips are fragile.*
2. Place the specimen on the slide. The specimen must be thin enough for light to pass through it.
3. Using a plastic dropper, place a drop of water on the specimen.
4. Gently place one edge of the coverslip against the slide so that it touches the edge of the water drop at a 45° angle. Slowly lower the coverslip over the specimen. If air bubbles are trapped beneath the coverslip, tap the coverslip gently with the eraser end of a pencil.
5. Remove any excess water at the edge of the coverslip with a paper towel.

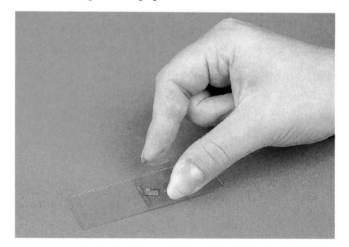

English and Spanish Glossary

absorption The process by which an object takes in, or absorbs, light. (p. 115)
absorción Proceso por el cual un objeto absorbe la luz.

accessory pigment A pigment other than chlorophyll found in plant cells. (p. 116)
pigmento accesorio Pigmento diferente de la clorofila que se halla en las células vegetales.

algae Plantlike protists. (p. 79)
algas Protistas con características vegetales.

algal bloom The rapid growth of a population of algae. (p. 84)
floración de algas Rápido crecimiento de una población de algas.

angiosperm A flowering plant that produces seeds enclosed in a protective structure. (p. 151)
angiosperma Planta con flores que produce semillas encerradas en una estructura protectora.

annual A flowering plant that completes its life cycle in one growing season. (p. 164)
anual Planta con flores que completa su ciclo de vida en una sola temporada de crecimiento.

antibiotic A chemical that can kill bacteria without harming a person's cells. (p. 62)
antibiótico Sustancia química que puede matar bacterias sin dañar las células humanas.

antibiotic resistance The ability of bacteria to withstand the effects of an antibiotic. (p. 63)
resistencia a antibióticos Capacidad de la bacteria a resistir los efectos de los antibióticos.

asexual reproduction A reproductive process that involves only one parent and produces offspring that are identical to the parent. (p. 52)
reproducción asexual Proceso de reproducción que implica a sólo un progenitor y produce descendencia que es idéntica al progenitor.

autotroph An organism that makes its own food. (p. 12)
autótrofo Organismo que produce su propio alimento.

auxin A plant hormone that speeds up the rate of growth of plant cells. (p. 161)
auxina Hormona vegetal que acelera el crecimiento de las células de la planta.

B

bacteria Single-celled organisms that lack a nucleus; prokaryotes. (p. 49)
bacteria Organismo unicelular que no tiene núcleo; procariota.

bacteriophage A virus that infects bacteria. (p. 41)
bacteriófago Virus que infecta bacterias.

biennial A flowering plant that completes its life cycle in two years. (p. 164)
bienal Planta con flores que completa su ciclo de vida en dos años.

binary fission A form of asexual reproduction in which one cell divides to form two identical cells.
fisión binaria Forma de reproducción asexual en la que una célula se divide para formar dos células idénticas. (p. 52)

binomial nomenclature The system for naming organisms in which each organism is given a unique, two-part scientific name indicating its genus and species. (p. 18)
nomenclatura binaria Sistema para nombrar organismos, en el cual a cada organismo se le da un nombre científico único de dos partes, que indica su género y especie.

bog A wetland where sphagnum moss grows on top of acidic water. (p. 123)
ciénaga Pantano en donde crecen los musgos esfagnáceos encima de agua ácida.

budding A form of asexual reproduction of yeast in which a new cell grows out of the body of a parent.
gemación Forma de reproducción asexual de las levaduras, en la que una nueva célula crece del cuerpo de su progenitor. (p. 90)

C

cambium A layer of cells in a plant that produces new phloem and xylem cells. (p. 142)
cámbium Una capa de células de una planta que produce nuevas células de floema y xilema.

cell The basic unit of structure and function in an organism. (p. 7)
célula Unidad básica de estructura y función en los seres vivos.

chlorophyll A green pigment found in the chloroplasts of plants, algae, and some bacteria. (p. 110)
clorofila Pigmento verde que se halla en los cloroplastos de las plantas, en algas y algunas bacterias.

chloroplast A plant cell structure in which photosynthesis occurs. (p. 105)
cloroplasto Estructura en las células vegetales en la que ocurre la fotosíntesis.

cilia The hairlike projections on the outside of cells that move in a wavelike manner. (p. 77)
cilios Proyecciones finas en el exterior de las células, que se mueven de manera ondulante.

classification The process of grouping things based on their similarities. (p. 17)
clasificación Proceso de agrupar cosas según sus semejanzas.

cone The reproductive structure of a gymnosperm.
cono Estructura reproductora de una gimnosperma. (p. 148)

conjugation The process in which a unicellular organism transfers some of its genetic material to another unicellular organism. (p. 52)
conjugación Proceso por el cual un organismo unicelular transfiere parte de su material genético a otro organismo unicelular.

contractile vacuole The cell structure that collects extra water from the cytoplasm and then expels it from the cell. (p. 76)
vacuola contráctil Estructura celular que recoge el agua sobrante del citoplasma y luego la expulsa de la célula.

controlled experiment An experiment in which all factors are identical except one. (p. 10)
experimento controlado Experimento en el que todos los factores son iguales excepto uno.

cotyledon A seed leaf; sometimes stores food. (p. 138)
cotiledón Hoja de una semilla; en la que a veces se almacena alimento.

critical night length The number of hours of darkness that determines whether or not a plant will flower. (p. 162)
longitud nocturna crítica El número de horas de oscuridad que determina si florece una planta o no.

cuticle The waxy, waterproof layer that covers the leaves and stems of most plants. (p. 106)
cutícula Capa cerosa e impermeable que cubre las hojas y los tallos de la mayoría de las plantas.

cytoplasm The region of a cell located inside the cell membrane (in prokaryotes) or between the cell membrane and nucleus (in eukaryotes); contains a gel-like material and cell structures. (p. 49)
citoplasma Región de una célula ubicada dentro de la membrana celular (en los procariotas), o entre la membrana celular y el núcleo (en los eucariotas); contiene un material gelatinoso y estructuras celulares.

day-neutral plant A plant with a flowering cycle that is not sensitive to periods of light and dark. (p. 162)
planta de día neutro Planta cuyo ciclo de floración no es sensible a la duración de los períodos de luz y oscuridad.

decomposer An organism that breaks down chemicals from dead organisms and returns important materials to the soil and water. (p. 56)
descomponedor Organismo que separa sustancias químicas de los organismos muertos y devuelve materiales importantes al suelo y al agua.

development The process of change that occurs during an organism's life to produce a more complex organism. (p. 9)
desarrollo Proceso de cambio que ocurre durante la vida de un organismo, mediante el cual se produce un organismo más complejo.

dicot An angiosperm that has two seed leaves. (p. 156)
dicotiledónea Angiosperma cuyas semillas tienen dos cotiledones.

dormancy A period when an organism's growth or activity stops. (p. 163)
dormición Período durante el cual se suspende el crecimiento o la actividad de un organismo.

embryo The young organism that develops from a zygote. (p. 138)
embrión Organismo joven que se desarrolla a partir de un cigoto.

endospore A small, rounded, thick-walled, resting cell that forms inside a bacterial cell. (p. 53)
endospora Célula pequeña y redonda de paredes gruesas que se encuentra en reposo, que se forma dentro de una célula bacteriana.

eukaryote An organism whose cells contain nuclei.
eucariota Organismo cuyas células contienen núcleo. (p. 28)

eutrophication The buildup over time of nutrients in freshwater lakes and ponds that leads to an increase in the growth of algae. (p. 86)
eutrofización Acumulación gradual de nutrientes en lagos y estanques de agua dulce que produce un aumento en el crecimiento de algas.

evolution The process by which species gradually change over time. (p. 23)
evolución Proceso mediante el cual las especies cambian gradualmente con el tiempo.

fertilization The joining of a sperm cell and an egg cell. (p. 107)
fecundación Unión de un espermatozoide y de un óvulo.

flagellum A long, whiplike structure that helps a cell to move. (p. 49)
flagelo Estructura larga con forma de látigo que ayuda a la célula para moverse.

flower The reproductive structure of an angiosperm. (p. 152)
flor Estructura reproductora de una angiosperma.

fossil A trace of an ancient organism that has been preserved in rock or other substance. (p. 32)
fósil Restos de un organismo antiguo que se ha preservado en la roca u otra sustancia.

frond The leaf of a fern plant. (p. 128)
fronda Hoja de un helecho.

fruit The ripened ovary and other structures of an angiosperm that enclose one or more seeds. (p. 155)
fruto Ovario maduro y otras estructuras que encierran una o más semillas de una angiosperma.

fruiting body The reproductive structure of a fungus that contains many hyphae and produces spores.
órgano fructífero Estructura reproductora de un hongo que contiene muchas hifas y produce esporas.(p. 90)

fungus A eukaryotic organism that has cell walls, uses spores to reproduce, and is a heterotroph that feeds by absorbing its food. (p. 88)
hongo Organismo eucariótico que posee paredes celulares, usa esporas para reproducirse y es un heterótrofo que se alimenta absorbiendo su comida.

gametophyte The stage in the life cycle of a plant in which the plant produces gametes, or sex cells.
gametofito Etapa en el ciclo de vida de una planta en la cual la planta produce gametos, es decir, células sexuales. (p. 110)

genetic engineering The process of altering an organism's genetic material to produce an organism with qualities that people find useful. (p. 167)
ingeniería genética Proceso por el cual se altera el material genético de un organismo para producir otro organismo con cualidades que se consideran útiles.

genus A classification grouping that consists of a number of similar, closely related species. (p. 18)
género Clasificación por grupo formada por un número de especies similares y muy relacionadas.

germination The sprouting of the embryo out of a seed; occurs when the embryo resumes its growth. (p. 140)
germinación La brotadura del embrión de una semilla; ocurre cuando el embrión prosigue su crecimiento.

gymnosperm A plant that produces seeds that are not enclosed by a protective fruit.
gimnosperma Planta cuyas semillas no están encerradas en una fruta protectora. (p. 146)

heterotroph An organism that cannot make its own food. (p. 12)
heterótrofo Organismo que no puede producir su propio alimento.

homeostasis The maintenance of stable internal conditions. (p. 14)
homeostasis Mantenimiento de condiciones internas estables.

hormone A chemical that affects growth and development. (p. 161)
hormona Sustancia química que afecta el crecimiento y el desarrollo.

host An organism that provides a source of energy or a suitable environment for a virus or another organism to live. (p. 41)
huésped Organismo que provee una fuente de energía o un ambiente apropiado para que viva un virus u otro organismo.

hydroponics A farming method in which plants are grown in solutions of nutrients instead of soil. (p. 166)
hidroponía Método de cultivo de plantas en el que se usan soluciones de nutrientes en vez de suelos.

hyphae The branching, threadlike tubes that make up the bodies of multicellular fungi. (p. 89)
hifas Delgados tubos ramificados que constituyen el cuerpo de los hongos multicelulares.

infectious disease An illness that can pass from one organism to another. (p. 60)
enfermedad infecciosa Enfermedad que puede pasar de un organismo a otro.

lichen The combination of a fungus and either an alga or an autotrophic bacterium that live together in a mutualistic relationship. (p. 95)
liquen Combinación de un hongo y una alga o bien una bacteria autótrofa, que viven juntos en una relación de mutualismo.

long-day plant A plant that flowers when the nights are shorter than the plant's critical night length. (p. 162)
planta de día largo Una planta que florece cuando las noches son más cortas que la longitud nocturna crítica de la planta.

monocot An angiosperm that has only one seed leaf.
monocotiledónea Angiosperma cuyas semillas tienen un solo cotiledón. (p. 156)

multicellular Consisting of many cells. (p. 7)
multicelular Que se compone de muchas células.

mutualism A type of symbiosis in which both partners benefit from living together. (p. 78)
mutualismo Tipo de simbiosis en la que ambos participantes se benefician de vivir juntos.

nonvascular plant A low-growing plant that lacks true vascular tissue. (p. 108)
planta no vascular Planta de crecimiento lento que carece de tejido vascular verdadero.

nucleus The dense area in a eukaryotic cell that contains nucleic acids, the chemical instructions that direct the cell's activities. (p. 27)
núcleo Área densa en una célula eucariota que contiene ácidos nucleicos, es decir, las instrucciones químicas que dirigen las actividades de la célula.

organism A living thing. (p. 7)
organismo Ser vivo.

ovary A flower structure that encloses and protects ovules and seeds as they develop. (p. 153)
ovario Estructura de la flor que encierra y protege a los óvulos y a las semillas durante su desarrollo.

ovule A plant structure in seed plants that produces the female gametophyte; contains an egg cell. (p. 148)
óvulo Estructura de las plantas de semilla que produce el gametofito femenino; contiene una célula reproductora femenina.

parasite An organism that lives on or in a host and causes harm to the host. (p. 41)
parásito Organismo que vive sobre o dentro de un huésped y le causa daño.

pasteurization A process of heating food to a temperature that is high enough to kill most harmful bacteria without changing the taste of the food. (p. 55)
pasteurización Proceso de calentamiento del alimento a una temperatura suficientemente alta como para matar la mayoría de las bacterias dañinas sin cambiar el sabor de la comida.

peat Compressed layers of dead sphagnum mosses that accumulate in bogs. (p. 123)
turba Capas comprimidas de musgos esfagnáceos muertos que se acumulan en las ciénagas.

perennial A flowering plant that lives for more than two years. (p. 164)
perenne Planta con flores que vive más de dos años.

petal A colorful, leaflike structure of some flowers.
pétalo Estructura de color brillante, en forma de hoja que tienen algunas flores. (p. 152)

phloem The vascular tissue through which food moves in some plants. (p. 137)
floema Tejido vascular por el que circula el alimento en algunas plantas.

photoperiodism A plant's response to seasonal changes in length of night and day. (p. 162)
fotoperiodicidad Respuesta de una planta a los cambios de día y noche por las estaciones.

photosynthesis The process by which plants and some other organisms capture and use light energy to make food from carbon dioxide and water. (p. 104)
fotosíntesis Proceso por el que las plantas y otros organismos captan energía luminosa y la usan para producir alimento a partir del dióxido de carbono y del agua.

pigment A chemical that produces color. (p. 79)
pigmento Sustancia química que produce color.

pistil The female reproductive part of a flower. (p. 153)
pistilo Parte reproductora femenina de una flor.

pollen Tiny particles (male gametophytes) produced by seed plants that contain the cells that later become sperm cells. (p. 137)
polen Partículas diminutas (gametofitos masculinos) producidas por las plantas de semillas que contienen las células que posteriormente se convierten en células reproductoras masculinas.

pollination The transfer of pollen from male reproductive structures to female reproductive structures in plants. (p. 149)
polinización Transferencia de polen de las estructuras reproductoras masculinas a las estructuras reproductoras femeninas de las plantas.

precision farming A farming method in which farmers use technology to fine-tune the amount of water and fertilizer they use to match the requirements of a specific field. (p. 166)
agricultura de precisión Método de cultivo en el que los agricultores usan la tecnología para determinar con precisión la cantidad de agua y fertilizante que emplearán, para suplir las necesidades de un terreno específico.

prokaryote An organism whose cells lack a nucleus and some other cell structures. (p. 27)
procariota Organismo cuyas células carecen de núcleo y otras estructuras celulares.

protist A eukaryotic organism that cannot be classified as an animal, plant, or fungus. (p. 75)
protista Organismo eucariótico que no se puede clasificar como animal, planta ni hongo.

protozoan An animal-like protist. (p. 75)
protozoario Protista con características animales.

pseudopod A "false foot" or temporary bulge of cytoplasm used for feeding and movement in some protozoans. (p. 76)
seudópodo "Pie falso" o abultamiento temporal del citoplasma, que algunos protozoarios usan para alimentarse o desplazarse.

R

red tide An algal bloom that occurs in salt water. (p. 85)
marea roja Floración de algas que se presenta en el agua salada.

reflection The process by which light bounces off an object. (p. 115)
reflexión Proceso por el cual la luz rebota en un objeto.

respiration The process of breaking down food to release its energy. (p. 51)
respiración Proceso de descomposición de alimentos para liberar su energía.

response An action or change in behavior that occurs as a result of a stimulus. (p. 9)
respuesta Acción o cambio en el comportamiento que ocurre como resultado de un estímulo.

rhizoid A thin, rootlike structure that anchors a moss and absorbs water and nutrients for the plant. (p. 123)
rizoide Estructura fina parecida a una raíz que sujeta un musgo al suelo, y que absorbe el agua y los nutrientes para la planta.

ribosome A tiny structure located in the cytoplasm of a cell where proteins are produced. (p. 49)
ribosoma Estructura diminuta ubicada en el citoplasma de una célula donde se producen las proteínas.

root cap A structure that covers the tip of a root, protecting the root from injury. (p. 141)
cofia Estructura que cubre la punta de una raíz y la protege contra daños.

S

seed The plant structure that contains a young plant inside a protective covering. (p. 137)
semilla Estructura de una planta que contiene una plántula dentro de una cubierta protectora.

sepal A leaflike structure that encloses the bud of a flower. (p. 152)
sépalo Estructura, parecida a una hoja, que encierra el botón de una flor.

sexual reproduction A reproductive process that involves two parents that combine their genetic material to produce a new organism, which differs from both parents. (p. 52)
reproducción sexual Proceso de reproducción que implica a dos progenitores que combinan su material genético para producir un nuevo organismo diferente a los dos progenitores.

short-day plant A plant that flowers when the nights are longer than the plant's critical night length. (p. 162)
planta del día corto Una planta que florece cuando las noches son más largas que la longitud nocturna crítica de la planta.

species A group of similar organisms that can mate with each other and produce offspring that can also mate and reproduce. (p. 18)
especie Grupo de organismos semejantes que pueden cruzarse entre ellos y producir descendencia fértil.

spontaneous generation The mistaken idea that living things arise from nonliving sources. (p. 10)
generación espontánea Idea equivocada de que los seres vivos surgen de fuentes inertes.

spore A tiny cell that is able to grow into a new organism. (p. 82)
espora Célula diminuta que, al crecer, puede convertirse en un nuevo organismo.

sporophyte The stage in the life cycle of a plant in which the plant produces spores. (p. 110)
esporofito Etapa en el ciclo de vida de una planta en la que la planta produce esporas.

stamen The male reproductive part of a flower. (p. 153)
estambre Parte reproductora masculina de una flor.

stimulus A change in an organism's surroundings that causes the organism to react. (p. 8)
estímulo Cambio en el entorno de un organismo que le hace reaccionar.

stomata The small openings on the surfaces of most leaves through which gases can move.
estomas Pequeñas aberturas en la superficie de casi todas las hojas, a través de las cuales pasan los gases. (p. 144)

symbiosis A close relationship between two organisms in which at least one of the organisms benefits. (p. 78)
simbiosis Relación estrecha entre dos organismos, en la que al menos uno de los organismos se beneficia.

taxonomy The scientific study of how living things are classified. (p. 17)
taxonomía Estudio científico de cómo se clasifican los seres vivos.

tissue A group of similar cells that perform a specific function in an organism. (p. 105)
tejido Grupo de células semejantes que realizan una función específica en un organismo.

toxin A poison that can harm an organism. (p. 61)
toxina Veneno que puede dañar a un organismo.

transmission The process by which light passes through an object. (p. 115)
transmisión Proceso por el cual la luz pasa a través de un objeto.

transpiration The process by which water is lost through a plant's leaves. (p. 145)
transpiración Proceso por el cual las hojas de una planta eliminan agua.

tropism The growth response of a plant toward or away from a stimulus. (p. 160)
tropismo Respuesta de una planta a un estímulo, que consiste en crecer hacia el estímulo o en la dirección opuesta.

unicellular Made of a single cell. (p. 7)
unicelular Compuesto por una sola célula.

vaccine A substance introduced into the body to stimulate the production of chemicals that destroy specific disease-causing viruses and organisms. (p. 65)
vacuna Sustancia introducida en el cuerpo para estimular la producción de sustancias químicas que destruyen a los virus y organismos específicos causantes de enfermedades.

vacuole A large sac-like storage area in a cell. (p. 105)
vacuola Gran área de almacenamiento parecida a un saco en una célula.

vascular plant A plant that has true vascular tissue. (p. 108)
planta vascular Planta que tiene tejido vascular verdadero.

vascular tissue The internal transporting tissue in some plants that is made up of tubelike structures.
tejido vascular Tejido de transporte interno en algunas plantas que está formado por estructuras parecidas a tubos. (p. 107)

virus A tiny, nonliving particle that invades and then reproduces inside a living cell. (p. 41)
virus Partícula diminuta no viva que invade una célula viva y luego se reproduce dentro de ella.

xylem The vascular tissue through which water and nutrients move in some plants. (p. 137)
xilema Tejido vascular por el que circulan agua y nutrientes en algunas plantas.

zygote A fertilized egg. (p. 107)
cigoto Óvulo fertilizado.

Index

Page numbers for key terms are printed in **boldface** type.
Page numbers for illustrations, maps, and charts are printed in *italics*.

Index

Page numbers for key terms are printed in **boldface** type.
Page numbers for illustrations, maps, and charts are printed in *italics*.

Acknowledgments

Acknowledgment for page 178: *The Corn Goddess* © Canadian National Museum of Civilization, author Diamond Jenness, 1956.

Illustration

Patrice Rossi Calkin: 44–45, 76–77; **John Edwards and Associates:** 23 insets, 43, 80, 116b, 138; **David Fuller:** 175; **Kevin Jones Associates:** 142; **Richard McMahon:** 118; **Karen Minot:** 26, 100, 162, 172; **Morgan-Cain & Associates:** 10, 11, 36t, 92, 144; **Laurie O'Keefe:** 23; **Stephanie Pershing:** 31; **Walter Stuart:** 89t, 123, 128, 176; **Cynthia Turner:** 156; **J/B Woolsey Associates:** 21, 22, 81, 90, 141, 152, 159. **All charts and graphs by Matt Mayerchak.**

Photography

Photo Research Sue McDermott
Cover image top, Lester Lefkowitz/Corbis; **bottom,** Zefa Biotic/Photonica

Page vi l, Dr. Brad Fute/Peter Arnold, Inc.; **vi m,** Dr. Linda Stannard, UCT/Photo Researchers, Inc.; **vi r,** Tektoff-RM/CNRI/Photo Researchers, Inc.; **vii,** Richard Haynes; **viii,** Richard Haynes; **x b,** USDA/S.S./Photo Researchers; **x t,** Courtesy of Cindy Friedman; **2,** Reinhard Dirscher/Alamy Images; **3,** Courtesy of Cindy Friedman.

Pages 4–5, Roland Birke/Peter Arnold, Inc.; **5 inset,** Richard Haynes; **6b,** Beatty/Visuals Unlimited; **6t,** Russ Lappa; **7br,** Biodisc/Visuals Unlimited; **7l,** Michael & Patricia Fogden/Corbis; **7tr,** Michael Abbey/Photo Researchers, Inc.; **8,** Norvia Behling/Animals Animals; **9l,** Steve Callahan/Visuals Unlimited; **9m,** Dan Suzio/Photo Researchers, Inc.; **9r,** Porterfield-Chickering/Photo Researchers, Inc.; **10,** Breck Kent/Animals Animals; **11,** Superstock; **12 inset,** Tom Brakefield/DRK Photo; **12–13b,** Stephen J. Krasemann/DRK Photo; **13 inset l,** Kennan Ward/Corbis; **13 inset r,** W. Perry Conway/Corbis; **14,** Michael Newman/ PhotoEdit; **15,** Russ Lappa; **16b,** Inga Spence/The Picture Cube, Inc.; **16t,** Russ Lappa; **17,** Biophoto Associates/Photo Researchers, Inc.; **18l,** Gerard Lacz/Animals Animals; **18m,** Gavriel Jecan/Art Wolfe, Inc.; **18r,** Ron Kimball Studios; **19,** Lynn Stone/Animals Animals; **21,** Thomas Kitchin/Tom Stack & Associates, Inc.; **24l,** Richard Day/Animals Animals; **24r,** Phil Dotson/Photo Researchers, Inc.; **25 all,** Russ Lappa; **27b,** Alan Schietzch/Bruce Coleman; **27 inset b,** BBoonyaratanakornkit & D.S. Clark, G. Vrdolijak/EM Lab, U. of C Berkeley/Visuals Unlimited; **27t,** Lennart Nilsson/Albert Bonniers Forlag AB; **27 inset t,** Eye of Science/Photo Researchers, Inc.; **28 inset l,** Carolina Biological/ Visuals Unlimited; **28 inset r,** W. Wayne Lockwood, M.D./Corbis; **28–29t,** Daniel J. Krasemann/DRK Photo; **29 inset l,** Photodisc/Getty Images, Inc.; **29 inset r,** E.R. Degginger/Animals Animals; **30,** Russ Lappa; **32l,** Biological Photo Service; **32r,** Reg Morrison/Auscape; **33,** Peggy/Yoram Kahana/Peter Arnold, Inc.; **34l,** W. Wayne Lockwood, M.D./Corbis; **34r,** E.R. Degginger/Animals Animals.

Pages 38–39, Dennis Kunkel/Phototake; **39 inset,** Richard Haynes; **40bl,** Institut Pasteur/CNRI/Phototake; **40br,** Lee D. Simon/Photo Researchers, Inc.; **40t,** Getty Images, Inc.; **41l,** Dr. Brad Fute/Peter Arnold, Inc.; **41m,** Dr. Linda Stannard, UCT/Photo Researchers, Inc.; **41r,** Tektoff-RM/CNRI/Photo Researchers, Inc.; **44–45,** Peter Minister/Dorling Kindersley; **46,** Esbin-Anderson/Omni-Photo; **47b,** Dr. Linda Stannard, UCT/Photo Researchers, Inc.; **47t,** Custom Medical Stock; **48,** Richard Haynes; **49b,** Geoff Brightling/Dorling Kindersley; **49t,** USDA/Visuals Unlimited; **50b,** David M. Phillips/Visuals Unlimited; **50r,** Oliver Meckes/Photo Researchers, Inc.; **50t,** Scott Camazine/Photo Researchers, Inc.; **51b,** Dr. Jeremy Burgess/Photo Researchers, Inc.; **51 inset b,** Dennis Kunkel/Phototake; **51l,** Steve Dunwell/Index Stock Imagery; **51 inset l,** Dennis Kunkel/Phototake; **51l,** Alan L. Detrick/Photo Researchers, Inc.; **51 inset t,** Photo courtesy of Agriculture and Agri-Food Canada ; **52b,** Dr. Dennis Kunkel/Phototake; **52t,** Dr. K.S. Kim/Peter Arnold, Inc.; **53,** Alfred Pasieka/Peter Arnold, Inc.; **54l,** StockFood/Raben; **54r,** Richard Haynes; **55l,** Dorling Kindersley; **55m,** J. C. Carton/Bruce Coleman; **55r,** Neil Marsh/Dorling Kindersley; **56b,** Ben Osborne; **56 inset,** Michael Abbey/Photo Researchers, Inc.; **56t,** John Riley/Getty Images, Inc.; **57,** David Young-Wolff/PhotoEdit; **59,** Richard Haynes; **60,** Richard Haynes; **61b,** Getty Images, Inc.; **61bm,** David M. Dennis/Tom Stack & Associates, Inc.; **61t,** Grapes/Michaud/Photo Researchers, Inc.; **61tm,** Richard Haynes; **62l,** Clouds Hill Imaging, Ltd.; **62r,** Dennis Kunkel/Phototake; **63,** Dr. Gary Gaugler/Photo Researchers, Inc.; **64,** Institut Pasteur/CNRI/Phototake; **65,** David Young-Wolff/PhotoEdit; **66–67 boy,** Richard Haynes; **66 stomach ulcers,** Veronika Burmeister/Visuals Unlimited; **66 tuberculosis,** Dennis Kunkel/Phototake; **66 cavities,** Dr. David Phillips/Visuals Unlimited; **66 pneumonia,** BSIP/Photo Researchers, Inc.; **66 strep throat,** Dr. Gary Gaugler/Photo Researchers, Inc.; **66 ear infection,** David M. Phillips/Photo Researchers, Inc.; **66 conjunctivitis,** Dr. Gary Gaugler/Visuals Unlimited; **66 meningitis,** Dr. Dennis Kunkel/Visuals Unlimited; **67 impetigo,** Dr. Stanley Flegler/Visuals Unlimited; **67r,** C. Swartzell/Visuals Unlimited; **68b,** Geoff Brightling/Dorling Kindersley; **68t,** Lee D. Simon/Photo Researchers, Inc.; **70l,** Dennis Kunkel; **70r,** Science Photo Library.

Pages 72–73, Michael Fogden/DRK Photo; **73 inset,** Richard Haynes; **74b,** Jan Hinsch/Science Photo Library/Photo Researchers, Inc.; **74t,** Science VU/Visuals Unlimited; **75b,** Gregory G. Dimijian/Photo Researchers, Inc.; **75m,** A. Le Toquin/Photo Researchers, Inc.; **75t,** O.S.F./Animals Animals/Earth Scenes; **76,** Astrid & Hanns-Frieder Michler/Photo Researchers, Inc.; **77,** Eric Grave/Photo Researchers, Inc.; **78b,** Oliver Meckes/Photo Researchers, Inc.; **78 inset,** Jerome Paulin/Visuals

Unlimited; **78t,** Layne Kennedy/Corbis; **79,** David M. Phillips/Visuals Unlimited; **80,** Sinclair Stammers Oxford Scientific Films/Animals Animals/Earth Scenes; **81,** Barry Runk/Stan/Grant Heilman Photography; **82 both,** David M. Dennis/Tom Stack & Associates, Inc.; **83b,** G.R. Roberts/Omni-Photo; **83t,** Dwight R. Kuhn; **84,** Doug Perrine/Hawaii Whale Research Foundation/Innerspace Visions; **85,** Sanford Berry/Visuals Unlimited; **85 inset,** Dr. David Phillips/Visuals Unlimited; **86,** Doug Sokell/Visuals Unlimited; **87,** Russ Lappa; **88b,** Michael Fogden/Animals Animals/Earth Scenes; **88t,** Russ Lappa; **89,** Fred Unverhau/Animals Animals/Earth Scenes; **90t,** Nobel Proctor/Science Source/Photo Researchers, Inc.; **90b,** David Scharf/Peter Arnold, Inc.; **91t,** Carolina Biological/Visuals Unlimited; **91bl,** Michael Fogden/Animals Animals/Earth Scenes; **91bl inset,** Scott Camazine; **91br,** Runk/Schoenberger/Grant Heilman Photography, Inc.; **91br inset,** E.R. Degginger/Photo Researchers, Inc.; **92l,** Viard/Jacana /Photo Researchers, Inc.; **92r,** Owen Franken/Corbis; **93bl,** Eye of Science/Photo Researchers, Inc.; **93br,** ISM/Phototake; **93t,** C. James Webb/Phototake; **94,** Photo courtesy of David Read; **95,** Rod Planck/Tom Stack & Associates, Inc.; **95 inset,** V. Ahmadjian/Visuals Unlimited; **96,** Richard Haynes; **97,** Richard Haynes; **98,** Michael Fogden/Animals Animals/Earth Scenes.

Pages 102–103, Norbert Rosing/National Geographic Image Collection; **103 inset,** Richard Haynes; **104,** Richard Haynes; **105l,** Michael J. Doolittle/The Image Works; **105 inset,** Runk/Schoenberger/Grant Heilman Photography, Inc.; **106,** Kjell B. Sandved/Photo Researchers, Inc.; **107,** Ludovic Maisant/Corbis; **108l,** Randy M. Ury/Corbis; **108r,** John Shaw/Bruce Coleman; **109bl,** Ron Thomas/Getty Images, Inc.; **109br,** Eastcott Momatiuk/Getty Images, Inc.; **109m,** Barry Runk/Stan/Grant Heilman Photography; **109tl,** R. Van Nostrand/Photo Researchers, Inc.; **109tr,** Brenda Tharp/Photo Researchers, Inc.; **110b,** Frans Lanting/Minden Pictures; **110tl,** Runk/Schoenberger/ Grant Heilman Photography, Inc.; **110tr,** Peter Chadwick/Royalty Free/Corbis; **113,** Lester Lefkowitz/Corbis; **114b,** Peter A. Simon/Corbis; **114t,** Richard Haynes; **115,** Christi Carter/Grant Heilman Photography; **116,** Runk/Schoenberger/Grant Heilman Photography; **117b,** Georg Gerster/Photo Researchers, Inc.; **117t,** Interfoto-Pressebild-Agentur; **118,** Biophoto Associates/ Photo Researchers, Inc.; **119,** Michael Keller/Corbis; **120,** Richard Haynes; **121,** Richard Haynes; **122t,** Russ Lappa; **122–123b,** J. Lotter Gurling/Tom Stack & Associates, Inc.; **123 inset,** Runk/Schoenberger/Grant Heilman Photography, Inc.; **124l,** Runk/Schoenberger/Grant Heilman Photography, Inc.; **124r,** William E. Ferguson; **125,** Richard Haynes; **126,** Richard Haynes; **128,** Milton Rand/Tom Stack & Associates, Inc.; **129l,** Runk/Schoenberger/Grant Heilman Photography, Inc.; **129r,** Gerald Moore; **130,** J. Lotter Gurling/Tom Stack & Associates, Inc.; **133,** Runk/Schoenberger/Grant Heilman Photography, Inc.

Pages 134–135, Barrett and MacKay; **135 inset,** Jon Chomitz; **136,** Russ Lappa; **137 both,** Phil Schermeister/Corbis; **138l,** Barry Runk/Grant Heilman Photography, Inc.; **138m,** Dave King/Dorling Kindersley; **138r,** Anna W. Schoettle, USDA Forest Service; **139bl,** D. Cavagnaro/Visuals Unlimited; **139br,** Frans Lanting/Minden Pictures; **139m,** Heather Angel/Natural Visions; **139mr,** Color-Pic/Animals Animals/Earth Scenes; **139ml,** John Pontier/Animals Animals/Earth Scenes; **139t,** J.A.L. Cooke/OSF/Earth Scenes; **140 background,** Color-Pic/Earth Scenes; **140 inset both,** Runk/Schoenberger/Grant Heilman Photography, Inc.; **141 background,** Color-Pic/Earth Scenes; **141l inset,** Max Stuart/Alamy; **141r inset,** Runk/Schoenberger/Grant Heilman Photography, Inc.; **142l,** Barry Runk/Stan/Grant Heilman; **142r,** Richard Shiell/Animals Animals/Earth Scenes; **143,** Darrell Gulin/Getty Images, Inc.; **145 both,** Dr.Jeremy Burgess/Photo Researchers, Inc.; **146,** Richard Haynes; **147b,** Ken Brate/Photo Researchers, Inc.; **147l,** Michael Fogden/Animals Animals/Earth Scenes; **147r,** Breck Kent/Animals Animals/Earth Scenes; **147t,** Jim Strawser/Grant Heilman Photography, Inc.; **149t,** Grant Heilman/Grant Heilman Photography, Inc.; **149t inset,** Breck P. Kent/Animals Animals/Earth Scenes; **149b inset,** Breck P. Kent; **149b,** Patti Murray/Animals Animals/Earth Scenes; **150,** Martin Rogers/Stock Boston; **151b,** Frans Lanting/Minden Pictures; **151t,** Russ Lappa; **153bl,** Ian Tait/Natural Visions; **153br,** Merlin D. Tuttle, Bat Conservation International; **153t,** Anthony Bannister/Animals Animals; **154l,** Perennou et Nuridsany/Photo Researchers, Inc.; **154ml,** Russ Lappa; **154mr,** Philip Dowell/Dorling Kindersley; **154r,** Jules Selmes and Debi Treloar/Dorling Kindersley; **155t,** Nancy Rotenberg/Animals Animals/Earth Scenes; **155b,** Dwight Kuhn; **157,** Alan Pitcairn/Grant Heilman Photography, Inc.; **158,** Richard Haynes; **160,** David Sieren /Visuals Unlimited; **161b,** E.R. Degginger; **161m,** Heather Angel/Natural Visions; **161t,** Barry Runk/Stan/Grant Heilman Photography; **163 both,** Scott Smith/Animals Animals/Earth Scenes; **164b,** Larry Lefever/Grant Heilman Photography, Inc.; **164m,** Mark E. Gibson/Corbis; **164t,** E. R. Degginger; **165,** Robert Frerck/Odyssey Productions, Inc.; **166b,** Arthur C. Smith III/Grant Heilman Photography, Inc.; **166–167t,** Patti McConville/Getty Images, Inc.; **168,** Richard Haynes; **169,** Richard Haynes; **170,** Ken Brate/Photo Researchers, Inc.; **174b,** Ed Simpson/Getty Images, Inc.; **174 inset,** Robert Frerck, Odyssey Productions, Chicago; **174–175t,** Monica Stevenson/Getty Images, Inc.; **176,** David Frazier Photo Library; **177,** Ed Bock/Corbis; **178b,** C.M. Dixon; **178t,** Tim Spransy; **179,** David Young Wolff/PhotoEdit; **180,** Tony Freeman/PhotoEdit; **181b,** Russ Lappa; **181m,** Richard Haynes; **181t,** Russ Lappa; **182,** Richard Haynes; **184,** Richard Haynes; **186,** Morton Beebe/Corbis; **187,** Richard Haynes; **189b,** Richard Haynes; **189t,** Dorling Kinderlsey; **191,** Image Stop/Phototake; **194,** Richard Haynes; **201,** Richard Haynes; **203 both,** Richard Haynes.